BIOTERROR

IN THE 21ST CENTURY

BIOTERROR
IN THE 21ST CENTURY

Emerging Threats in a New Global Environment

Daniel M. Gerstein

NAVAL INSTITUTE PRESS
Annapolis, Maryland

Naval Institute Press
291 Wood Road
Annapolis, MD 21402

Library of Congress Cataloging-in-Publication Data
Gerstein, Daniel M., 1958-
  Bioterror in the 21st century / Daniel M. Gerstein.
    p. cm.
  Includes bibliographical references and index.
  ISBN 978-1-59114-312-3 (alk. paper) — ISBN 978-1-59114-313-0 ((pbk.) :
alk. paper) 1. Bioterrorism. I. Title. II. Title: Bioterror in the twenty-first century.
  HV6433.3.G47 2009
  363.325'3—dc22
                                        2009025842

Printed in the United States of America on acid-free paper

14 13 12 11 10 09   9 8 7 6 5 4 3 2
First printing

*To my wife Kathy and
daughters Sarah and Rachel,
who never fail to inspire me and
cause me to want to do better.*

Contents

Tables and Figures

Foreword

On September 11, 2001, America was attacked in a way few of us will forget. The images of the terrorist-controlled airplanes flying into buildings in New York and Washington, DC, and falling into a field in Pennsylvania left an indelible impression. We quickly discovered who the culprits were, took steps at airports and on airplanes to prevent a reoccurrence, and moved against the organization responsible.

A few weeks later, Americans were again the victim of an attack, but this time a biological weapon was hidden within the ubiquitous interchange of everyday mail. It took seven years for the Federal Bureau of Investigation (FBI) to publicly identify a suspect. While mail coming to government buildings in Washington is now treated, prevention on a larger scale is much more difficult.

The anthrax attack in the fall of 2001 has had far-ranging consequences in the efforts to protect Americans, and far-ranging consequences on the national psyche, but it may be just a foretaste of what is to come.

A host of studies and reports published before 9/11 warned of the potential use of nuclear, biological, or chemical weapons in the United States. While the destruction and consequences of a nuclear detonation would be in a category all its own, many who have studied the issues believe biological weapons pose the greatest danger.

Generally, biological weapons are easier to acquire than nuclear arms and can be lethal to an enormous number of people. They can hide among the population for a period, then spread widely as people and other carriers move about the country and even internationally, as the 2009 swine influenza has demonstrated, while health-care professionals attempt to diagnose the problem. Of course, the category "biological weapons" covers many different pathogens with a wide variety of characteristics, thus making prevention and preparation even more difficult.

Dr. Gerstein notes biological weapons stand at the intersection of two trends that provide tremendous benefits for humankind: (1) greater connectivity, which facilitates more communication and ease of movement, and (2) the biological revolution, in which new drugs and therapies are extending and improving life for millions. But he goes to the heart of the matter when he writes, "The very capabilities that show such promise for increasing the longevity of humans and the quality of life of humankind have the potential to be combined in ways that could threaten and perhaps even doom the human race."

The challenge is to understand the threat we face, put it into perspective, and develop policies to deal with it appropriately. We should not overreact, which might divert our efforts from other threats that require our attention. We should plan and prepare, however, for the real possibility—many would argue probability—such weapons will be used against us again, and to far greater effect.

The pace of developments makes it difficult for policy makers and policy implementers to stay abreast of the threat. That is why Dr. Gerstein's comprehensive but readable review of the subject is so welcome and so needed. It is a major contribution to an important subject that should spur sensible and thoughtful action.

CONGRESSMAN MAC THORNBERRY (R-TEX.)

Acknowledgments

No project of such magnitude could possibly be the work of a single person, and this one is no exception. This project began years ago with the many opportunities afforded to me to work on national security and defense issues. I will forever be indebted to my many mentors throughout almost three decades of professional assignments and educational opportunities in this field. The list includes soldiers, U.S. government civilians, educators, and policy experts who took time to teach me *how* to think, and not *what* to think. In this way, they contributed in untold ways to the completion of this effort.

This book began as a dissertation. I would like to specifically thank the members of my committee for the wisdom and insights they have provided to the effort. My committee chair, Dr. Reuben Brigety II, provided great insight into asking the right questions and pushing me to take a systems approach to this complex issue. Dr. Gregory Koblentz assisted me in the early stages of development of the topic and in the difficult policy questions associated with bioterror. Dr. Robert Baker was instrumental in teaching me the science behind biological warfare, as well as in providing me with a practical understanding of the nexus between biotechnology and bioterror. Dr. Ivan "Sascha" Sheehan guided my efforts to deal with the question of terrorism—specifically bioterror. In particular, Dr. Sheehan guided my understanding of the psychological aspects that motivate these individuals and groups. Ms. Kay Goss was instrumental in providing insights into the homeland security doctrine in the United States, and in how that doctrine would be used in the event of a bioterror event.

I would also like to thank my acquisitions editor at the Naval Institute Press, Adam Kane, who provided the direction for converting a dissertation into a book. This is no small task, and his dedication and perseverance helped to make the final product more relevant and readable.

I would also like to thank a number of friends and colleagues who have suffered through my musings and questions during the course of this project. Col. Chris Shoemaker, USA (Ret.), assisted greatly through one difficult period. Several colleagues have also been involved in discussions about the study methodology and in the reading of drafts. Their suggestions have immeasurably improved the final product. In this regard, I would like to thank Larry Loveless, Andrew Fulton, Lara Henry, and Dr. Jonathan Chanis.

Several individuals from within the biodefense community have also assisted greatly in this work. In particular, I would like to thank William C. Patrick III and Joel McCleary. Several others have been instrumental, but they wish to remain anonymous.

Into the Abyss

The gravest danger our Nation faces lies at the crossroads of radicalism and technology. Our enemies have openly declared that they are seeking weapons of mass destruction, and evidence indicates that they are doing so with determination. The United States will not allow these efforts to succeed.

White House, *National Security Strategy of the United States*, September 17, 2006

Much has been written about the potential for a bioterror attack. Since the 2001 anthrax attacks in the United States, the lore surrounding the potential for a catastrophic and deadly bioterror attack has become an integral part of the future national security landscape. As we consider the potential for such an attack, several questions come to mind: Where would terrorists obtain the biological material for use in an attack? Would they be able to process the material in a meaningful way so it could be dispensed effectively and efficiently? Do biological weapons have the significant capability often attributed to them? Would there be any signs either during the weapons development or during dispersal that we could target? Do we have the necessary response capability? Finally, would we be ready? The following fictional scenario will begin to frame some of these difficult questions:

The year 2020, Underground Revolutionary Front (URF) Headquarters, Houston, Texas. The URF's goal is the destruction of the institutions of global governance, causing national governments to fail and international systems such as the United Nations (UN) to demonstrate their fecklessness in the face of a global crisis. In pursuit of their goals, the URF examined a wide variety of possible attack scenarios. They had many targets from which to choose: they could attack the seats of government power, or military forces to demonstrate their ability to strike the base of power. They could attack shopping malls and financial institutions for their psychological impact. Whichever target was selected, their attacks would be timed to inflict the maximum number of casualties, have great symbolic effect, and strike fear in the hearts of governments and people.

While their objectives were clear, the question always came back to how to perpetrate such an attack. They could use conventional capabilities such as assault rifles and explosives, but that seemed so mundane. Sure, this type of attack could inflict tens or even hundreds of casualties in a very short period, but the attackers would undoubtedly be killed, too. With the antiterrorist countermeasures that had been built into government office buildings, the likelihood of being able get into position and launch this type of assault effectively was greatly diminished in the almost twenty years since the events of 9/11.

What about the use of weapons of mass destruction (WMDs)? Would WMDs be possible? Nuclear weapons would be nearly impossible to acquire. The Nunn-Lugar Cooperative Threat Reduction (CTR) program had been highly successful in containing the weapons and fissile material from the former Soviet Union. Even the use of crude radiological devices was problematic. The signature made it impossible to accumulate a large quantity of radiological material, even for use in a "dirty bomb." And such an attack would be highly inefficient and difficult to predict the effects with any certainty. The best they could hope for from this type of attack would be to make a radiological cocktail that caused a significant decontamination effort. Still, the amount of material needed and the likelihood of a meaningful attack made this type of assault less desirable.

Chemical weapons would certainly be a possibility. Many necessary precursor chemicals would be easy to acquire. Even crude weapons such as chlorine gas can have a significant disruptive effect. Chemical weapons effects are reasonably predictable based on factors such as the type of chemical, method of dispersal, and meteorological conditions at the time of release. They can certainly cause a large numbers of casualties, but such an attack requires a considerable amount of material to have a reasonable effect. Still, the laws governing commercial chemical precursors had been significantly tightened, spearheaded by the U.S. Department of Homeland Security (DHS) and in conjunction with the chemical industry, which was initially skeptical of the efforts.

What about biological weapons? Now, that could be interesting. A little bit of material can have a significant effect, but the material is hard to work with and unpredictable. It also degrades quickly in the environment and is highly sensitive to its surroundings. And there are so many types of germs one could use: which to choose? In the end, the URF would discover that, while there are many different pathogens, the selection for their purposes was limited by what was "available."

The URF leadership wanted to mount a catastrophic attack that would kill millions in several target countries. But this would require a highly contagious pathogen, dispersed in several locations around the world nearly simultaneously. Smallpox (*Variola major*) would be an ideal weapon with its high infectivity and lethality, but unfortunately it was "taken off the market" with the eradication of the disease in the late 1970s; the only known virus stores are in the United States and Russia under tight control. What about Ebola, the horrific disease introduced to the world in 1976, which killed with extraordinary efficiency with a 90 percent mortality rate? This pathogen would be difficult to acquire, given the remote locations where it occurs naturally and the time between outbreaks. It would also be too dangerous to handle and likely result in the death of URF members attempting to process and weaponize the virus. While the URF could live with these acceptable losses, even one Ebola death would likely alert the government of the impending attack.

In the end, the URF would decide to use an ancient germ that was well known in the history of humankind and the world of disease— the plague. Two pandemics provide ample evidence of its potential: Justinian's Plague in the middle of the 6th century killed more than 100 million people, and the Black Death in the middle 14th century killed between a fourth to more than half of the population.

For the attack, the URF decide to employ the *Yersinia pestis* bacteria in an aerosol, causing the pneumonic form of the disease, which is highly efficient for human-to-human transmission. The URF also decided to let the bacteria travel on the global transportation networks by dispersing the pathogen in multiple locations—they had thought about this technique since reading about a bioterror exercise—Atlantic Storm—in which smallpox virus was dispersed in six locations—five transportation hubs and a market—to begin the deadly journey around the globe.

Plague is attractive as a biological weapon for a number of reasons. It is a naturally occurring disease that appears with some frequency around the world, although, of course, it is more likely to appear in underdeveloped areas. The primary sources of the disease in humans are infected fleas and contact with the droppings of infected rats. It has a short incubation period of one to three days, requires immediate treatment within twenty-four hours, resembles the common influenza in the early stages, and is considered to cause 100 percent mortality for the pneumonic variant of the disease if treatment with antibiotics does not occur soon after exposure.

Despite plague being a naturally occurring pathogen, there was still the question of where to get the original bacteria. A good biological warfare (BW) weapon begins with a good biological agent, and not all the bacteria are equally effective in causing disease or even in allowing human-to-human transmission. Collecting and processing naturally occurring samples would involve considerable expertise and testing, carrying its own risk. If the URF could get "good bacteria" from which to begin their program, they were confident they could care for and prepare it for dispersal. At least they could eliminate some of the risk by starting with a high-quality pathogen.

It was good fortune that the URF had its "headquarters" in Houston close to the University of Texas Medical Branch (UTMB) in Galveston, one of only a handful of BSL-4 (biosafety level 4) facilities in the country able to handle the most deadly pathogens known to humankind, including those designated as Category A agents by the Centers for Disease Control and Prevention (CDC). It was also fortunate that the effects of Hurricane Ike that had scored a direct hit on Galveston in 2008 were still being felt almost ten years later, because it was this fact that caused one of the scientists at UTMB to allow himself to become an unwilling participant in the most significant and terrifying bioterror attack in world history.

The relationship between a URF terrorist and the UTMB scientist began as a "chance" encounter on the tennis court. The scientist, "Sam," was pleased to have found a good doubles partner, "George," who also shared his vocation in biotechnology. George was not a bacteriologist, but was working on setting up a series of national laboratories. As their friendship grew, they began to discuss their work. George was "surprised" to learn Sam worked on plague, and had lots of questions for Sam. George was "fascinated" by the history of the disease and continued to extract more information. Sam was eager to talk about what he knew. He had a passion for his work, and it was not often he had a chance to carry on this sort of a dialogue with someone who was so interested.

Providing some basic biosafety information and laboratory security material to his friend seemed quite innocuous at the time, but would have dire consequences later. Over the course of several years, George continued to gain Sam's trust and confidence and their discussions grew more candid. By the time George asked for a sample of *Yersinia pestis* bacteria, Sam was in too deep. He had already been photographed providing information to George, some of which would likely be judged to be sensitive. There would be an investigation, and Sam would undoubtedly lose his job. Besides, there was another issue of concern: George had been helpful in assisting Sam with an issue involving a citation Sam received for driving while intoxicated. Sam had been surprised how much pull George had with the local police, and it had been fortuitous that George had pulled on to the scene just after Sam had failed the field sobriety test.

Once the material had been acquired, several URF members with basic laboratory skills were able to grow the bacteria in sufficient quantities for the attack scenarios they had planned. Using standard centrifuges and commercially available drying equipment, the team began the task of readying the deadly pathogen for release.

Through similar good fortune, George's fellow URF compatriot had a relationship with a person with expertise in aerosol techniques. George was able to fashion an aerosol system attached to a small canister filled with *Yersinia pestis* bacteria. The courtesy drivers at the five international airports, including three in the United States, did not know they were spreading plague as they drove their golf carts throughout the airport. As a symbolic measure, attacks were also launched against the U.S. Capitol and the UN's headquarters in New York.

The attacks were launched nearly simultaneously in early November, the beginning of the yearly influenza season, and the initial cases went misdiagnosed as the seasonal influenza. It was not until a number of the first victims died that suspicions were raised. In fact, even after a large number of deaths, the press continued to report a particularly virulent influenza that season. Eventually, the national and global epidemiological systems sensed that a bioattack had occurred. However, this realization came on Day 4 after 10,000 deaths in thirty-five nations. More than 200,000 people were infected and several hundred thousand others had been exposed in the first few days following the attack. Unfortunately, the worst was yet to come.

Because pneumonic plague had been released within the transportation network, anyone traveling during the attacks or immediately thereafter was potentially exposed. Global public health authorities began advising all passengers displaying influenza-like symptoms to get medical evaluation and treatment. As the disease spread, other forms of transportation such as buses and trains became conveyances for the spread of the plague. Travelers took the disease home and spread it to family members who took the disease to their schools, churches, and places of work.

The global, bioterrorist-caused pandemic continued for months, with cases popping up periodically during this time. In all, 500,000 people died worldwide with 50 million infected. The outcome would have been much worse but for new treatments, particularly New Age antibiotics, that worked to reduce mortality and morbidity.

As with all major catastrophic events, a number of lessons were learned, resulting in changes in the public health and biosurveillance systems. For many, these lessons came much too late.

Could such a scenario occur? What does it demonstrate about potential proliferation possibilities and attack scenarios? And what does it say about the nexus between globalization, terrorism, and biotechnology? This illustration represents a single scenario. However, any number of scenarios employing different pathogens, methods of transmission, and points of attack are possible. The goal of this book is to examine the potential for such a bioterror attack and to expose some of the important seams in biodefense today. While the problems we face in biodefense are not intractable, they are certainly complex and highly challenging, as we will see.

The confluence of globalization, terrorism, and biotechnology presents a real and dangerous threat to humankind. Each individual component is experiencing unprecedented—even exponential—growth. When examined collectively, they present a potentially serious challenge to U.S. national security, as well as to our scientific, government, and cultural systems.

Today, civilizations, nations, and peoples are increasingly connecting, mixing, and clashing. The catalyst for these increased interactions is globalization, resulting from advances in communications, transportation, and information technologies. Goods, services, and people traverse great distances and connect, even across national borders, with increasing regularity. Events occurring halfway around the world can and do affect our daily lives. Physical distance as a measure has lost much of its relevance, and has been replaced with virtual proximity. We know more about the world and about each other now than people have at any time in history.

All of this connectedness places great strains on our nation's security. The relationships that have defined the world since the development of the concept of the nation-state have evolved and, in a real sense, eroded. While the world has gotten smaller and faster, the systems we have relied on for our national security have seen little change. Such is the case with the National Security Act of 1947, which established many of the key mechanisms designed to deal with the Cold War world emerging at the conclusion of World War II. The same is true for multinational organizations such as the UN that were specifically created as international fora for states to resolve differences and promote the common good. The problem is not that the nation-state has become irrelevant in this new highly globalized and connected world, but rather that many of the structures and mechanisms applicable within a state-to-state dialogue have little relevance in the state-to-transnational actor (or terrorist) dialogue. And such is clearly the case with regard to gaining an understanding of the likelihood of a terrorist using biological weapons to attack the United States.

In this 21st-century environment, we find a greater variety of threats and vulnerabilities as well as a wider array of actors prepared to work against U.S. interests. Transnational and even subnational entities have emerged with interests, goals, objectives, and even capabilities that heretofore have been the exclusive purview of the nation-state. This diffusion of power comes at a time when new transnational organizations, including terrorist groups, are arising. These organizations have demonstrated global reach, nefarious intentions, and increasing capabilities to act against the interests of the United States and its allies.

Evidence also suggests terrorists are looking for new, innovative, and more-destructive capabilities to promote their causes and attack those state and nonstate actors they believe are threatening to them and their ideals. We are witnessing a new wave of terrorism, terrorism that has become increasingly violent and increasingly transnational. The U.S. embassy bombings in Africa, the 9/11 terrorists attacks against the United States, and the London and Madrid train bombings provide ample evidence of these new and disturbing trends.

As with globalization and terrorism, biotechnology is also experiencing great change. In this field, in fact, change is arguably more dramatic. Many key technologies are experiencing annual growth rates of 400 percent. And many of these new technologies are emerging and proliferating before their full impact is understood, and well before laws and policies are in place to ensure their use for peaceful purposes. Entire new areas of study are emerging that show great promise for humankind, as well as for the potential for their misuse. One such example is genomics, which officially started with the Human Genomic Project in 1989. It took that project an entire decade to decode the human genome. Later, using these new capabilities, it took only three weeks to decode the severe acute respiratory syndrome (SARS) virus in 2003 at the height of the SARS pandemic. The proliferation of this knowledge has provided ever-increasing opportunities for scientific breakthroughs as well as for employing biological technology for less-than-noble purposes. Consider, for instance, the potential for employing this technology for the manipulation of a pathogen to alter its virulence or improve its stability when deployed as a weapon.

In examining the issue of the potential for a significant bioterror attack in the future, two main schools of thought prevail. One school argues the threat of a biological attack perpetrated by a terrorist is imminent and the time to prepare is now. The other argues the threat has been exaggerated and the focus of our efforts and resources on bioterrorism detracts from other more-pressing and even greater threats. The purpose of this volume is to confront directly the question of the potential for a terrorist or group of terrorists to conduct an attack against the United States using biological weapons.

Bioterror has become an extremely topical and highly charged issue since the anthrax attacks in the United States of October and November 2001, now commonly called the Amerithrax attacks. Entire lines of business and courses of study have evolved as a result. Since 2001, more than 150 degree programs have been developed in emergency management at major universities, and almost 100 degree and certificate programs have been developed in homeland security. Other courses of study in biodefense have emerged that focus exclusively on the threat in this area. The United States has spent more than $56 billion on biodefense initiatives since 2001. Pronouncements and assertions based on wild exaggerations and minimalist judgments are equally abundant and cover both ends of the spectrum. In truth, neither brings us any closer to understanding the difficult problem that biodefense—specifically bioterror—poses.

In all likelihood, the danger lies somewhere in the middle between the two extremes, but how can we be sure? The question that guides this analysis revolves around gaining an understanding of the facts that drive this issue and ultimately might lead to realistic assessments about the likelihood of a bioterror attack and the actual danger we might face from such an attack. However, this analysis is less about predicting future behavior with any certainty than it is about understanding three issues: (1) the framework within which this globalization-terrorism-biotechnology nexus continues to allow for more dangerous capabilities to proliferate, (2) the motivations that would drive each of the actors, and (3) the potential outcomes with regard to the use of BW by terrorists.

Several important trends will frame the issue of the potential for a future bioterror attack. Globalization will continue at or above the current pace, and more people around the world will feel its effects, both good and bad. The erosion of the nation-state will have serious consequences, and resulting instability and conflict—including terrorism—will continue to present a serious challenge, albeit not an existential threat to the United States. However, driven by the desire to gain greater visibility and promote their causes, terrorists will continue to increase the number and lethality of their attacks.

Terrorists will act in ways they consider rational, even if this rationality is not obvious to outsiders. They will maintain a core *raison d'être* that will propel their actions and modulate their behavior to positively influence their constituencies. This will be very important, as in the case of moderating behavior. Terrorists generally will be disinclined to engage in large-scale attacks with large numbers of civilian casualties (i.e., death, disease, and morbidity greater than one thousand people) because this would tend to negatively influence their support base. This is not meant to imply that some terrorists, perhaps those that are highly insular, would not desire to conduct a mass casualty attack. Rather, the implication is that deterrence as a concept still has application, even with hardened, determined terrorists.

There has been and will continue to be an increase in biotechnological capabilities that will allow for greater access to potentially dangerous capabilities and knowledge that represents an important lowering of thresholds. This proliferation has serious implications on the potential for a major bioterror attack. This means that, as the capabilities for a terrorist to conduct a bioterror attack are becoming more readily available, we must look for other ways to positively influence terrorists to moderate their behavior with regard to biological weapons. In other words, we must affect their intentions, making the cost-benefit calculus one-sided to convince the potential bioterrorist that use of these types of capabilities represents a threat to their existence that will not be allowed under any circumstances.

In this regard, counterthresholds (in both capabilities and motivations) exist that will interact to make the potential for a large-scale bioterror attack not particularly likely in the near future. Just as we have observed with regard to state use of WMDs, in particular biological weapons, a threshold exists that tends to moderate behavior. The historical precedents concerning terrorist use of BW suggest a similar, albeit not absolute, threshold for nonstate actors. Additionally, developing capabilities for such an attack will prove to be technically challenging for terrorists for the foreseeable future and not in keeping with their goals and objectives. Therefore, with the increased availability of knowledge and capabilities, the potential for small-scale attacks (i.e., death, disease, and morbidity of fewer than one thousand people) will be very real. However, mounting a large-scale BW attack using advanced capabilities would present a number of challenges that would be difficult to overcome in the near-term. Therefore, we should not consider bioterror to be an existential threat at this time.

Over time, however, the technical hurdles will diminish and the tendency toward larger, more-spectacular attacks will likely increase the potential for a large-scale bioterror event. While predicting such an attack with certainty is not possible, we must understand the proliferation of technology, increasing connectedness of the world, and a propensity toward more-spectacular attacks suggests the probability of such a large-scale bioterror attack will increase in the future.

An infinite number of scenarios employing different pathogens, methods of transmission, and points of attack are possible. The goal of this book is to examine the potential for a bioterror attack and to expose some of the important seams in biodefense today. While the problems we face in biodefense are not intractable, they are certainly complex and highly challenging.

CHAPTER ONE

The 21st-Century Environment

Globalization

Globalization is the emergence of a global society in which economic, political, environmental, and cultural events in one part of the world quickly come to have significance for people in other parts of the world. It is the result of advances in communication, transportation, and information technologies.[1]

Some may question why examination of the potential for a bioterrorist attack should begin with a discussion of globalization. For the author, the logical linkages are so strong that separating globalization from terrorism and biotechnology would be impossible; to do so would result perhaps in an irrelevant distinction. It is from this perspective that our investigation begins.

A broad definition, such as the one presented above, is likely to come as a surprise to many who see globalization as a relatively new phenomenon and more related to advances in information technology than to communications and transportation. However, this definition serves as a reminder that globalization is measured in thousands of years and not just in the past several decades of the Information Age. The pre–Industrial Age saw a progression of globalization in linear terms. Increases were evolutionary and the pace could be characterized as steady and modest. A woman born in 1650 who died in 1700 likely saw improvements, yet few startling or revolutionary changes that could be considered life altering, in her lifetime. Most of the world lived in what could be considered an agrarian society. Few lived in cities; most tended the land or hunted and gathered in a subsistence form of existence. An average man would likely live his entire life within a single fifty-mile radius, never venturing far from home. There were historical examples of exploration and conflict in distant lands, but these involved a very small percentage of the total population.

The gradual pace of the pre–Industrial Age period was replaced with an exponential progression in technology, communications, and transportation during the industrial age. In the 240 years or so from the 1750s to the 1990s, humankind went from travel by foot and horse to space travel and even virtual travel through the use of video teleconferencing. Regular movement across the globe through commercial air travel, starting in the 1950s, allowed people to cross and even move between continents in hours instead of days. Indeed, during the past fifty years, the rate of change has been more dramatic than at any other time in human history.

This globalization, however, has not just affected technology, communications, and transportation. Many second- and third-order repercussions have resulted from this movement of peoples and cultures. Disease is one of the areas that has been and will continue to be impacted in dramatic ways by globalization. Just as people move around the world with increasing regularity, so too do bacteria and viruses, exposing more and more people to exotic diseases, and, perhaps more important, exposing populations to pathogens and vectors they may be unable to combat with their naïve immune systems. The worst yellow fever epidemic in the United States, for example, occurred in the late 19th century. It resulted from a globalization chain that began with ships from Africa carrying a deadly cargo of *Aedes aegypti* mosquitoes infected with a highly virulent strain of the virus. The ships docked in Cuba and subsequently transferred their yellow fever "cargo" to other ships and crews bound for the United States. The failure to quarantine and decontaminate these ships upon their arrival in the United States allowed infected crews to enter the country accompanied by the infected mosquitoes. The result was catastrophic and nearly destroyed the population of Memphis, Tennessee, in 1878. Ultimately, the epidemic claimed the lives of 5,000 of the city's 40,000 inhabitants, and displaced another 15,000 as they fled to avoid the seemingly unstoppable disease.

Given the pervasiveness of globalization, it should come as no surprise that many recent studies have attempted to understand this force and the challenges and opportunities that will be faced by nations, societies, and peoples in a globalized 21st-century world. One such study, "Mapping the Global Future," is a report from the National Intelligence Council's 2020 Project. It was prepared based on consultations with "nongovernmental experts throughout the world." In assessing the impact of globalization, the report develops several important trends that serve as harbingers of the effects of globalization. The study team concluded the following:

1. We see globalization—growing interconnectedness reflected in the expanded flows of information, technology, capital, goods, services, and people throughout the world—as an overarching "mega-trend," a force so ubiquitous that it will substantially shape all the other major trends in the world of 2020.

2. The world economy is likely to continue growing impressively. By 2020, it is projected to be about 80 percent larger than it was in 2000, and average per capita income will be roughly 50 percent higher. Of course, there will be cyclical ups and downs and periodic financial or other crises, but this basic growth trajectory has powerful momentum behind it.

3. Yet the benefits of globalization won't be global. Rising powers will see exploiting the opportunities afforded by the emerging global marketplace as the best way to assert their great power status on the world stage. Those left behind in the developing world may resent China and India's rise, especially if they feel squeezed by their growing dominance in key sectors of the global marketplace. And large pockets of poverty will persist even in "winner" countries.

4. The greatest benefits of globalization will accrue to countries and groups that can access and adopt new technologies. Indeed, a nation's level of technological achievement generally will be defined in terms of its investment in integrating and applying the new, globally available technologies—whether the technologies are acquired through a country's own basic research or from technology leaders.

5. The expected next revolution in high technology involving the convergence of nano-, bio-, information and materials technology could further bolster China and India's prospects.

6. More firms will become global, and those operating in the global arena will be more diverse, both in size and origin, more Asian and less Western in orientation. Such corporations, encompassing the current, large multinationals, will be increasingly outside the control of any one state and will be key agents of change in dispersing technology widely, further integrating the world economy, and promoting economic progress in the developing world.

7. An expanding global economy will increase demand for many raw materials, such as oil. Total energy consumed probably will rise by about 50 percent in the next two decades compared to a 34 percent expansion from 1980–2000, with a greater share provided by petroleum.[2]

While most of these trends can be considered positive or at least neutral, there is another side to globalization—a "dark side"—that cannot be ignored. Globalization can be thought of as "super-sizing" global requirements that potentially will have dramatic effects on peoples, cultures, and nations. Demands for energy will continue to increase as nations wrestle to develop their economies and capacities. The same is true for populations where globalization, coupled with advances in health and medicine, has contributed to increased longevity, placing an even greater strain on the planet's resources and the social systems that must sustain these growing *and* aging populations. Information is also in ever-increasing demand. Twenty-four-hour-a-day news channels beam information across the globe, depicting both the good and the bad with increasing regularity and, perhaps more importantly, with few editorial constraints. The number of Internet users is expanding exponentially with demand exceeding capacity. Information is a readily available commodity.

"Mapping the Global Future" also provides some interesting commentary with regard to this "dark side" of globalization, and prospects into the year 2020.

- The nation-state will continue to be the dominant unit of the global order, but economic globalization and the dispersion of technologies, especially information technologies, will place enormous new strains on governments.
- Even as most of the world gets richer, globalization will profoundly shake up the status quo—generating enormous economic, cultural, and consequently political convulsions.
- Weak governments, lagging economies, religious extremism, and youth bulges will align to create a perfect storm for internal conflict in certain regions.
- The likelihood of great power conflict escalating into total war in the next 15 years is lower than at any time in the past century, unlike during previous centuries when local conflicts sparked world wars.
- Countries without nuclear weapons—especially in the Middle East and Northeast Asia—might decide to seek them as it becomes clear that their neighbors and regional rivals are doing so [for their deterrent value].[3]

If globalization in the Industrial Age was about power and production, globalization in the Information Age is about reach and velocity. It is a real and powerful force that cannot be contained. Even if we wanted to reverse its effects, any actions taken to do so would only temporarily halt this juggernaut. In this globalized world, requirements drive the development of capabilities and in turn the new capabilities create new demands or requirements. The cycle continues at an ever increasing rate with no end in sight. Inevitably, this leads to competition. Competition fuels tensions, which in turn fuels conflict. Sometimes this clash is waged state to state, while at other times it is waged as asymmetric conflict involving nonstate and even transnational actors.

Terrorism

> Over the past three decades, terrorists have multiplied the number of their victims by an order of magnitude every 15 years. In the 1970's, the bloodiest incidents involved tens of fatalities. By the '90's, hundreds were killed and the incidents increased. In 2001, the number reached the thousands, and today we fear scenarios in which tens of thousands might die.
>
> BRIAN JENKINS, RAND[4]

In analyzing the likelihood of a bioterror event, gaining an understanding of the potential principal actor involved in perpetrating the act is essential. Several questions seem to frame most discussions of terrorism: What is terrorism? Are terrorists rational people or mass murderers? Why do groups and individuals turn to terrorism? What is the future of terrorists and terrorism? Is terrorism as a tactic on the rise? If so, when will it ever wane? These fundamental issues are critically important to assessing the likelihood of a future bioterrorist attack.

Inevitably, the first major issue one confronts when examining the topic of terrorism is the lack of an agreed definition. This may seem a frivolous complaint until one realizes that not having a definition contributes to incoherent policies in the United States as well as in other countries. In many cases, when attempting to understand or define a term, it can be useful to examine the history of the issue to gain a better understanding. In this case, our examination does not provide much clarity. Whether one considers the perpetrators of a violent act as criminals, insurgents, freedom fighters, or terrorists is an important issue with broad implications for international cooperation, law enforcement, and national security. In this regard, some of the confusion has its roots in the rather long and meandering history of terrorism.

The term "terrorist" can be traced to the French Revolution, during which the *régime de la terreur*, or reign of terror, had a positive connotation: it was used to define a "people's movement" to reestablish order following the uprisings of 1789. Ironically, these foundations were closely aligned with the ideals of "virtue and democracy," and the actions of the *régime de la terreur* were "neither random nor indiscriminate as terrorism is often portrayed today, but was organized, deliberate, and systematic."[5]

The Industrial Revolution gave rise to a new era of terrorism. The socioeconomic changes of this period led to a new brand of terrorism born of the "alienation and exploitive conditions of nineteenth-century capitalism."[6] During this period, one of its leaders, Carlo Piscane led a revolt against Bourbon rule, believing that violence was necessary for gaining visibility for the cause and gaining popular support.

Over time, terrorism evolved. Around the turn of the 20th century, a series of assassinations, including the assassinations of Czar Alexander II in 1881 and of President William McKinley in 1901, provide examples of this evolution. The perpetrators of these acts were anarchists with an ideology bent on using assassination as a means of achieving revolutionary change. At approximately the same time, a new influence was emerging, one in which "the motivation was neither anti-monarchial nor anarchist, but nationalist and separatist." In fact, on the eve of the First World War, "terrorism still retained its revolutionary connotations."[7] By the 1930s, terrorism was used less to depict revolutionary or separatist movements than it was to describe the use of force by totalitarian states such as Germany, Italy, and Russia against their populations.

During World War II, terrorism regained the revolutionary connotations most typically associated with it today. The 1960s and 1970s saw a continuation of terrorism in a revolutionary context, the 1980s saw terrorism as a means for "destabilizing the West as part of a global conspiracy," and the 1990s saw a blurring of the term with narcoterrorism and the "gray area phenomena." The subcategorization of this "gray area" was meant for "highlighting the increasingly fluid and variable nature of subnational conflict in the post–Cold War era," and terrorism came to be seen as a threat of nonstate actors to the stability of nations.[8]

While this history explains terrorism's evolution, some experts today simply divide terrorism into two categories—old and new—with the major distinction between them the use of indiscriminate violence. So-called old terrorists shied away from the use of indiscriminate violence because to do so tended to "reduce their claims of legitimacy and alienate them from supporters thereby reducing their access to new recruits and funding."[9] In contrast, new terrorists display a willingness to use excessive indiscriminate violence. One author comments, "Some believe that the willingness to use extreme violence shows that new terrorists do not have an organization or state sponsor to protect, so they see no reason to limit their violence as they do not fear a backlash."[10] A further difference is that old terrorism was largely secular, while new terrorism is increasingly seen as being linked to religious fanaticism.

Today, there is a pervasive feeling among many experts that terrorism can be broken down into pre-9/11 and post-9/11 terrorism. The writings as well as the rhetoric of the political leaders clearly demonstrate this discontinuity. Immediately in the aftermath of the attacks, President George W. Bush declared, "This is a new kind of evil . . . [and we] will rid the world of the evildoers. . . . Our war on terror begins with al-Qaeda, but it does not end there."[11] The statement highlights this discontinuity. The declaration of a global war on terror (GWOT) served to underscore this new type of conflict.

The question of state sponsorship raises an interesting issue, requiring some additional consideration and ultimately factors heavily into the later analysis concerning the potential for a bioterror attack. In the modern era of terrorism, we have witnessed numerous terrorist organizations that have received state support and at times have functioned as proxies for a state. For example, a number of states (including Iran, Lebanon, and Syria, to name a few) have provided support to Hezbollah, although the support has not been constant and has evolved based on the Hezbollah issues of the day. One overarching unifying theme has been the desire to see or bring about the destruction of Israel. It was Hezbollah that was attributed with the suicide bombing of the U.S. Marines barracks in Lebanon in 1983 that killed 241 people.

With regard to an al-Qaeda–like threat—such as that which has become the post-9/11 focus of attention—one observer notes that to operate as it did prior to 9/11, al-Qaeda would need the sponsorship of a state, but also cautions, "[T]here is no reason to think that Al-Qaeda and the International Islamic Front can't change their way of functioning so that the services of a state are no longer critical."[12]

Given this meandering history of terrorism, it should come as little surprise that establishing an absolute definition of terrorism has been elusive and the source of great debate both within the United States and internationally. The manifestation of this lack of a definition has led to considerable confusion and disagreement. The result is that terms such as "guerillas," "insurgents," and "terrorists" are used almost interchangeably.

This is unhelpful and confuses the issue. To confuse the issue even further, some have argued that terrorism can be considered in almost the same category as violent crime rather than in the same category as warfare.

Another aspect of terrorism important for gaining an understanding of the potential for a bioterrorist attack is the question of rationality. Several important considerations assist in understanding this issue. For instance, what may appear as indiscriminate violence to victims, the global community and governments, likely has a clear purpose. In fact, terrorists use violent means and conduct lethal attacks while, in their minds, working to achieve rational objectives.

Contributing to the question of rationality and in an effort to gain a greater understanding of the mind of the terrorists, many theories have been proffered. They range from the psychopathological, which begins from the standpoint that the terrorists are insane, to the rational choice theory, which allows that the pursuit of terrorism is a choice made to achieve goals and objectives, to sociological theories, which attempt to explain terrorists based on the conditions under which they live.[13]

Some have taken a less complicated approach and ask simply whether poverty and despair are the underlying causes of terrorism. Others have asserted that the general oppression of people—most recently Islamic peoples—or social injustice and inequality have led to increased militancy in Islam. While the cause of this increased militancy continues to be debated, the overarching question of the rationality of terrorism seems to have waned, with most now recognizing the actions of terrorists as rational at some level.

Jessica Stern's book, *Terror in the Name of God: Why Religious Militants Kill*, is one such definitive work on the subject, and aims to understand the causes and organizational dynamics of terrorism. Based on her interviews with terrorists, she has catalogued a wide variety of actors involved in both domestic and international terrorism activities. She has identified alienation, humiliation, demographics, history, and territory, among others, as causes of terrorism. What emerges from her book is a vivid picture of highly motivated and determined individuals and groups that have reached a point where resorting to violence is perceived to be the only or at least the best course of action to achieve their desired outcomes.

Stern's observations are directly related to understanding the potential for large-scale terror attacks. She describes clearly the importance of maintaining the ideological and financial support base for their activities. While large-scale attacks are spectacular and gain publicity, they can also be detrimental if the acts are perceived by supporters to be directed against inappropriate targets or to be causing indiscriminate casualties. Her description of terrorists "fighting for market share in the same way that firms or humanitarian organizations do,"[14] developing mission sets that change over time, building resilient networks, and fighting to recruit members at all levels of the organization, stands in stark contrast to the notion that terrorists are simply indiscriminate mass murderers.[15]

Another terrorism expert, Louise Richardson, in her book *What Terrorists Want: Understanding the Enemy, Containing the Threat*, examines the issue of rationality of action. She concludes that terrorists want to achieve the "three Rs: revenge (for perceived injustices), renown (the attention of the world), and reaction (disproportionate enough to perpetuate a sense of moral outrage)."[16] This is an important characterization, in the sense that it again confirms an underlying rationale for terrorists' actions and motivations and suggests that an overreliance on violence against terrorists could have the unintended consequence of causing a greater desire for revenge and perhaps even a greater desire for more violent and disproportionate actions by the terrorists. It also provides insights into the thinking that could cause terrorists to want to resort to WMDs.

The previous discussion was meant to establish authoritatively that terrorism is a rational act and that we must attempt to understand this rationality to have any hope of dealing with terrorism or those that seek to employ violent means to achieve their goals and objectives. In fact, in "Rational Extremism: Understanding Terrorism in the Twenty-First Century," David Lake attempts to come to grips with this idea of rationalism.[17] In a novel approach, he suggests there might be some way to alter the bargaining range such that there would be some common ground that would define a range of outcomes acceptable both to the terrorists and to the object of their rage. Think of a continuum that includes a range of possible outcomes. At the polar ends are the most extreme positions of the parties, in this case the terrorist at one end and the U.S. government at the other. The terrorist wants to promote his cause and achieve a set of objectives using a variety of means. This may entail the use of tactics ranging from political discourse to extreme violence. At the other polar end, the U.S. government wants to promote peace and prosperity, ensure the security of its citizens and people, and prevent terrorists attacks and violent demonstrations. The question is whether there would be a range of mutual behavior deemed acceptable for both parties.

Of course, the intent is not to enter into face-to-face negotiations with terrorists, but rather to identify potential areas where accommodations which could be made or situations mitigated that would lead to a reduction in tensions and underlying causes that lead to terrorist attacks. This is a highly theoretical construct; the application of such a concept would undoubtedly be difficult and perhaps impractical. Still, the idea of identifying potential risk-reduction techniques similar to what was done in the Cold War between the United States and the Soviet Union is intriguing.

Another important issue that contributes to the question of the potential for a bioterror attack is related to the structure of terrorist cells and their support base. The U.S. Army Training and Doctrine Command (TRADOC) published "A Military Guide to Terrorism in the Twenty-First Century" in August 2007 that depicts a four-level, pyramidal organizational structure with leaders, operational cadre, active supporters, and passive supporters. While these four levels are depicted as distinct, in reality things are not nearly so clear. Undoubtedly, movement occurs between the levels. For example, a sympathizer can take a more active role providing support to the level of active supporter for a particular operation, but then, following that event, return to the role of sympathizer or passive supporter.[18] It is this structure and the need to maintain support that can serve as an important moderating influence against the use of biological weapons. As alluded to previously, the implication is that a fine line exists between employing levels of violence that could diminish support or "just enough" violence (or activity) to gain visibility for the terrorists' causes.

The effect of terrorism on the United States' psyche and national policies is undisputable. The question we might ask is whether this fixation is reasonable and prudent, given 9/11 and what we have seen and experienced since. Today, it is virtually impossible to find a U.S. security policy document that does not address the terrorist threat. Both the National Security Strategy (NSS) of the United States and the National Strategy for Homeland Security (NSHS) feature terrorism as a significant focus. Entire organizations solely charged with addressing the issue, such as the National Counterterrorism Center (NCTC), have emerged. Billions of dollars have been spent to analyze the issue and mitigate the threat. So, with all this attention, perhaps the relevant questions are these: Have these efforts been worthwhile? and Are they based on the realities we are facing?

As we consider the potential for a bioterror attack, we see several troubling trends emerging in the post-9/11 environment. These trends are likely to shape terrorism for the foreseeable future. We are witnessing a networking of terrorists using technology to become allies of convenience and not necessarily ideologically aligned. Under the leadership of Osama bin Laden, al-Qaeda has become a sort of franchise. What is important about this trend, as will be discussed in Chapter 4, is that the potential for a large-scale bioterror attack is directly related to the support infrastructure and resources available to the potential perpetrators. In other words, we will see that the technical requirements associated with mounting a successful large-scale bioterror attack will be limited to a very small, well-financed, and unique subset of terrorist groups.

One such group that has expressed the desire to acquire WMDs and that has taken active steps in this regard is al-Qaeda, which is undergoing a troubling metamorphosis. Osama bin Laden's role as an operational leader of al-Qaeda has been eclipsed by his more prominent role as titular head of a global terrorist network. The loosely aligned subgroups may not have the same goals and objectives—other than a desire to attack the West and essentially reverse the effects of globalization—but they are willing to align to fight their common enemy.

The development of virtual networks by the terrorists has dramatically improved the efficiency and effectiveness of their organizations. It has also provided less opportunity for counterterrorist attacks on locations where large numbers of terrorists are likely to be hiding. Ever-increasing information technologies are "enabling the new terrorists to communicate covertly and to bridge distances more easily."[19] In short, the general trend toward the terrorists' use of information technologies has increased, and will likely continue to do so in the future.

Another general trend almost universally noted by terrorism experts is the use for nefarious purposes of technologies and capabilities designed for peaceful purposes and the benefit of humankind. The attacks of 9/11, using civilian airliners as missiles and their loaded fuel tanks as the payload, provide a vivid exclamation point for this assertion. The effect of this trend has been to increase the reach of the terrorist and his ability to launch coordinated attacks using these new technologies. The simultaneous attacks on the U.S. embassies in Tanzania and Kenya in 1998 provide another data point supporting this enhanced capability to conduct coordinated, complex attacks.

Attacks are also becoming more overt, with open warfare in some areas such as the Philippines, Iraq, and Afghanistan. In such regions, terrorists are acting and even organizing more like paramilitary forces than what we might traditionally think of as terrorist organizations. They now use strategies and tactics that are a mix of terrorist and conventional warfare capabilities, and adjust rapidly to evolving situations. In fact, in both Iraq and Afghanistan the distinction between terrorism and insurgency is virtually impossible to discern.

The London bombings and Madrid train bombings certainly provide evidence of a trend toward increased lethality and the sharing of capabilities. Tactics and techniques are migrating between organizations in terms of learning what works for one group and transplanting those tactics for use by another terrorist group. The U.S. military has seen this migration between Iraq and Afghanistan with deadly improvised explosive devices (IEDs), which have been used with great effect for remote attacks on convoys and soldiers.

Along with the migration of strategies and tactics, another troubling trend is the incorporation of advanced capabilities and weapons. One source notes, "[T]wo new approaches are particularly alarming to intelligence officials: efforts to use surface-to-air missiles and attempts to acquire chemical, nuclear, or biological material."[20] Other advanced systems are also being incorporated into terrorists' arsenals.

Examination of the statistics regarding terrorism can also be important for providing a context for understanding terrorism. In his 2002 book, *Terrorism, Asymmetric Warfare, and Weapons of Mass Destruction: Defending the U.S. Homeland*, Anthony Cordesman provides some telling statistics concerning terrorist attacks. The data he uses concentrate on the period from 1987 to 1999. In looking at many of the graphs and tables, one would likely draw erroneous conclusions and almost certainly a perception that does not appear to align to the current focus on terrorism. In one single measure, "Terrorist Incidents Involving Americans versus Total Incidents," Cordesman depicts trends in both measures as negative, indicating a reduction in the number of all terrorist attacks and those targeting Americans.[21] Of course, this data set does not include the 9/11 attacks or the London and Madrid bombings that have seemingly ushered in a new era, or at least a new highlighting of terrorism as one of the preeminent national security threats the United States faces today.

In one comparison, the U.S. Department of State (DOS) and RAND/ MIPT compiled data concerning terrorism fatalities are compared, providing some interesting differences. In Figure 1–1, international terrorism fatalities from 1968 to 2004 are depicted.[22] The disparity in the graphs demonstrates the data are highly sensitive to the definitions used, the incidents included, and the counting rules used.

The data demonstrate the yearly number of international fatalities resulting from terrorism averaged fewer than five hundred from 1973 to 1998, when the number spiked due to the embassy bombings in Africa in 1998, and the attacks of 9/11 in the United States in 2001. The data do not

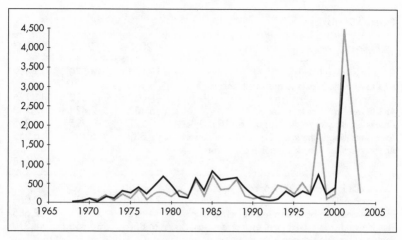

FIGURE 1-1 International Terrorist Fatalities, 1968–2004 (U.S. DOS RAND/MIPT data)

include the Madrid and London bombings in 2004 and 2005, respectively, which were also high-casualty attacks.[23]

DOS has included on their website enlightening information on terrorism attacks in 2005, 2006, and 2007. The rationale provided for only reporting these three data sets is that the metrics and definitions have been revised since 2004 and therefore a comparison between these three years and earlier periods would not be consistent. In compiling the information, the NCTC used a "panel of experts" and a broader definition of "terrorism," rather than the more narrow definition associated with "international terrorism" (Figure 1–2).[24]

Several important notes are in order. First and foremost, the data cannot be compared directly with the earlier DOS and RAND/MIPT databases depicted in Figure 1–1. The differences in definitions prohibit direct comparison. Additionally, operations in Iraq and Afghanistan tend to skew the data. For example, the numbers of terror attacks in Iraq and Afghanistan in 2007 were 6,212 and 1,127, respectively. Therefore, of the total 14,449 attacks in 2007, 7,339—or more than 50 percent—occurred in these war-torn nations.

A discussion of the moral justification for the conflicts and the issue of whether these attacks were related to the ongoing insurgency or for terrorists' motivations is well beyond the scope of this effort. In looking at the data, however, one must recognize that a large percentage of the data remains highly open to interpretation. Still, the data do indicate several important developments. The number of attacks per year is increasing. Additionally,

Overall Statistics

Attack Breakdown	2005	2006	2007
Terror attacks worldwide	11,156	14,570	14,499
Attacks resulting in at least one death, injury, or kidnapping	8,032	11,322	11,125
Attacks resulting in at least one death	5,137	7,434	7,258
Attacks resulting in the death of at least 10 people	227	295	355
Attacks resulting in the injury of at least one person	3,839	5,798	6,259
Attacks resulting in the kidnapping of at least one person	1,154	1,349	1,158
People killed, injured or kidnapped as a result of terror attacks	74,309	75,211	72,066
People worldwide killed as a result of terror attacks	14,616	20,872	22,685
People worldwide injured as a result of terror attacks	24,853	38,455	44,310
People worldwide kidnapped as a result of terror attacks	34,840	15,884	5,071

NCTC Key Observations

- Approximately 14,500 terrorist attacks occurred in various countries during 2007, resulting in over 22,000 deaths

- Compared to 2006, attacks remained approximately the same in 2007 while deaths rose by 1,800, a 9 percent increase from 2006's number

- Largest number of reported attacks and deaths occurred in Near East and South Asia, which accounted for about 87 percent of the 335 casualty attacks that killed 10 or more people—only 45 casualty attacks occurred in Africa, East Asia & Pacific, Europe & Eurasia, and Western Hemisphere

- Of the 14,499 reported attacks, almost 43 percent—about 6,200—occurred in Iraq where approximately 13,600 fatalities—60 percent of the worldwide total—were reported for 2007

- Violence against non-combatants in Africa, particularly related to attacks associated with turmoil in or near Somalia, Kenya, and Niger, rose 96 percent in 2007, totaling 835 attacks in comparison to approximately 425 attacks reported for 2006

- Fighting in Afghanistan intensified during 2007, resulting in 1,127 attacks and a 16 percent increase over the approximately 970 attacks reported for 2006

- The number of reported attacks in 2007 fell in the Western Hemisphere by 42 percent, in Europe and Eurasia by 8 percent, and in South Asia by almost 7 percent

FIGURE 1-2 Department of State Terrorism Statistics, 2005–2007

the number of killed and injured has greatly increased, although the impact on Americans is minimal. For example, in 2007, *only* nineteen Americans were killed, with two killed in Afghanistan and seventeen killed in Iraq.

The data also indicate that in most terrorist attacks—9,200 of the 14,449 attacks in 2007—64 percent could not be attributed to a particular person or group. A wide variety of means have been employed in these attacks, including guns, bombs, chemical weapons, and IEDs. The lethality of the attacks is also on the rise. This can be seen in the 50 percent increase in the number of attacks from 2005 to 2007 that have killed ten or more people. The targets also varied greatly and included schools, mosques, transportation networks, vehicles, and property.

In concluding this section, a fair assessment is that recent trends indicate a new era in terrorism has begun, arguably beginning with the bombing of the U.S. embassies in Kenya and Tanzania. The manifestation of the new terrorism has been an increase in violence, a willingness to target large symbolic targets, and a corresponding increase in global awareness and response to terrorism. The increased violence and number of attacks are cause for concern because they highlight an increased propensity toward high-profile, high-lethality terrorist events using a wide variety of available means. Still, it is important to understand that the total number of people killed, injured, or kidnapped as a result of terrorism is extremely low as a percent of the world population.

Another important question concerns the "lifecycle" of terrorist groups. This has implications on both our current war on terror as well as on the likelihood of future WMD attacks. A 2008 RAND study asks the interesting question, How do terror groups end? The study examines the history of eliminated terrorist groups in the hopes of learning lessons about the potential for countering al-Qaeda. In a particularly noteworthy portion of the analysis examining 268 eliminated terrorist groups worldwide, the study concludes 43 percent were eliminated through politics, 40 percent through policing, 10 percent through victory, and only 7 percent through military force. The study also found,

> [R]eligiously motivated terrorist groups took longer to eliminate than other groups but rarely achieved their objectives; no religiously motivated group achieved victory during the period studied; size significantly determined a group's fate. Groups exceeding 10,000 members were victorious more than 25 percent of the time, while victory was rare for groups below 1,000 members; and terrorist groups from upper-income

countries are much more likely to be left-wing or nationalist and much less likely to be motivated by religion.

Out of the 648 total groups active since 1968, 244 terrorist groups still existed in 2006, and 404 had ended. Of the 404 groups that ended, 136 (or 28 percent) ended because of splintering.[25]

The RAND study has important implications for our bioterror question. The fact that negotiation and law enforcement were able to eliminate 83 percent of terrorist organizations suggests understanding the objectives and rationality of the organizations can be an important part of managing and defeating terrorism. It also suggests the prosecution of the initial stages of the GWOT, which tended toward treating the issue as a military campaign, might have been relying too heavily on military efforts and outcomes.

Another important finding of the RAND study that ultimately contributes to our bioterror question concerns the linkages between the motivations of the terrorist group (i.e., policy change, territorial change, regime change, desire for empire, and social revolution) and the possibility of a settlement. Groups that seek less-drastic outcomes such as policy change were more likely to fall into the 83 percent that could be affected through law enforcement and negotiation, while those with more-drastic objectives were less likely to be dissuaded using these tools.

The RAND study also serves as a harbinger of the inherent difficulties in attempting to counter and ultimately eliminate the al-Qaeda terrorist threat. Al-Qaeda is a religiously based organization with more than 10,000 members, including all of the splinter groups, although actual membership is unknowable. This implies that this threat involving the hard-core elements of al-Qaeda will likely prove to be difficult to eradicate. Still, the RAND analysis does have some important implications for the splinter groups that fall under the larger al-Qaeda umbrella and may be more prone to be positively influenced by nonmilitary efforts.

Conclusions

The relationship between terrorism and globalization may be, in many regards, a "chicken or the egg" question: Did globalization cause terrorism, or was terrorism a new type of conflict enabled by globalization?

In a 2005 Congressional Research Service (CRS) study on terrorism, several important emerging trends concerning globalization and terrorism are noted. First, globalization has allowed terrorists to move toward a "loosely organized, self financed, international network of terrorists."[26]

Second, a strong trend toward religiously or ideologically based terrorism has emerged. Third, a new terrorist type with links between different organizations that may include "military training, funding, technology transfer or political advice" has been gaining prevalence.[27] The study also notes a troubling trend toward the proliferation of WMDs, while highlighting the effect globalization has on combating terrorism noting, "[e]fforts to combat terrorism are complicated by a global trend towards deregulation, open borders, and expanded democracies."[28] This study is particularly noteworthy because the methodology for compiling these CRS studies involves drawing heavily from U.S. government official reports, thus providing an overview of how the government interprets this particular issue.

Several principles concerning globalization and terrorism emerge from this chapter. First, halting globalization—or, in other words "unglobalizing"—is not a reasonable expectation. All trends strongly suggest further integration is more rather than less likely, and globalization will continue at an ever-increasing rate. This in turn leads us to conclude terrorism will continue to be a fixture on the global scene. However, this does not mean the terrorism of today will remain exactly the same. In fact, the increased number and lethality of the means available suggest we are going to see more violence and ever-more-spectacular attacks.

Second, terrorists have underlying and rational causes for their actions. Therefore, terrorism is not simply a random act of violence directed against civilian targets. At times, the attacks may appear random and perhaps may not make sense to the governments and peoples affected by them, but they will be rational in the minds of the terrorists. This is an important finding as we begin to examine the potential for terrorists' use of WMDs. This underlying rationality can be useful because it suggests that, if we are able to engage terrorists in such a way as to place at risk things they value, then it might be possible to avoid unthinkable scenarios such as a large-scale bioterror event.

Third, terrorists have very different, highly stylized motivations, structures, support bases, and capabilities. They do not function as a set of monolithic actors. The very nature of the terrorist—whether a lone actor or part of a transnational group—will play a role in his ability to perpetrate large-scale acts of violence. Speaking in terms of likelihood, in general a single actor or small group has less probability than a large group of being able to conduct a large-scale attack.

A useful delineation as we continue to examine the potential for a bioterrorist attack is to categorize terrorists as traditional, waning, or apocalyptic. The *traditional terrorist* uses a range of activities from politics to violence in pursuit of his objectives. This terrorist will be highly sensitive to retaining the support of the base. The *waning terrorist* began by using violence, but over time has moved toward becoming a political entity and therefore tending away from high-violence and high-profile attacks. *Apocalyptic terrorists* are those with an ideology and intentions that will make it less likely that they will be concerned with gaining constituent support or avoiding high-casualty attacks. The term "apocalyptic" is not necessarily intended to identify these terrorists as moving toward the apocalypse in a literal sense, but rather that they have high-violence strategies they will undertake regardless of the actions of the adversary. While not attempting to identify the cause of the terrorist actions, this delineation focuses on the potential of the lone terrorist or terrorist organization to be dissuaded based on a desire to maintain support for their causes and the degree to which each is likely to find the use of WMDs acceptable for attempting to achieve its respective cause.

In developing these three categories, we must consider that an over-whelming number of terrorist groups fall into the traditional and waning groups. In fact, the numbers of apocalyptic terrorists groups are measured in ones and twos. In Chapter 2 of this book we will discuss Aum Shinrikyo as being in this category. Another group in this category might be the Covenant, the Sword, and the Arm of the Lord (CSA). It is also possible there are splinter groups from terrorist organizations such as al-Qaeda also in this category, although no evidence supports this categorization.[29]

Another important aspect of international terrorist groups is the nature of the issues and objectives. Most—well over 95 percent—are single-issue groups focused on a specific area. Examples include the Revolutionary Armed Forces of Colombia (FARC), a narcoterrorist organization, and the Liberation Tigers of Tamil Eelam (LTTE), a separatist movement focused on gaining independence from Sri Lanka that was defeated in 2009.

As we prepare to examine in the next chapter biowarfare and bioterrorism, it is useful to think about the future of terrorism. In this regard, the field is mixed. One leading author makes the following emphatic observation: "The September 11 attack has created a resolve in America and elsewhere to end international terror once and for all."[30] This is an almost hopeful statement indicating great determination to end terrorism. Of course, there is no universal acceptance of this pronouncement, and events since 9/11 do not necessarily support this conclusion, given the emergence of elements such as al-Qaeda in Iraq (AQI), and the manner in which the GWOT has been prosecuted.

Another author notes ominously, "The globalization of terrorism is perhaps the leading threat to long-term stability in the twenty-first century."[31] This sentiment has a strong following among many Western national leaders, governments, and populations. However, this calculus appears to be based on perceptions, partial information, and emotional responses rather than on an analytical review of the threat we face and the degree to which terrorism can or cannot be considered an existential threat.

While the exact nature of terrorism is hard to predict with certainty, almost a foregone conclusion is that dramatic advances are likely to occur in biotechnology and medicine over the next several decades that will directly relate to the potential for a bioterror attack.

CHAPTER TWO

Biotechnology and Biowarfare:
Two Sides of the Same Coin?

Overview

Humankind has benefited greatly from advances wrought by globalization. Perhaps in no field has this benefit been more clearly demonstrated than in biotechnology, yet it is at this critical intersection between globalization and biotechnology where we find the potential for the "perfect storm." The very capabilities that show such promise for increasing the longevity of humans and the quality of life of humankind have the potential to be combined in ways that could threaten and perhaps even doom the human race.

The seemingly breakneck speed with which the world continues to globalize only serves to accelerate the potential for the proliferation of BW capabilities and a bioterror attack. These trends will have a dramatic impact on the formulation and execution of strategies for thwarting an attack from a WMD. This is particularly true in the field of biowarfare (more specifically bioterrorism) and biodefense, which are two sides of the same coin.

This analysis has been deliberately limited because it concentrates on biotechnology and biowarfare threats as they apply to humans. The concept of biowarfare also applies to agriculture with regard to both plants and animals. In fact, many of the potential pathogens that could be used in a bioterror attack are epizoonotic—diseases of animals that can be transmitted to humans. Despite this close relationship, this analysis will not delve into agroterrroism in detail: that is a separate field of study with a different set of threats and vulnerabilities and worthy of in-depth study beyond our scope.

The Basics

Microbes are inherent in all life forms. Microbes include bacteria, viruses, protozoa, algae, and fungi. While some microbes are responsible for causing disease, many others serve vital functions supporting all forms of plant and animal life. One textbook on microbiology puts it this way:

> Microbes have dominated Earth for more than three billion years and are the basis for all other life-forms. Microbes account for more than 60 percent of all the Earth's organic matter and weigh more than 50 quadrillion metric tons. Microbes are everywhere and constitute nine out of ten cells in the human body. There are uncounted millions of different kinds of microbes, but only a few thousand cause disease in plants and animals.[1]

The focus of biowarfare is to find pathogens that can be effectively delivered to cause disease in an intended target.

Disease is a part of life and intrinsic in the continuous natural selection process in which there are clear winners and losers. Species able to adapt and evolve become strengthened through the process of natural selection, while species unable to adapt and evolve become losers over time, are selected out, and ultimately become extinct.

For most of human history, precious little was known about disease. While it has been understood for thousands of years that there were forces at work that caused sickness, surprisingly little was known about the instruments by which diseases were spread or the manner in which they functioned within the host. Despite not understanding the exact mechanisms of infection, there were numerous historical examples of the deliberate spread of disease as part of the history of conflict. Early and oft-cited examples include the use of arrows dipped in blood or decomposing bodies by Scythian archers as early as 400 BC, the use of animal carcasses to contaminate the water in wells, and the hurling of animal carcasses into the camps and castles of adversaries.

So while the mechanisms of disease were not known, cause-and-effect relationships were understood, if only at a rudimentary level. The perpetrators had no scientific rationale for how and why they worked, only that certain actions promoted disease and had a negative effect on the enemy. This changed in the middle of the 19th century, when a group of scientists began to delve into the causes of and cures for the diseases of the day. For the first time, scientists began to understand disease. In fact, the spread of disease became a topic of great debate among those responsible for public health and medicine. Early theories held disease was spread by bad air, thus the more foul the air smelled, the more likely it caused disease. With greater scientific understanding of disease and more-rigorous analytical techniques, the mysteries were beginning to be unraveled.

British physician John Snow used observation and mathematical techniques to determine the cause of cholera outbreaks in London, tracing the cause to a contaminated well. German physician Rudolf Virchow, who created the field of cellular pathology, promoted the idea that disease begins at the cellular level. French chemist and microbiologist Louis Pasteur developed a process for rendering safe through boiling products that contained harmful bacteria. German physician Robert Koch promoted a rigorous way in which to understand disease and developed a set of postulates that still form the basis for much of the work in disease research today. In fact, much of what we call modern medical techniques was being investigated in Europe in the middle to end of the 19th century.

In the United States, little of this cutting-edge research was occuring, although toward the late 19th century a group of American scientists began to collaborate and learn from the revolution that was ongoing in Europe. John Barry's book, *The Great Influenza*, provides a riveting account of the state of American medicine on the eve of the 1918 Spanish influenza pandemic, which killed more than 50 million people worldwide.

> Not until late—very late—in the nineteenth century, did a virtual handful
> of leaders of American medical science begin to plan a revolution that
> transformed American medicine from the most backward in the devel-
> oped world to the best in the world. When it [the Great Influenza] came,
> they placed their lives in the path of the disease and applied all of their
> knowledge and powers to defeat it.[2]

The discussion of disease and the strides made in the period from the middle of the 19th century to just prior to the start of the 1918 pandemic are certainly impressive. Even more impressive, however, are the extraordinary technological breakthroughs that have occurred since then.

In this post-1918 pandemic ninety-year period, advances in medicine and biotechnology have continued in leaps and bounds. Whole new fields of study have been developed, and progress has been measured in increased longevity and quality of life. Diseases have been eradicated. Common ailments previously considered deadly can be cured using remarkable "wonder drugs." We are able to transplant organs to extend life for those afflicted with life-threatening disease. These examples are some of the more prominent illustrations, but the progress certainly has not stopped there. Generally, these advances in biotechnology have been used to the benefit of humankind. As with all technological advances, however, at some point there are those inclined to use these capabilities to the detriment of society.

While not attempting at this point to discuss biowarfare, we need to understand a certain amount of science in order to understand the manner in which bacteria, viruses, and toxins cause disease. These three disease-causing agents act in very different ways and have vastly different mechanisms of action. Even within the three categories, the individual mechanisms of action for potential pathogens are quite different. For example, *Bacillus anthracis* and *Francisella tularensis*, the causative bacterial organisms for anthrax and tularemia, respectively, are very different in their disease-causing capabilities, potential outcomes, and even treatments, although they also have some striking similarities.

Bacteria

Bacteria are living organisms. They are composed of a nucleus, cytoplasm, a plasma membrane, and a cell wall. The nucleus contains genomic material including deoxyribonucleic acid (DNA), a nucleic acid that contains the genetic instructions used in the development and functioning of all known living organisms; and ribonucleic acid (RNA), a nucleic acid made from a long chain of nucleotide units that translates proteins and is essential for life.

Upon introduction into a host, bacteria have a number of mechanisms for gaining entry into the cells. Once inside the cells, they can have very different effects. *Bacillus anthracis* binds to the host cell, where it is absorbed. After penetrating the cell membrane, the bacteria begin the production of toxins that will be responsible for killing cells and doing significant damage to many of the major organs of the body. The incubation period and the long-term prognosis varies depending on the route of infection, the virulence of the bacteria and the dose received. For inhalational anthrax, the death rate approaches 100 percent for doses above 8,000 bacteria if left untreated. *Francisella tularensis*, which causes the disease tularemia, or rabbit fever, is also absorbed by the cell, forming an endosome. Once it penetrates the cell, the bacteria continue to multiply in the macrophages, which are part of the host's immune system, until these structures become engorged and eventually burst. At that time, the bacteria are released, where they are spread to the regional lymph nodes and to other organs of the host, including the lungs, kidneys, spleen, and liver. The effect is to do major tissue damage that results in death of the host. The incubation period is up to twenty-one days and again varies by dose and virulence. However, unlike anthrax that requires 8,000 organisms for a lethal dose, for tularemia, it can be as low as 10–50 organisms. For both inhalational anthrax and tularemia, the initial symptoms are similar to influenza.

Viruses

In contrast, viruses are not living organisms and are therefore metabolically inert. They also have a much less complex structure than bacteria and rely on the host for their mechanisms of action. Viruses are composed of genetic material, either DNA or RNA, contained within a viral capsule and proteins that have a variety of functions for the virus. These functions include the building of the structures in which the virus's genomic material resides and the binding of the virus to the host cell. Once bound to the host cell, the virus's genomic material is absorbed and travels to the cell's nucleus. Because a virus is not a living organism, it relies on the host cell's machinery to function. Therefore, the virus operates by "hijacking" the host's cellular machinery and interfering with normal cell functions.

Just as with bacteria, each virus has distinct mechanisms of action. In the case of Sin Nombre virus, responsible for causing the hantavirus pulmonary syndrome (HPS) that has been found naturally occurring in the southwest United States, the disease begins with the inhalation of the viral particles found within the feces of infected indigenous rodents. Once inhaled, the virus goes through a long, silent incubation period of anywhere from seven to twenty-eight days, during which there is viral replication in the cells of the lungs and lymph nodes and transport to the spleen. In these early stages, the spleen becomes inundated with virons. As the disease progresses, the cells of the immune system begin to secrete mediators in an attempt to resolve the disease and protect the host. This leads to pulmonary edema, progressing to lung capillary leakage. The lung is clearly the most affected organ in this disease. In severe hantavirus cases, there is also a profound impact on the heart, with myocardial dysfunction common in terminal patients. The imminent death of the patient can be predicted according to when the patient goes into shock. For recorded cases in the United States, patients arriving at the hospital in shock died in eleven of fourteen cases. In contrast, if shock follows patient admission to the hospital, ten of twelve patients survived.

In contrast to Sin Nombre virus, dengue is caused by a virus transmitted by infected vectors such as mosquitoes or ticks. After the host is infected, there is a two- to seven-day incubation period. After that, the host develops a fever, bone pain, anorexia, nausea, weakness, respiratory symptoms, and sometimes a rash. In severe cases, the disease can progress to a dengue hemorrhagic fever, which has considerably higher mortality rates than simple dengue. In contrast to the high mortality associated with the HPS, dengue has mortality rates of 10 percent without treatment and 0.1 percent with treatment.

Toxins

Toxins are derived from living organisms and can have bacteria, plant, fungi, or animals as sources. While they are similar in mechanism of action to chemical poisons, the distinguishing characteristics are (1) poisons are not derived from living organisms, whereas toxins are; and (2) toxins are considered to be a "small molecule," meaning they can be synthesized.

In the case of botulinum neurotoxin, the toxin is derived from the organism *Clostridium botulinum* and can be prepared in a laboratory. While botulinum neurotoxin can result from the introduction of the live organism, it can also be prepared as a purified toxin and introduced into the host. In this purified form, it will be even more effective and have a more rapid onset. In an aerosol form, the toxin will be absorbed by the lungs and cause the disruption of the neurotransmitters responsible for contracting of muscles, with the most affected muscles those responsible for respiration. Therefore, without mechanical ventilation and other supportive care, the victim normally dies.

Just as with bacteria and viruses, toxins have discrete mechanisms of action. As a contrast to botulinum neurotoxin, consider the purified toxin from *Vibrio cholerae*, the organism responsible for causing the disease cholera. In its purified form, the toxin will be absorbed by the host cell where it will begin to pump out chlorine molecules and water from the cell, creating an electrolyte imbalance and loss of fluids, which, if not halted, will result in cell death. In an aerosol form, the victim would rapidly succumb to pulmonary edema (drowning) because the fluid collects in the lungs, preventing normal breathing.

Summary of Disease-Causing Pathogens

Bacteria, viruses, and toxins are all composed of or derived from biological material and are therefore highly sensitive to the environment, including ultraviolet light, wind, and rain. They will also be sensitive to disinfectants and sterilization. The result is that these disease-causing pathogens have a natural lifespan in the environment—a biological clock, if you will—which means that, over time, either the material will die without being introduced into a host or will lose effectiveness. Of course, this too is highly dependent on the type of pathogen and its formulation or preparation. In the case of anthrax, which occurs in spore form, this degradation is negligible, while for a virus such as the one responsible for causing HIV/AIDS, the lifespan outside a host is short lived.

Introduction to the Immune System

A discussion of bacteria, viruses, and toxins would not be complete without a complementary introduction to the immune system. While an in-depth discussion of the human immune system would fill volumes, well beyond our scope, it is useful to understand the role of the host's immune system in fighting disease. The immune system has two major components: the nonspecific and specific subsystems.

Nonspecific Subsystems

The nonspecific is always turned on and has the capability to detect and act on foreign bodies detected as "nonself" as they are introduced into the host. For very low exposures, the nonspecific immune system—led by the killer T cells—can normally resolve the exposure. If so, the host will likely not even be aware of the introduction of a pathogen. However, some pathogens such as the Marburg virus have a very low requirement for effective exposure, which can be as low as three to five virons. Therefore, even a small exposure can be deadly.

Specific Subsystems

The specific immune system is, as the name implies, directly related to specific antigens and therefore must be conditioned to become functional. This conditioning is essentially the manner in which vaccines work as they provide a stimulus against a specific microbe. The catch is that the specific immune system requires a period of activation in order to get the antibodies or B cells to effective strength for providing protection against an antigen. Furthermore, over time protection can degrade depending on a variety of factors. This is also why, for certain diseases such as chicken pox, an individual will normally only contract the disease once, after which he or she has lifelong immunity because the antibodies remain capable of attacking these secondary viral exposures. The degree to which the specific immune system is stimulated may require that, for certain vaccines, an effective regimen may include multiple inoculations, as in the case of the anthrax vaccine, which requires a series of six shots to gain full protection.

The immune system is naturally regulated. Therefore, certain triggers are required for turning up or down the immune response. Some bacteria and viruses are able to evade the immune system as one of their mechanisms of action. An example is the Ebola virus, which is thought to have a gene that renders it invisible to the nonspecific immune system. Therefore, the virus replicates unfettered and unbeknownst to the first line of defense, the nonspecific part of the immune system. By the time the immune system finally detects the virus, it has progressed too far to be controlled by the nonspecific portion and prior to the full activation of the antibodies from the specific immune system. In this critical period, the victim normally succumbs to the Ebola virus, which has a mortality rate of approximately 90 percent and no effective treatment other than supportive care.

Additionally, at times the regulators do not act properly and the immune system can be overstimulated, which can cause a cytokine storm resulting in major damage to the host's biological systems by the release of these immune system elements. This overreaction by the immune system has been a recurring theme in trying to understand why the 1918 pandemic seemed to disproportionately affect people in their late teens into middle age, while having a lower mortality rate in infants and the elderly.

Biotechnology

Some experts claim we have left the Information Age and are entering the Age of Biotechnology. The validity of this claim, of course, is highly subjective and certainly open to many interpretations and questions, not the least of which is whether the Information Age has "officially" ended. Still, the sentiment is both interesting and a cause for reflection. Biotechnology is one of the weapons developed by humans to wage war against the elements of disease that could potentially do harm. However, as one author noted, "Every major technology—metallurgy, explosives, internal combustion, aviation, electronics, nuclear energy—has been intensively exploited, not only for peaceful purposes, but also for hostile ones."[3] It is from this perspective we begin the discussion of biotechnology and biowarfare, two sides of the same coin.

Like information technology, which is driven by Moore's Law, there is an "X" factor driving this unprecedented growth in biotechnology, particularly in such fields as genetic engineering and molecular biology.[4] In a 2003 article, Rob Carlson described this growth in what has become known as Carlson's Law. He demonstrated that the growth in biosequencers and biosynthesizers is exponential and even greater than the growth being experienced in information technology.[5] Projecting these findings across the biotechnology field, Carlson contends these developments are likely to lead to revolutionary advances that will make today's horrific diseases obsolete, to the development of gene therapies that will fundamentally alter people's lives, and to man-machine interfaces that will give individuals superhuman capabilities. While these areas of research and exploration hold great promise for public health and disease prevention, the same technologies have the potential to be misused by terrorists bent on threatening populations. It is within this critical nexus brought about by the proliferation of information and biological capabilities that we find a potentially catastrophic convergence.

In looking to the future of biotechnology in early 2008, Ray Kurzweil, the author of *Fantastic Voyage*, was being interviewed by television moderator John McLaughlin on NBC during the Sunday morning talk shows. While discussing the progress that had been made in biotechnology as well as the likely future of this field, he emphasized the future impact advances in biotechnology will have on average Americans. He noted that, while it took fifteen years to sequence the HIV/AIDS virus, the SARS virus was sequenced in just three weeks. He also identified advances in RNA research that had yielded incredible results for RNA interference (RNAi) that would essentially block disease-promoting genes, perhaps eliminating certain categories of disease.

Interestingly, Kurzweil also touched on the subject of nanotechnology, declaring that in twenty to thirty years nanotechnology will function in humans, assisting in prevention of disease and repairing damaged human tissue. This last area, he contended, would extend human life to 150 years and perhaps longer. While such claims seem highly futuristic, there is reason to believe he is on to something. In making such bold predictions, Kurzweil identified an area in biotechnology that has experienced and will likely continue to experience record growth in an extremely compressed period.[6]

Arguably, no other major field of study is currently experiencing such a significant exponential rise in knowledge and capabilities. The Federation of American Scientists (FAS) assessment, which comes originally from the "Militarily Critical Technologies List Part II: Weapons of Mass Destruction Technologies" (see Figure 2–1), provides insights into the rate of change of several key technologies selected both for their applicability for use in the biotechnology field and for use in developing and manufacturing biological weapons.[7] The information in the chart has been coded to reflect not only the key technologies, but also the rate of change for each. Consider the field of vaccine development which depicts the rate of development from

1940 to 1970 as doubling every five years. From 1970 to 1980, the rate increased fivefold such that the time to double the capabilities in the field of vaccines was one year. Over the twenty-year period from 1980 to 2000, the time to double in capability decreased to six months. This translates to advances in vaccine development, sensors, personal protection, and pathogen masking. Another field, DNA engineering, which was not even in existence until 1982, has doubled in capacity every six months from 1982 to 2000. This area is critically important to a wide variety of biotechnical advances, including gene therapy, vaccine development, and sensors, as well as ominously increasing the virulence of a pathogen. The same is true for encapsulization and stabilization, which have potential for enhancing personal protection and therapeutics, as well as for making BW weapons more effective and stable in the environment.

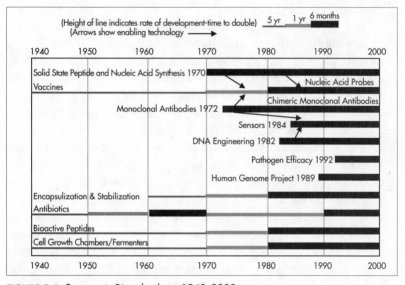

FIGURE 2-1 Progress in Biotechnology, 1940–2000

In another study that examines the future of biotechnology, the Institute of Medicine (IOM) and the National Research Council (NRC) of the National Academies jointly sponsored an analysis by the "Committee on Advances in Technology and the Prevention of their Application to Next Generation Biowarfare Threats." The results of the study, *Globalization, Biosecurity, and the Future of the Life Sciences*, were published in 2006.[8] The volume approaches the issue of globalization with a strict focus on the

KEY FINDINGS

1. The committee endorses and affirms the policies and practices that, to the maximum extent possible, promote the free and open exchange of information in the life sciences.
2. The committee recommends adopting a broader perspective on the "threat spectrum."
3. The committee recommends strengthening and enhancing the scientific and technical expertise within and across the security communities.
4. The committee recommends the adoption and promotion of a common culture of awareness and a shared sense of responsibility within the global community of life sciences.
5. The committee recommends strengthening the public health infrastructure and existing response and recovery capabilities.

FIGURE 2-2 Results of "Globalization, Biosecurity, and the Future of the Life Sciences" study.

effect of biotechnology on humankind. The five overarching findings are provided in Figure 2–2.

From the tone of the findings, the message is clear. The committee expresses collective concern about trends in biotechnology. These concerns are measured not in platitudes and assertions, but rather in facts that make the compelling case the state of biotechnology has increased dramatically with no reason to believe these trends will not continue. Furthermore, this proliferation has come at a time when few control measures exist to place reasonable limits on the efforts. The study underscores the community's belief that we must think differently about the "threat spectrum," because the greater availability of knowledge and capabilities has led to a dangerous proliferation, making BW capabilities more readily available.

In a section titled "Emerging Technologies," the authors of *Globalization, Biosecurity, and the Future of the Life Sciences* discuss several technologies that did not even exist a decade ago, yet are maturing with such rapidity that the potential exists for developing cures for major diseases in the near future. One such example is the same RNAi that Kurzweil spoke of, which has the potential to cure some diseases, including cancer. This technology uses interfacing and binding molecules to cleave and destroy sequence-specific RNA, thus interrupting one of the mechanisms by which certain viruses cause disease. RNAi also has application in functional genomics, allowing the blocking of the expression of genes: if the genes responsible for disease are blocked, it might in turn be possible to prevent the disease.[9] Of course, this same technology could also make it possible to enhance the effectiveness and virulence of BW pathogen.

Nanotechnology was identified as another example of a rapidly emerging field with great promise. The committee noted, "in just five years, nanotechnology has catapulted from being a specialty of a handful of physicists and chemists to a worldwide scientific and industrial enterprise."[10] The committee goes on to say the industry will reach $1 trillion in the United States by 2012.

Nanotechnology—also sometimes known as DNA nanotechnology —has potential for manipulation of DNA at the lowest levels by using nanoparticles for a variety of tasks, including detecting disease, repairing genes, and even developing smart drugs that can target the disease-causing pathogens. With regard to these enhancements, nanotechnology will undoubtedly expand into such areas as nanoparticle drug delivery, future applications of molecular nanotechnology (MNT), and nano-vaccinology.

Concerning advances in biotechnology, the committee uses descriptions like "successive serendipitous discoveries" and "practically impossible to determine where the next breakthroughs might happen" to describe a system experiencing this meteoric rise.[13] Several key statistics are cause for reflection and lead to the serious issue of the proliferation of potentially dual-use technologies. The National Academies study has done a country-by-country assessment of the state of biotechnology in fourteen nations across the globe, and has concluded that advanced capabilities are proliferating extremely rapidly as measured in terms of research conducted, patents filed, and the number of scientists being trained, among other key determinants of technological progress. The international component of the biotechnology revolution means any efforts to moderate behavior and protect potentially dual-use technologies from further proliferation will need to be international, because the United States certainly does not have exclusivity in these emerging biotechnology areas.

We are even seeing major changes in some of the more routine areas of biotechnology with extraordinary results. In the early 1980s, the field of sequencing of DNA was a tedious job involving untold hours. Today, we find the sequencing of an organism's genomes has been decreased since 1994 by several orders of magnitude in terms of time and cost.[11] Furthermore, in 1990 DNA sequencing per base pair cost $10. Today, cost for that sequencing is $0.01.[12] Emerging technologies such as DNA sequencing for determining the gene sequence of genomic material, DNA synthesis in which DNA is created synthetically, and protein structural synthesis are all becoming commonplace. They are widely practiced and affordable.

The explosion in biotechnology has allowed many of these key areas of interest to go from theory to the lab to the field in highly compressed timeframes. One such example is polymerase chain reaction (PCR), which was discovered in 1983 by Dr. Kary Mullis. His discovery earned him the

Nobel Prize in Chemistry. This technology has become routine and has become the basis for a wide variety of equipment, testing, and capabilities from rational drug design to biosensors that monitor the air in cities across the United States.

These rapid, expansive, and seemingly unregulated biotechnical enhancements have yielded dramatic increases in standards of living and quality of life. People are living longer and leading more-productive lives. Life expectancy for Americans has increased from 59.7 years in 1930 to 77.8 years in 2005.[14] The same trends are evident throughout the globe, although the benefits vary greatly by country based on the environment, health care, societal norms, and other factors.

New public health and medical capabilities also have contributed measurably to improvements in quality of life. Vaccines have virtually eliminated previously widespread diseases such as measles, mumps, and rubella. Another disease, smallpox, has been eradicated, with the only known stores of the virus in Russia and the United States in controlled and highly protected environments. New Age pharmaceuticals targeting inherited conditions such as high cholesterol, diabetes, and heart disease show continued potential for medical benefit.

Another interesting aspect of biotechnology is globalization's effect on biological organisms. With the increasing connectedness of the world, large flows of people, animals, and products regularly cross national borders, exposing naïve populations to potentially dangerous pathogens. Furthermore, humans venturing into remote areas that heretofore have been largely uninhabited are also exposing populations to novel pathogens. In this regard, the NRC and the IOM ask, "Beating nature: Is it possible to engineer a 'better' pathogen?" The implication is clear. Nature's ability to adapt, including its ability to adapt bacteria, viruses, and fungi, may far outstrip humankind's ability to engineer such a weapon.

As evidence of this potential, consider bacterial diseases such as the plague or tuberculosis. The plague comes from the *Yersinia pestis* bacterium and is estimated to have killed more than 100 million people in the middle of the 6th century during Justinian's Plague. Tuberculosis, which is caused by *Mycobacterium tuberculosis*, even today kills approximately 2 million people a year worldwide. The same can be said for viruses such as the 1918 Spanish influenza type A, estimated to have killed from 50–100 million people worldwide, and the viral hemorrhagic diseases such as Marburg and Ebola, that kill with devastating speed and horror. While the overall number of deaths from these hemorrhagic viruses is small to date, they have certainly demonstrated great virulence and potential for far greater mortality with rates, as high as 90 percent for Ebola.

This ability of people to traverse the globe and the increasing interactions that result have serious implications for the spread of disease. One analysis concludes that in 1850 it took approximately 360 days to circumnavigate the globe. By 1875, that figure had been reduced to 150 days through advances in shipbuilding technology. With the introduction of steam engines on ships, by 1925 the time had been reduced to fifty days. With the introduction of aircraft, the time has been reduced to days or even hours. At the same time, the world's population has increased from 200 million in 1850 to more than 6 billion today. One can conclude from this that we have a greater ability to circumnavigate the globe and there are considerably more people that could potentially do so.[15] While it draws no direct conclusions with respect to the potential for the spread of disease, the increased mobility of the population and the overall growth of the population indicate more people will encounter each other. This will undoubtedly expose naïve populations to new forms of disease and facilitate the spread of disease. It also places an increased strain on international, national, regional, and local health departments, as well as those responsible for monitoring population flows including the U.S. Customs and Border Protection (CBP) agency. In effect, this provides one more data point concerning the "dark side" of globalization.

Therefore, even in the absence of a biowarfare threat, naturally occurring pathogens cause risks to plant and animal life, including humans. We see this on a daily basis throughout the world with cholera outbreaks following natural disasters, endemic disease caused by poverty, and epizoonotic diseases that can threaten both animals and humans.

The SARS outbreak that rapidly spread across the world in a compressed timeframe in late 2002 and 2003 demonstrates the potential for the global spread of disease. The outbreak infected 8,096 people worldwide, resulting in 774 deaths worldwide as listed in the World Health Organization's (WHO) April 21, 2004 concluding report.[16] The highly pathogenic respiratory virus with a mortality rate of more than 9 percent demonstrates the potential for new and exotic diseases to rapidly emerge and surprise even the experts.[17]

More recently, a dengue fever epidemic in Brazil in the latter part of 2007 and early months of 2008 infected more than 40,000 people and killed several hundred, demonstrating the potential for large-scale outbreaks. To further illustrate the power of naturally occurring disease, consider the millions of deaths per year due to tuberculosis, malaria, and HIV/AIDS, the three largest lethal pandemics in the 21st century so far. Together they kill more than 6 million people annually, demonstrating the effectiveness and global reach of disease today.

The swine influenza global emergency discovered in April 2009 provides another important example. This outbreak had as its epicenter Veracruz, Mexico. However, as the news of the epidemic spread, more people who had influenza-like illness went to hospitals and were screened for the emerging disease. Early statistics indicated only Mexico and the United States reported cases to the WHO. Within 72 hours of initial news coverage, however, more than ten nations had reported cases and all could be traced back to sources in Mexico through travel or contact with individuals who had recently traveled to Mexico. Only within a globalized world with ever-increasing connectedness could such rapid spread across the world be possible.

Certainly, increases in biotechnology contribute to humankind in a variety of ways, but we must note that, just as with the discussion of globalization, a dark side of biotechnology exists where the potential for these same technologies to be turned against society in the form of a bioattack. Advances in science and technology have made possible the enhancement of the virulence of a pathogen and even the potential for the development of "designer" pathogens. A *Washington Post* article, "Custom-Built Pathogens Raise Bioterror Fears," discusses an experiment in which a molecular geneticist was able to create the "first live, fully artificial virus in the lab."[18] The virus was developed from nonliving components using specialized equipment and chemicals at a university laboratory at the State University of New York (SUNY) at Stony Brook. Dr. Eckard Wimmer, the scientist who developed the artificial poliovirus, made the point that, while this was a first step using a relatively simple virus, the future would undoubtedly see viruses such as Ebola and smallpox created in a similar manner.

In yet another harbinger of what the future holds, the same article discusses the potential for a growing business in commercial gene synthesis. A British scientific journal wanted to make the point about the ease with which potentially dangerous genetic sequences could be obtained. Of the twelve companies contacted, only five stated they screened customer orders prior to shipping the information and material.

By way of an exclamation point concerning advances in biotechnology, in reports surrounding the identification of the likely perpetrator of the Amerithrax attacks, much was made of how significant advances in genomics and other key technologies made the rapid differentiation of various strains of anthrax possible and assisted in identifying the suspect. Dr. Bruce Ivins, who committed suicide in 2008 prior to formal charges being filed for an alleged criminal connection to the attacks, is the only suspect in the case as of this writing. These technologies did not even exist at the time of the Amerithrax attacks.

Biowarfare

History has demonstrated that research in biology, even when conducted without any military application in mind, may still contribute to the production of biological weapons. Indeed, people knew how to intentionally spread illness long before naturalists discovered that germs caused disease.[19]

The history of BW can be traced to antiquity, including the oft-cited siege of Caffa on the Crimean peninsula in the 14th century, the use of arrows that had been dipped in manure or rotting corpses against enemies during medieval times, and the catapulting of human corpses and animal carcasses into enemy encampments and fortifications during the Crusades. During the U.S. Civil War, General Johnston's troops poisoned water by dumping animal carcasses in ponds. The use of smallpox-infected blankets against the Indians during the settling of the western United States is yet another example of the use of biological weapons. While these examples are instructive, they do not reflect well-defined programs designed to develop and use biological weapons, nor do they provide much insight into the potential threat of a bioattack in today's environment. To examine this question, a more relevant point of departure is the history of modern biological weapons.

In this regard, the Japanese experiences in the period before and during World War II provide a useful starting point. Japanese Unit 731 served as the focal point for these efforts, experimenting with a number of agents and using several, including plague-infected fleas over China, aerosolized anthrax, and typhoid bacteria. The United States, the United Kingdom, and the former Soviet Union had BW programs beginning post–World War II. Worthy of note is that these "modern" programs were developed in the post-1925 Geneva Convention protocol era. The Geneva Convention "prohibited the use of chemical and biological agents, but not the research and development of these agents."[20]

While the United States had been a party to the negotiation, it was not until forty-five years later the treaty was ratified by President Gerald Ford. The U.S. biological and chemical programs continued to be developed and were viable during this intervening period. With regard to biological weapons, this changed in 1969 when President Richard Nixon decided to "unilaterally and unconditionally renounce biological weapons." This included the "destruction of the entire U.S. biological weapons stockpile and the conversion of all production facilities to peaceful purposes."[21]

To put the issue of BW into perspective and relate it to the overarching issue of globalization discussed in Chapter 1, the National Academies study provides a vivid description of the impact of biotechnology on the BW threat.[22] Figure 2–3 highlights the beginning of the "modern" biowarfare period beginning in the 1940s. In this depiction, the Pre-Genomic Era prior to 1999 and the sequencing of the first human genome indicate a threat from traditional agents predominantly. Only in the later years of this period did genetically altered traditional agents join traditional agents as threats to humankind. As the world has moved farther into the Genomic Era, genetically altered agents and a new category called advanced biological agents combine with the traditional threats to depict a steep linearly increasing threat. While this is a theoretical construct and not an absolute depiction, the idea that biotechnology will experience this meteoric growth must be considered in any future global BW scenarios. Although positive effects will continue to include greater longevity, better quality of life, and reduced infant mortality, this continued proliferation of biotechnology will also make knowledge, equipment, and capabilities more readily available to an increasingly large number of people, some of whom may have less than noble purposes.

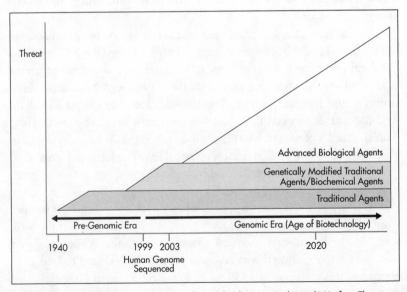

FIGURE 2–3 Timeline Describing Impact of Biotechnology on Biological Warfare Threat

Other potential concerns center on the accidental misuse of these capabilities and the potential for genetically engineered pathogens to "escape" or be used in an attack with potentially devastating consequences. Consider the case of a National Institutes of Health (NIH) study in which an ultravirulent strain of mousepox virus, a relation to the smallpox virus in humans, was developed. Dr. Mark Butler, professor of molecular microbiology and immunology at St. Louis University, used as a reference a 2001 published Australian study in which a lethal variant of the mousepox virus was created by manipulating the wrong gene in the attempted development of a sterilization treatment for mice. Butler replicated the experiment hoping to identify an effective sterilization treatment and inadvertently developed a variant of the mousepox that was twice as lethal as the Australian variant. Of particular concern is that both of these viruses were created mistakenly by activating the wrong gene in the experiment.[23] This anecdote points to another concern, too: the ready availability of information that can be used inappropriately. Furthermore, it provides a vivid reminder that something extraordinary occurred with the sequencing of the first human genome in 1999, with implications going well beyond "simple" science. In many regards, this event can be considered the ushering in of a new era, the Age of Biotechnology, as well as the potential for a new era in biowarfare.

What Is BW?

The sparse history of biowarfare means discussions of the topic invariably revolve around several capstone incidents and scenarios developed to explain and underscore the potential for BW. Two oft-quoted sources provide great headlines for catching one's attention concerning the potential for a BW attack. The numbers are staggering: if even a fraction of the death and devastation were to be unleashed, these events would dwarf the 9/11 terrorist attacks by orders of magnitude.

Scenario #1. In 1970, a World Health Organization (WHO) expert estimated casualties following a theoretical release of 50 kilograms of anthrax spores from an aircraft over an urban population of 5 million people. It estimates there would be 250,000 casualties, of which 100,000 would die without proper treatment.

Scenario #2. A later (1993) report by the US Congressional Office of Technology Assessment looked at a scenario involving release of 100 kilograms of anthrax aerosol upwind of the Washington DC area. It estimated that this would cause at least 130,000 deaths and possibly as many as 3 million. An economic model developed by the Centers for Disease Control and Prevention recently estimated a cost of $26.2 billion per 100,000 people exposed to a bioterrorist attack.[24]

BW uses naturally occurring pathogens including bacteria, viruses, and fungi, or toxins derived from biological sources to cause disease and death in a targeted population. Figure 2–4 provides a synopsis of the distinguishing characteristics of biowarfare and some indication of why biological weapons may be of interest to some nations and potentially to terrorists.[25] While Figure 2–4 provides an overview of BW highlights, the exact effect of each pathogen is highly dependent on a variety of factors. Likewise, the use of a pathogen for a particular attack scenario must be tied to an intended outcome. As an example of the potential variance, the time for symptoms to occur will be highly dependent on the characteristics and exact pathogenesis of a particular agent. Even for the same pathogen, the prodromal (or incubation) period can vary greatly. Additionally, the delivery method will have a major impact on the time required for symptoms to occur. An example would be the differences between an oral challenge through the gastrointestinal tract versus an inhalational cholera attack. In the case of the oral route, the onset would be typically two to three days, although there have been cases were the symptoms occur in two to three hours. For an inhalational cholera attack, however, the incubation could be measured in minutes and hours, depending on the dose received.[26]

BIOLOGICAL WEAPONS HIGHLIGHTS

- Biological weapons are unique because they are made up of pathogenic organisms that can reproduce and cause infection (and death) in a large number of hosts.
- It takes hours to days for symptoms of exposure to appear.
- Biological weapons are relatively inexpensive to produce.
- All of the equipment used to produce biological agents is dual use, with applications in the pharmaceutical, food, cosmetic, and pesticide industries.
- Dissemination and dispersion are key to the effective employment of | biological weapons.
- Many toxic organisms are subject to destruction by external forces (e.g., sunlight, explosives).

FIGURE 2–4 Biological Weapons Highlights (The Militarily Critical Technologies List Part II: Weapons of Mass Destruction Technologies, U.S. Department of Defense, Office of the Under Secretary of Defense for Acquisition and Technology, February 1998)

The range of pathogens and scenarios also leads to a sense of attractiveness. Consider the nearly unlimited number of combinations that could be employed in a BW attack. Attempting to protect against all or even a large subset of these potential attacks would be very costly and of questionable utility. Additionally, the potential for large-scale mortality and morbidity using a modest amount of biological material also lends a certain attractiveness to biological weapons. The WHO and the Office of Technology Assessment (OTA) scenarios presented above underscore this potential.

Complicating any efforts to limit BW proliferation are several factors: (1) BW pathogens are naturally occurring, (2) the equipment for production is dual-use, and (3) the costs associated with development and production are modest. Strong evidence supports concerns about the potential for biotechnology capabilities to be employed in ways to render them suitable for use as weapons against populations, cities, animals, and crops. Several studies from a number of communities confirm this belief and indicate the growing nature of this threat due to advances in biotechnology. A 1996 U.S. Department of Defense (DoD) report identifies five potential types of novel biological agents, including microorganisms:

1. genetically modified to produce a toxin of venom;
2. engineered to be resistant to antibiotics, vaccines, and standard therapeutics;
3. modified to have enhanced aerosol and environmental stability;
4. altered to complicate identification and detection; and
5. some combination of the previous four types.[27]

Another 1997 study by the NRC and the IOM identified the potential for pathogens with designer genes, binary biological weapons and stealth virus to avoid detection.[28] These studies along with National Academies assessment (Figure 2–3) and the Progress in Biotechnology (Fig. 2–1) provide important insights into the nature and magnitude of potential BW capabilities and threats we are likely to face in the future.

Bioweapons makers must consider numerous factors when developing their weapons. Will the agent be a bacteria, virus, or toxin? Should it be contagious or non-contagious? A lethal or incapacitating agent? How will it be deployed? Above all, for the weapon to be effective, the concentration, dose, and susceptibility of the target must be considered. A useful model commonly taught within one university biodefense program provides insights into the process that could be used in developing a BW capability. The relationships expressed as a formula for the Effectiveness of

Biological Warfare (BWef) are

$$BW_{ef} = f\{A, D, F, M, MT\}, \text{ where}$$

A = Choice of agent

D = Deployment method

F = Formulation

M = Manufacturing process, and

MT = Meteorological and terrain conditions.[29]

Knowledge, while not depicted explicitly, is implied as a prerequisite for anyone wanting to develop BW capabilities. Furthermore, many of the capabilities discussed previously as part of "*Militarily Critical Technologies List Part II: Weapons of Mass Destruction Technologies*" would be useful in gaining and perfecting BW capabilities.

In the development of BW, understanding the linkages between the components becomes imperative. The choice of agent (A) and deployment method (D) relate closely to the operational parameters of the intended attack. Selecting the wrong agent for the intended effect can doom the effort from the start. Selecting an incapacitation agent if the goal was to kill large numbers of people would not allow the perpetrator to achieve his goal. Formulation (F) and manufacturing process (M) can be used to refine the agent to enhance its capabilities as a weapon or provide characteristics that better support the attack parameters. Examples would be engineering the pathogen to be more virulent or perhaps for it to have greater stability in the environment. In fact, engineering pathogens to be more virulent using recumbent technologies is a specialized skill that would be highly useful for executing a large-scale attack. Other emerging technologies such as DNA engineering, encapsulization, and nucleic acid synthesis all are specific capabilities requiring advanced biological knowledge that would also likely contribute to preparations for an attack in the future. Obviously, the incorporation of these types of techniques would in turn translate into a higher probability of success for the perpetrator of the attack.

Likewise, the ability to develop scenarios that account for meteorological and terrain conditions will be fundamental to achieving a successful attack. Even with excellent laboratory techniques, if agents are not employed properly based on weather and terrain, the attack will be suboptimal or perhaps even ineffective, because these agents are highly sensitive to the environment, including ultraviolet light and wind conditions. Furthermore, they will experience normal biological decay that must be considered by an attacker.

Illustrative scenarios can assist in understanding the balance between the factors. For example, while anthrax has received a good deal of press since the 2001 attacks in the United States, this agent is of most use against a point target or population that has not been vaccinated. Anthrax can even be used to make large areas uninhabitable until a thorough decontamination is conducted. However, other pathogens present an even more difficult scenario to defend against. Consider the case of a pathogen that has documented human-to-human transmission, is highly contagious, and has been genetically modified to have higher pathogenity and a shorter incubation period.

One example, a postulated scenario used in BW exercise Dark Winter, uses a deliberate release of smallpox, a highly pathogenic agent eradicated as a naturally occurring disease in 1979 after a decade-long effort spearheaded by the WHO. A detailed account of the findings is contained in Appendix B. The reason why a smallpox attack is of such concern is its highly infectious nature coupled with its high mortality rate. Additionally, given the eradication of smallpox and the discontinuation of the vaccination program, few would have immunity to the disease. It is further worthy of note that, for the smallpox vaccine to be effective, it should be given prior to the outbreak of symptoms and preferably even before exposure. The genetic manipulation of the virus into a super-smallpox variant with higher virulence would be even greater cause for concern. It has been reported the Soviet Union made such biological modifications as part of their state BW program. In one such experiment, they were known to have genetically engineered a combination of *Variola major* (smallpox) and Venezuela equine encephalitis (VEE).[30]

What History Tells Us

The use of science and technology for nefarious purposes with large numbers of dead and dying as an outcome is certainly a horrific scenario to contemplate, but in dealing with threats and scenarios it can be useful to examine the historical precedents to gain perspective and context for understanding these weapons and their capabilities.

The use of biological weapons since the 1940s when the "modern" Age of Biological Warfare began provides surprising little data on which to base such an analysis. The National Academies' report lists seven instances of the use of BW weapons:

1. 1940–41 Japanese use of BW in China in the Hangzhou and Nanjing provinces

2. 1957–63 in Brazil, against Indian tribal populations
3. 1981 in the United Kingdom, when commandos used anthrax against a research facility
4. 1984 in Oregon, United States, when the Rajneeshee cultists used salmonella against citizens, among other BW attacks
5. 1989 in Namibia during a covert operation by South Africa
6. 1990–93 in Japan, when the Aum Shinrikyo cult attempted to use a variety of agents against citizens
7. 2001 in the United States, when a terrorist used anthrax-filled letters to attack several targets[31]

The number of attempted attacks in this more than sixty-year period provides interesting insights into the potential for use of BW in the future. Of particular note is that these referenced attacks were characterized as "authenticated" but did not include events such as the poisoning of Bulgarian dissident Georgi Markov in 1978, the attempted use of these agents for what would be considered criminal activity such as the poisoning of a rival, or the many hoaxes that occur on a fairly regular basis.[32]

Milton Leitenberg from the Center for International and Security Studies at the University of Maryland provides a historical perspective concerning BW development. In his published a report, "An Assessment of Biological Weapons Threat to the United States,"[33] he provides an assessment compiled from a variety of sources, including the U.S. Non-Compliance document, the 1993 Russian Foreign Intelligence Report, and his own judgments to arrive at a unique analysis that lists the states suspected of having programs as of January 2001.[34] What is unique about this analysis is his attempt to categorize the various state programs based on the level of activity, including offensive research and development (R&D), testing, production, stockpiling, and alleged use. He concludes that up to eleven countries had offensive R&D programs: China, Egypt, Iran, Iraq, Israel, Libya, North Korea, South Africa, the former Soviet Union, Syria, and Zimbabwe. Of these countries, only China, Iraq, Israel (probably), North Korea, and the former Soviet Union had testing programs, with two other countries (South Africa and Zimbabwe [formerly Rhodesia]) noted as question marks in terms of previous testing activities. All countries with the exception of Syria and perhaps Zimbabwe were assessed to have some production and stockpiling of BW material. Only three countries—South Africa, the former Soviet Union, and Zimbabwe—are alleged to have used BW. Not on this list, but mentioned by other sources, are Bulgaria, Cuba, Sudan, and Taiwan; and Pakistan, which the U.S. Central Intelligence

Agency (CIA) suspects of having biological weapons research. It is noteworthy the analysis does not include information on Brazil, Canada, France, Germany, Japan, the United Kingdom, and the United States, which are all known to have had BW programs.[35]

Historical references provide ample evidence of the potential for biological weapons to inflict large numbers of casualties and even render large areas uninhabitable until a thorough decontamination has been conducted. It is believed the Japanese BW experiments in the 1930s and 1940s caused disease and killed thousands of Chinese and Allied prisoners with anthrax, plague, cholera, and typhoid. The U.K. BW program was also quite robust, with one of the most oft-cited examples of open-air testing at Gruinard Island off the coast of Scotland in 1942. These tests determined, "weight for weight, anthrax could be one hundred to one thousand times more potent than any chemical weapon of the time."[36] A secondary effect was to render the island uninhabitable for almost fifty years. It took a major decontamination effort using millions of gallons of seawater and bleach to eliminate the anthrax spores from the area.

Arguably, the most robust of all state programs was that of the Soviet Union, which continued in earnest from the 1930s until the early 1990s. The Soviets melded their civilian and military biotechnical capabilities into a highly secretive program, which included hundreds of facilities and thousands of scientists. The oft-cited Vozrozhdeniye (Rebirth) Island in the Aral Sea is the prototypical open-air testing facility. Even today, after closure and significant decontamination at the expense of the United States as part of the Nunn-Lugar Cooperative Threat Reduction Act, Vozrozhdeniye Island remains a significant health hazard. Mortality rates and health statistics from the region indicate significant anomalies, such as high levels of arsenic, continuing to lead to low life expectancy and high infant mortality even after billions of dollars have been invested in clean-up efforts.

Much of what was learned about the program came from a number of Soviet defectors. One example is the information provided by Dr. Ken Alibek, who served as the deputy for Biopreparat, the organization responsible for leading much of the BW development program.[37] The Soviet program included all aspects of BW weapons design from laboratory work to open-air testing to development of the delivery systems that would transport the deadly cargo thousands of miles to the intended targets. The Soviets reportedly had developed the capability to launch BW-capable intercontinental ballistic missiles. For ensuring the availability and viability of the weapons, the Soviets had factories for BW production at

Stepnogorsk in Kazakhstan and at six other facilities that could rapidly produce large amounts of the weaponized BW material from the seed stocks they maintained.

One noteworthy event provides evidence of the program the Soviets had developed, the secrecy surrounding the program, and the potential lethality of the weapons. In 1979, an accidental release of anthrax occurred from a weapons production facility in the Soviet Union in the city of Sverdlovsk. The outbreak occurred over a sixty-day period. It originally was attributed publicly to contaminated meat, but in the Age of Perestroika, President Boris Yeltsin acknowledged the accidental release was from a weapons production facility. The incident is well documented in the Alibek book. The release was apparently caused by the inadvertent removal of a filter used in the end-stage production of the bacterium spores into appropriately sized particles for aerosolizing through the process of milling. The filter was essentially the last line of defense preventing the weaponized spores from release to the outside air. The release formed a highly predictable plume and subsequent dispersion pattern based on meteorological data at the time. The "contaminated meat" caused 96 people to become ill and 66 to die, according to accounts in Alibek's book. Another source suggests that the casualties may have exceeded 1,000 military and civilian deaths, although the mischief today continues to be shrouded in mystery.[38] The length of time from the release of the spores to the final infections provides evidence of the hardiness of the anthrax spores, and their ability to cause infections. While the initial release created a plume in the atmosphere sickening many of the night shift workers on duty within the affected area, later infections resulted from the spores being reaerosolized in the days and weeks after the original release. It is interesting to note one assessment: the Parliamentary Office of Science and Technology states the release "exposed 15,000 workers at the plant and at least 50,000 people living in the surrounding area to an aerosol of anthrax spores."[39] This suggests one of several possibilities: the exposures were very low in most of the cases, the agent may not have been as virulent as believed by the Soviet Union, or the lethal dose (LD) requirements for anthrax are higher than have been suggested in some analyses.

The experimentation by the former Soviet Union included efforts to develop resistant forms of disease and to increase the lethality of their pathogens. One account in which an antibiotic strain of anthrax was examined is provided below:

[S]cientists found that a plasmid with the genes for resistance to tetracycline, one of the most potent and widely effective of all antibiotics. In a
Petri dish, they mixed small quantities of B. *thuringiensis* with anthrax,
cultivated the two strains together, and then placed them in a test tube
with tetracycline to see if the anthrax bacteria would survive. The antibiotic killed most of the anthrax bacilli, but a few cells survived. Most of
these had incorporated the antibiotic-resistant genes from B. *thuringiensis*
into their own genetic structure. These new cloned cells could now be
used to create tetracycline-resistant strains of anthrax.[40]

The program began to be dismantled in the early 1990s, yet remnants
remain today in various states of disrepair in a number of countries
formerly part of the Soviet Union. Work continues under the Nunn-Lugar
program to destroy the last vestiges and ensure even the knowledge gained
through the program is no longer used for development of BW.[41]

Therefore, if one were to take the Leitenberg analysis and combine
it with the CIA input and the other known programs that have been
well documented in the literature on the subject, one would find twenty-
two nations that have at one time or another in the modern Age of
Biotechnology (i.e., since the 1940s) had some type of BW program. The
exact nature of many of these programs remains elusive, with many of the
details uncertain at best.

It would certainly be possible to delve more deeply into the question of
state-sponsored programs, but one is unlikely to get closer to ground truth
in this area. Suffice it to say that a bit more than twenty nations have had
varying levels of activity with regard to BW programs. However, one trend
worth considering is that the number of BW-capable states is decreasing.
Note, for instance, that Iraq has been found to not have biological weapons
in the aftermath of the 2003 invasion, and Libya agreed to divest all its
WMD capabilities and provide information concerning previous work in
this area.

Building a State BW Program

Despite the apparent decrease in the number of nations attempting
to develop BW weapons, examining the requirements for building such
a program can still provide a useful starting point for understanding the
equipment, technologies, capabilities, and facilities would be required. In
Chapter 3, these requirements will be compared to the requisite steps a
terrorist might need to take to gain such a deployable BW capability.

One such analysis for developing a state BW capacity comes from the OTA. In their analysis, the OTA developed a proliferation pathway for state actors that lists five main elements:

1. R&D
2. agent production
3. munitions design, testing, and building
4. delivery systems acquisition
5. operational capability acquisition[42]

Figure 2-5 provides a graphic overview of this five-step process, including each step's subordinate elements. This proliferation pathway identifies a typical industrial process required from early research through the fielding and lifecycle support for a major weapons system.

WMD DEVELOPMENT STEPS FOR STATE ACTORS

- Conduct Research and Development
  - Obtain microbial seed stock for standard or novel agent
  - Manipulate genetic characteristics (optional)
  - Test suitability for weapon purposes
  - Develop and pilot-test production process
- Produce Agent
  - Mass produce and harvest agent
  - Induce spore formation or freeze-dry
  - Microencapsulate agent
  - Store agent under refrigeration
- Design, Test, and Build Munitions
  - Area delivery: sprayer system or point delivery, cluster bomb or warhead
  - Field test
  - Mass produce
  - Fill munitions
  - Stockpile munitions
- Acquire Delivery System
  - Adapt aircraft, artillery, missiles, etc., as necessary
  - Establish logistical network
  - Acquire individual and collective BW defenses, including vaccines
  - Develop strategic and tactical BW battle plans
  - Train troops to use BW munitions and operate in a BW environment
- Acquire Operational Capability
  - Integrate munitions with delivery system
  - Integrate weapon systems into military forces

FIGURE 2-5 WMD Development Steps for State Actors (Office of Technology Assessment)

The methodology described in the report articulates a formal acquisition process for developing state BW capabilities. It provides a detailed exhaustive listing of those developmental activities for a state program. The process is flexible enough, however, to allow for tailoring it to respond to individual state preferences. For example, some of these steps could be combined or perhaps even eliminated for more-modest state programs.

In fact, many of the component elements such as "develop and pilot-test production process" within the first step—R&D—have greater applicability for a large-scale weapons program. They would not necessarily be required for relatively small-scale or investigative programs. The same can be said of the "acquire individual and collective BW defenses, including vaccines" in step 4, acquire delivery system. This step might go well beyond the minimum requirements for an early-stage state program. Of note is that any of these steps combined with the intent to develop an offensive BW capability would violate the Biological Weapons Convention (BWC) and international norms against the use and development of biological weapons capabilities. More on both the BWC and international norms will be discussed in detail later in this chapter.

A major weapons system acquisition program would be designed based on a requirements generation process and result in a system with specific measurable and predictable capabilities. Defense planners would likely not be satisfied with developing a system that may or may not reliably have the required effect. In contrast, a small-state program (or even a terrorist cell) would likely have a sliding scale in terms of outcomes and might be willing to accept an attack using a pathogen that may not be particularly toxic or invasive, and thus be satisfied with simply achieving inflicting terror on the target population or government without killing significant numbers of people. The desired outcome in terms of scale, mortality, and destruction will likely drive the rigor with which a state would conduct its BW program. Programs focused on achieving only a psychological effect would likely have a lower threshold for rigor in their developmental programs, while those attempting to achieve specific "battlefield" effects would likely have greater rigor and perhaps even follow more closely a large-scale state BW developmental process.

The FAS provides another perspective on the set of requirements for weapons production for a biological weapon. Their programmatic requirements are much less detailed and can be thought of as minimum required steps in a BW program. Their three stages are:

1. A biological agent must first be chosen and acquired. In the case of toxins, the production method must be acquired.
2. After growing and multiplying to sufficient quantities, various selection and modification procedures can alter certain traits and characteristics of the organism.
3. The agent is then prepared for delivery.[43]

This model clearly reflects a minimalist approach to BW weapons development and perhaps could be considered more in line with a small-state, nonstate, or terrorist program. The FAS model suggests the threshold for developing biological weapons can be quite low. The implication is that with the right information and access to pathogen seed stock, the development of a biological weapons capacity does not require much in the way of equipment or facilities.

The two basic steps for BW development identified in the "Military Critical Technologies" reference are (1) production, and (2) stabilization, dissemination, and dispersion. The design elements for production include containment, purification equipment, sterilization equipment, and ventilation and filtration systems. Equipment required for production include containment facilities with the appropriate barriers that protect workers, fermenters with a capacity greater than one hundred liters, centrifugal separators capable of processing five-liter batches, and cross-flow filtration equipment capable of processing twenty-liter batches. Stabilization, dissemination, and dispersion equipment includes freeze-drying equipment, aerosol inhalation chambers, delivery systems, and spray tanks to allow bomblet dissemination, warheads for missiles, and development and use of accurate short-term weather prediction.[44]

Acquisition of the seed stock for a state would not appear to be a significant hurdle either. This does not imply *all* pathogens would be readily available, but rather, with high probability, that a state would likely be able to acquire a highly pathogenic biological substance that could be weaponized. A number of sources are possible. The pathogen could be naturally harvested and, through biological engineering, modified to have the characteristics desired for the operational scenarios envisioned. A state would also likely have access to these pathogens through legitimate sources such as the ATCC (originally the American Type Culture Collection), which has a ready stock of thousands of samples for use in legitimate studies and processes. Only states with demonstrated questionable behavior in the past would likely find it difficult to legally obtain these materials. A state would also likely have the national capacity to develop this material either by growing the substances, as in the case of the toxins, or by using recombinant technologies to synthesize biological material for use in a BW program. While the state of recombinant technologies today would likely limit the ability to synthesize these pathogens, the rate of change in the field of biotechnology will lower thresholds and make these capabilities more readily available.

To complicate matters for those aiming to limit BW proliferation, since these weapons are based on biological pathogens, a very small amount of seed stock can be grown to a large amount of product suitable for use in a BW. The trick, so to speak, is to begin with the seed stock either through direct acquisition or modification, using specialized techniques to develop a pathogen that fits within the scenario or operational range of delivery parameters envisioned for the weapon.

Earlier we stated that some 20 nations had at one time had BW programs. The difficulties in establishing certainty in this area is directly related to the dual use issue. For both moderating behavior and discerning whether a nation has a BW program, one must consider that the technologies used in the development of a weapons program also have direct application in the pharmaceutical, food, cosmetic, and pesticide industries, as well as the obvious linkages to the fields of biotechnology and medicine. This complicates determining the purpose of sites where biotechnology is being used and therefore requires a degree of extrapolation to make a determination as to the exact nature of the work being done. Furthermore, the cost to develop even a "large-scale" facility for producing a BW is quite modest. "Biological Weapons Technology," published by the DoD in 1998 in their document "Militarily Critical Technologies List Part II: Weapons of Mass Destruction Technologies," says a vaccine plant would cost approximately $50 million, but a less-elaborate fermentation plant could be built for about $10 million, clearly well within the funding of most countries.[45] The basic equipment, while somewhat specialized, is not difficult to acquire, given its dual-use nature in a variety of medical and legitimate commercial activities.

Attempts to Moderate Behavior

The NRC and the IOM report, *Globalization, Biosecurity, and the Future of the Life Sciences*, characterizes biological weapons as easy and cheap to produce; highly diverse, with more than twenty pathogens suitable for use in BW; and difficult to detect. With this assessment, it should come as no surprise that there is significant difficulty associated with attempts to control proliferation or moderate behavior.[46]

Moderating behavior with regard to biological weapons can be thought of as efforts to deter or dissuade nations from developing biological weapons programs and more generally WMD programs, and from developing nonproliferation and counterproliferation (N/CP) activities. Deterrence and dissuasion are designed to prevent some action from occurring, in this case the acquisition of biological weapons. Deterrence can be achieved either by convincing a would-be aggressor the attack will fail—"deterrence by denial"—or by giving the impression success would be achieved at an excessive price—"deterrence by punishment."[47] Dissuasion can be achieved by persuading a state, group, or individual not to engage in some behavior or action.

Within the context of biological weapons, the intent of deterrence and dissuasion is to convince a party potentially interested in developing BW that the political costs would far exceed the likely benefit accrued from possessing these capabilities. The difficulty in this approach is that many states that want to acquire WMD capabilities do so to deter their potential adversaries within a regional context. They see ownership of WMDs as a way to offset shortfalls in conventional capabilities, or perhaps as a way to cause an adversary to refrain from attacking their nation.

An inherent difficulty in deterrence or dissuasion with regard to the acquisition of biological capabilities is that a nation would have to be convinced the simple act of possessing BW capabilities or weapons would be detrimental. This amounts to developing an argument designed to alter policy based on self-selection. Once a national decision is made to acquire BW capabilities, the strategy would need to change to incorporate N/CP activities to halt or hinder BW programs.

The DoD defines nonproliferation and counterproliferation as follows:

Nonproliferation: Those actions (e.g., diplomacy, arms control, multilateral agreements, threat reduction assistance, and export controls) taken to prevent the proliferation of weapons of mass destruction by dissuading or impeding access to, or distribution of, sensitive technologies, material, and expertise.

Counterproliferation: Those actions (e.g., detect and monitor, prepare to conduct counterproliferation operations, offensive operations, weapons of mass destruction, active defense, and passive defense) taken to defeat the threat and/or use of weapons of mass destruction against the United States, our military forces, friends, and allies.[48]

The definitions make clear that activities for both nonproliferation and counterproliferation are interagency and require combined contributions from several cabinet-level departments, agencies, and organizations working in a coordinated manner to achieve the intended results. Three of the preeminent actors in this regard are the DOS, the DoD, and the Intelligence Community (IC). Each of these has a strategy for dealing with these concerns. We will explore the DoD's strategy below.

The DoD strategy—the National Military Strategy to Combat Weapons of Mass Destruction—provides an instructive depiction of efforts to stem proliferation (Figure 2–6).[49] It portrays the relationships between counterproliferation, nonproliferation, and consequence management for WMDs, describing a continuous process in which counterproliferation and nonproliferation are used in complementary ways to reduce the potential for use of WMDs, reduce the effects if WMDs are used, and respond appropriately to eliminate future threats. It is always to the United States' advantage to remain on the left side of the diagram: that is, it is to our advantage to prevent, dissuade, deny, deter, and defeat a WMD threat. In the event this is not possible and an attack does occur, we must then have the capacity to defend, respond, and recover, as well as to take appropriate action to reduce, destroy, and reverse any proliferation trends.

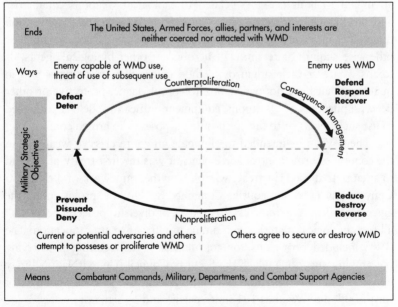

FIGURE 2–6 Strategic Military Framework for Combating WMDs.

Historically, a major tenet of our NSS has been based on the use of multilateral and bilateral arms control agreements to moderate behavior, limit weapons holdings, and control dangerous technologies. Examples include the Strategic Arms Limitation Talks (SALT) and the Intermediate-Range Nuclear Forces Treaty (INF), which limits long-range and eliminates intermediate-range nuclear weapons, respectively; the Chemical Weapons Convention (CWC), which eliminates chemical weapons; and the BWC, which prohibits offensive biological weapons capabilities. Treaty verification regimes coupled with requirements to modify certain perceived threatening behaviors form an important aspect of all effective arms control agreements.

Related programs such as the CTR regimes were developed during the post–Cold War era as part of the efforts of the Defense Threat Reduction Agency (DTRA) under the Nunn-Lugar legislation. These efforts are designed "to lessen the threat posed by WMDs, to deactivate and to destroy these weapons, and to help the scientists formerly engaged in production of such weapons start working for peace."[50] The efforts were focused on the threat from former Warsaw Pact nations, although recently the program has been broadened to include other nations where indications of potential proliferation have surfaced.

The roots of U.S. BW N/CP can be traced to the Cold War. The BWC attempted to limit activities related to biological weapons capabilities and production. Article I states, "Each State Party to this Convention undertakes never in any circumstances to develop, produce, stockpile or otherwise acquire or retain: (1) Microbial or other biological agents, or toxins whatever their origin or method of production, of types and in quantities that have no justification for prophylactic, protective or other peaceful purposes; (2) Weapons, equipment or means of delivery designed to use such agents or toxins for hostile purposes or in armed conflict."[51]

The BWC was intended to eliminate an entire class of weapons. In the context of arms control agreements, it was the first treaty of its kind to attempt to do so. The treaty was built on the framework of the Geneva Conventions cited previously. Contained within the provision of the agreement were requirements "to destroy, or divert to peaceful purposes" all such biological material within nine months of treaty ratification. The BWC included provisions for consultations, "cooperating in carrying out any investigations which the Security Council [United Nations] may initiate," and for information exchanges. By way of a reference point, as of early 2009, the BWC has 161 states-parties and 14 signatory states.[52]

Unfortunately, the BWC failed to contain a critical aspect of arms control treaties, a verification regime. It is under this context that the BWC, with the best of intentions, has failed to positively affect the norm against biological weapons. In fact, since the BWC entry into force (EIF), the number of nations with BW programs has grown. However, during the period from EIF to the present, establishing "ground truth" has proven to be problematic, with a wide variance in assessments, even of which nations have acquired BW capabilities.

For example, at the time of the BWC entering into force in 1975, four nations were believed to have BW: China, South Africa, the Soviet Union, and the United States.[53] However, in 1989, CIA Director William Webster announced, "at least 10 countries" were developing BW weapons.[54] Then in 2005, one source suggests seven nations had programs: China, Egypt, Iran, Israel, North Korea, Russia, and Syria.[55] Another indicates concern about "compliance for ten or so countries with the treaty and concerns about the biological weapons programs in a few countries that are not party to the treaty."[56] And of course earlier, Milton Leitenberg's analysis arrived at approximately 20 nations that at one time had BW programs.

In examining this question of state proliferation in 1995 in Senate hearings, the OTA listed seventeen countries that were "suspected of manufacturing biological weapons.[57] This statement reflects an increase in the estimated number of likely BW capable states at the time of the signing of the BWC and the statement by CIA Director Webster in 1989. The question of the actual number of BW-capable states was then and remains now a difficult one, as the data indicate. The lack of a viable BWC verification regime coupled with the ease of masking a BW program has most certainly contributed to this shortfall.

The lack of a verification regime in the BWC was due not to an act of omission, but rather to the difficulties associated with establishing an intrusive inspection and compliance monitoring system that would undoubtedly include defense facilities, civilian laboratories, and pharmaceutical companies. Such a requirement would be resource intensive in terms of time, cost, and personnel; ripe for industrial espionage; and of questionable utility, given the nature of biological weapons development, including the dual-use nature of biotechnology research.

To understand the extreme difficulties with developing a verification regime for the BWC, consider Figure 2–7, which was included in congressional testimony by Col. David Huxsoll, then director of the U.S. Army Medical Research Institute of Infectious Diseases (USAMRIID). In testimony to the U.S. Senate Committee on Governmental Affairs in

May 1989, Colonel Huxsoll discussed the difficulties in early-stage work of differentiating between a vaccine development program and a BW weapons program. While there will be some telltale signs in the early stages, it is only in the later stages of vaccine or BW weapons development that intent becomes clear.[58]

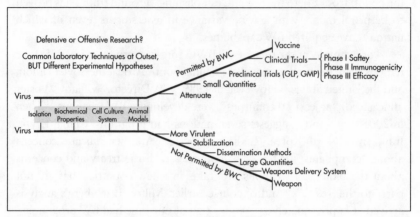

FIGURE 2-7 Offense or Defense? It's Hard to Tell.

In fact, many of the steps are identical in the early stages. Even in the later stages, differentiating between actions, equipment, and techniques for attenuating the pathogen to make it less virulent for use as a vaccine or more virulent for use as a weapon are difficult to discern. Similarities even exist in the testing of vaccines and weaponized material to determine effectiveness. In Figure 2–7, one differentiation appears to be in the quantities of material produced. The vaccine development branch suggests quantities would be small, while the weapons development branch suggests quantities would need to be large. However, even this differentiation is misleading. In the manufacturing of vaccines, it is not uncommon to see large amounts of biological material that would be required for developing the capacity for mass vaccinations.

The international framework for controlling the proliferation of biological weapons production capabilities, many of which are dual-use, does little to stem the flow of these technologies, the equipment required, or the source material necessary for developing biowarfare potential. Additionally, proliferation of the knowledge for bioweaponeering, also part of the dual-use conundrum, has become an issue because it, too, is becoming more readily available. Ultimately, international efforts, including BWC, although necessary and laudable, must be examined in light of the emerging international environment to determine if they are sufficient and what changes will be required to reduce BW proliferation and the potential for use of these weapons.

In a telling assessment of the environment in which the BWC was developed and ratified, one expert notes about the treaty, "When it was signed in 1972, scientists were not considered likely to develop biological weapons on their own, but at the behest of their governments. However, the perception that scientists are just tools of their governments changed with the increased powers of biotechnology and the increased interest in bioterrorism by nonstate actors." The same author notes, "the ability to use biology to do harm is no longer the province of teams of scientists and large budgets, but a possibility for a trained scientist working alone at the bench."[59] Given this recognition, efforts are under way to increase accountability for scientists with new provisions for bioethics, control of pathogenic material, and limiting the proliferation of key technologies and capabilities. Still, it points to a serious proliferation pathway that will be difficult to manage.

While over the years there has been considerable criticism of the BWC, and in particular the lack of its verification regime, one author notes the BWC has had an important positive effect: "The BWC stamped biological warfare as an illegitimate, immoral way to wage war. The moral force of the agreement has not extended to every nation—there are countries that almost certainly have biological weapons programs—but no country openly displays their biological weapons program."[60] This statement becomes very important in considering the potential for moderating behavior with respect to national biological weapons programs. It will also be important as we transition to the discussion of the potential for a bioterror attack.

Several other nonproliferation initiatives have been established to reduce the potential for these capabilities to be misused. The Australia Group (AG), formed in 1985, is a body of approximately forty like-minded nations that collaborate to restrain proliferation through a series of licensing measures on chemicals, biological agents, and dual-use equipment. A similar program is the Proliferation Security Initiative (PSI) announced by President George W. Bush in 2003. This initiative is designed as a cooperative measure with nine European allies, Australia, and Japan to interdict WMD trafficking. Still, the general proliferation of equipment, capabilities, and knowledge significantly limits the effectiveness of these initiatives in this increasing globalized world in the emerging Age of Biotechnology. One expert notes ominously, "The kind of trade control represented by the AG and PSI may be less effective in relation to biological weapons agents and equipment than it is for either chemical or nuclear arms."[61]

In examining these arms control policies, several common threads emerge. Arms control agreements enacted during the Cold War era were characterized as being international treaties under which signatory nations had detailed responsibilities for compliance, verification, and confidence building. They were state-to-state agreements with limitations applied primarily to military capabilities; they were not intended to restrict civilian activities. The notable exceptions were the CWC and BWC, which were based on the dual-use potential of the material and capabilities. These conventions made certain activities related to chemical and biotechnology unlawful.

The end of the Cold War has had serious negative consequences for biological weapons proliferation. The Soviet scientists that were once employed in state-sponsored labs found themselves no longer employed, and with highly marketable skills of great value to many in the commercial sector as well as to those seeking to develop a biological weapons program. The material that was under some degree of control in the Soviet bioweapons program is now not as closely guarded, nor is the information on developing these capabilities held or guarded today as state secrets.[62] To close this potential avenue of proliferation, the United States enacted the Nunn-Lugar Act, designed "to lessen the threat posed by weapons of mass destruction, to deactivate and to destroy these weapons, and to help the scientists formerly engaged in production of such weapons start working for peace."[63]

Even the United States, which is a signatory of the BWC, has conducted questionable work within the field of BW that has caused concern within the international community. From 1997 to 2001, three separate initiatives— projects *Clear Vision*, *Bacchus*, and *Jefferson*—examined various aspects of BW proliferation. *Clear Vision* involved fielding and testing a Soviet-type model bomblet for dispersing bacteria. *Bacchus* examined the potential for developing an anthrax-type weapon using readily available capabilities and equipment. *Jefferson* examined the potential for developing a resistant strain of anthrax bacteria. While each of these programs could easily be associated with an offensive BW program, one must look carefully at the intent in determining whether they were indeed a violation of the BWC.[64] Still, the issue is difficult, as Ken Alibek points out: "When you 'start modeling or mimicking actual weapons, you come into very sensitive areas' that can imply offensive preparations, especially if the details are kept secret."[65] In fact, these programs have caused difficulty for the United States with regard to BWC compliance. Additionally, the United States has not been supportive of efforts to strengthen the BWC because it would undoubtedly have negative impacts on "defensive" programs such as *Clear Vision*, *Bacchus*, and *Jefferson*, as well as general concerns by pharmaceutical companies and others about industrial espionage.

These three projects are not the only experiments that have been conducted during our nation's BW history. In fact, the history of the U.S. offensive biological warfare program can be traced back to fall 1941 when the Army began to examine the potential for employing biological weapons. Intelligence reports suggested that Germany and Japan might be preparing to launch a biological attack, making Allied efforts crucial for better understanding of potential effects and defensive preparations, and as deterrence. Early U.S. efforts focused on anthrax and botulinum toxin as well as pathogens that target livestock. In 1945 the United States reached an ominous milestone when the cloud chamber project that allowed for aerosol testing became operational at Fort Detrick.[66] Liaisons with key British and Canadian counterparts allowed for collaboration on BW development and information sharing, which was important to early U.S. efforts.

The early 1950s saw an expansion in the program in terms of both operational capability and development of the policy that could eventually result in the use of BW weapons by the United States. The first open-air tests were conducted off the coast of Norfolk using a BW simulant, *Bacillus globigii*. Open-air testing off the coast of San Francisco was also conducted during this period using both *Bacillus globigii* and *Serratia marcencens*. In the *Bacillus globigii* test, 130 gallons was released 2 miles offshore. It is estimated that 400,000 would have been infected and that lethal doses would have been seen as far away as Berkeley, CA. The intent of these tests was to examine the dispersion patterns and ultimately predict the potential for casualties. Development and expansion of BW facilities at Fort Detrick, Pine Bluff Arsenal, and Dugway Proving Ground continued. In one such test at Dugway, three individuals involved in testing *Coxiella burnetii*, the agent responsible for Q-fever, were infected from a distance of 43 miles from the release of the agent. This agent is highly infective with a single inhaled organism enough to cause an incapacitating disease. All three were treated and recovered.

The Army's experimentation with BW expanded to include tests with actual BW pathogens under Operation Whitecoat in 1955. The tests were designed to determine human susceptibility to *Coxiella burnetii*, the organism that causes Q-fever. In fact, one report states, "Between 1954 and 1967, at least seven different biological agents were produced: *Brucellis suis, Pasteurella [Fransicella] tularensis, Coxiella burnetii*, Venezuelan equine encephalitis [VEE], *Bacillus anthracis*, botulinum toxin, and *Staphylococcus enterotoxin* B [SEB].[67]

In the 1960s the open-air testing was expanded through a series of experiments under the Project 112 program. The sea testing was conducted under Project Shipboard Hazard and Defense (SHAD). The program was designed to understand the vulnerabilities of U.S. warships to chemical and biological weapons. One of the series of tests was codenamed Shady Grove and involved testing using *Bacillus globigii, Coxiella burnetii*, and *Pasteurella tularensis*. Ships and personnel were sprayed from an A-4B aircraft fitted with specially designed tanks. In all, Shady Grove consisted of twenty-five trials in the Pacific Ocean and another ten at Eglin Air Force Base, in Florida.[68]

In another Project 112 experiment, codenamed Red Cloud, the U.S. Army conducted experiments to gain an "understanding of biological decay and animal infectivity data on aerosols of *Francisella tularensis* (wet and dry forms) disseminated in a frigid field environment." In these experiments, bomblets were dropped from fixed towers and allowed to hit spruce trees to simulate actual envisioned operational conditions. These tests involved both monkeys and human subjects.[69] In all, Project 112 had planned for over one hundred tests; however, documentation indicates that approximately fifty were conducted.[70]

In *Lab 257*, an account of the BW programs at Plum Island off the coast of Long Island, Michael Christopher Carroll highlights several other tests conducted by the DoD, including special operations forces from Fort Detrick running "vulnerability tests" using suitcases to disperse *Serratia marcencens*, and a later experiment in 1966 using three *Bacillus subtilis*–filled light bulbs tossed into a New York subway to gauge the effects and dispersion patterns. In the case of the latter experiment, the assessment was than, had actual anthrax been used rather that the simulant, a million passengers would have been killed.[71]

The end of the U.S. offensive biological warfare program came in 1969, when President Nixon renounced the development, production, stockpiling, and use of biological warfare agents. However, this announcement came after a series of policy reviews by the Johnson and Nixon administrations and diminishing congressional support as the Senate Armed Services Committee voted to zero out funding, and amendments to the spending bills eliminated open-air testing in July 1969.[72] Before the end of the program, open-air tests in a variety of climates from arctic to temperate to tropical had been conducted and in a variety of settings including at sea and on land. The results have been catalogued and still contribute to our understanding of BW possible effects and dispersion patterns. Much of the history of the U.S. offensive program remains shrouded in secrecy and intrigue, even years later.[73]

Work in the United States for defensive BW continues today in government, commercial, and academic institutions. However, as we have seen, sorting tests, experiments, and programs in offensive or defensive activities is not a trivial matter.

The need to assess biological programs in terms of intent clearly complicates the determination of whether a particular project is a commercial activity that uses pathogens in a program such as vaccine development, a defensive BW activity, or an offensive BW program. Judging intent has been and will continue to be complex and highly subjective, and therefore will make developing definitive assessments concerning biotechnology-related programs challenging.

This leads to the unavoidable conclusion that in examining programs using biological material it is problematic, to say the least, to determine if a program is defensive, thus permitted under the BWC, or offensive, thus resulting in a violation of the convention. Furthermore, it makes determination of offensive versus defensive, in many respects, more *art* than *science*.

The ability to make this determination will become even more difficult as technology matures. Consider genetic engineering techniques that use recombinant technology in vaccine development. These techniques show great promise, as has been discussed previously. In this process, "the 'virus' genome is converted from RNA to DNA, manipulated to remove the genes thought to cause pathogenicity and converted back to RNA for vaccine production."[74] However, the potential most certainly exists for reversing the outcome such that a more potent pathogen would be created and reintroduced for use as a BW weapon. A cursory review of the work would likely not provide insight as to whether offensive or defensive work was being conducted.

One conclusion concerning the BWC is clear. The treaty has not and will not be able to alter BW proliferation activities in its current form and with its current provisions. Given the treaty's inability to address state BW proliferation, the ability to police nonstate activities is even less assured. If the BWC is not effective, how can one explain the trend toward a reduction in the number of states attempting to develop these capabilities?

One recent case study involving Libya, a state formerly aiming to acquire WMDs, renouncing these activities is enlightening. In attempting to explain the cost-benefit of this action, one analysis provides the conclusions seen in Table 2-1.[75]

TABLE 2-1 Libya's Decision to Renounce WMDs

Action	Cost (–)	Benefit (+)
Libya ending its WMD capability	• Reduce deterrence • Loss of status symbol • Possible security deficit	• Ease of international sanctions, financial benefits • Demonstrate goodwill, make positive gesture to the international community
Libya retaining its WMD program	• Sanctions continue • Libya isolated politically and economically • Country under constant pressure for being a WMD proliferator • WMD program no longer a financial burden • Economic costs to maintain WMD programs	• Retain political status symbol • Increased security

Of course, the data in the table are highly subjective and reflect an outsider's interpretation of the cost-benefit analysis. Still, the table is worthy of consideration. If the analysis is to be believed, Libya made a strategic assessment, determining the loss of deterrence and "prestige" was outweighed by the lifting of sanctions and the return to good standing within the community of nations. This is also an important development in that Libya has been identified frequently as a state sponsor of terrorism. Therefore, this announcement reflects one less potential proliferation channel for any terrorist actor formerly aligned with Libya.

The Dual-Use Conundrum

We have already alluded to the dual-use issues that advances in biotechnology have brought to the forefront of the proliferation issue, but this is an area that requires further elaboration because it lies at the heart of the dilemma we face. Colonel Huxsoll, in his testimony to the U.S. Senate Committee on Governmental Affairs in May 1989, highlighted that, in the early stages, the development of vaccines and weapons share common procedural paths. The equipment required for the two processes are also common. The major differences occur with regard to the end state of the processes, as well as to the intent of the actor. This sentiment will be a recurrent theme underlying the dual-use issue.

The NRC and the IOM, in their publication, *Globalization, Biosecurity, and the Future of the Life Sciences*, provide a useful graphic that elaborates on the complexities of the dual-use issue. This publication further helps to explain why the dual-use issue is so difficult to manage.[76] The fields of pharmaceuticals, medicine, agriculture, and biomaterials are identified as requiring specific biotechnologies, yet each also uses technologies that can be incorporated into a BW weapon. The obvious example is gene therapy, which can be used in the treatment of disease for the repair of defective genes, and which has great application in the manipulating of genes in a pathogen to change the pathogenicity or stabilization characteristics. Beginning from a common starting point, then, one can arrive at very different conclusions with very little that distinguishes the processes (Figure 2–8).

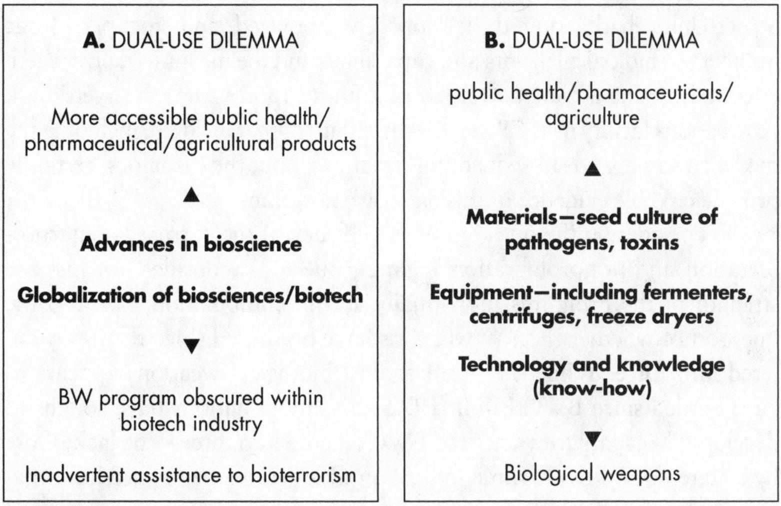

A. DUAL-USE DILEMMA

More accessible public health/ pharmaceutical/agricultural products

▲

Advances in bioscience

Globalization of biosciences/biotech

▼

BW program obscured within biotech industry

Inadvertent assistance to bioterrorism

B. DUAL-USE DILEMMA

public health/pharmaceuticals/ agriculture

▲

Materials—seed culture of pathogens, toxins

Equipment—including fermenters, centrifuges, freeze dryers

Technology and knowledge (know-how)

▼

Biological weapons

FIGURE 2–8 The Dual-Use Issue (from *Globalization, Biosecurity, and the Future of the Life Sciences*)

A complicating issue is that the requirements for biotechnology efforts are fairly common and can be contained within a modest facility with little measurable signature. Unlike reprocessing nuclear material, which requires highly specialized equipment with exact tolerances, biological weapons programs can be developed with common, off-the-shelf equipment, most of which can be found at local hardware stores and laboratory supply companies.

Consider that even in a legitimate commercial pharmaceutical plant that occupies 100,000 square feet of space, a small investigative BW capability could be contained within a one-hundred-square-foot space or ten-foot-by-ten-foot room, making it unobtrusive and difficult to identify as containing activities that would be in violation of the BWC. To identify those activities would be like trying to find the proverbial "needle in a haystack."

So What about State Programs?

Coming back to the BWC by way of a final conclusion and as a transition to the next section, anecdotal evidence of the BWC's success or lack thereof can be found in references and testimonials published since the end of the Cold War. Ken Alibek in his book, *Biohazard*, paints a grim picture of the degree to which the Soviet Union disregarded the BWC despite having signed the agreement.[77] If his assertions are to be believed, the former Soviet Union had acquired, developed, weaponized, and stockpiled large numbers of biological agents and capabilities and the means to deliver them effectively.[78] The accidental release of anthrax spores from the Sverdlovsk bioweapons facility in 1979 and the aftermath of that incident, including the media coverage and subsequent information about the casualties, certainly provide credible evidence of this extensive program.

In considering the question of the efficacy of the current counterproliferation and nonproliferation regimes, one must consider not just the strength of the programs individually and in combination, but also the question of whether the BW weapons have been used since the treaty entered into force. While the norm against biological weapons appears to have eroded since BWC EIF in 1972—and more nations have sought to develop BW capabilities since the BWC entered into force—the lack of use by a state does provide some indication of a deterrence or threshold that has moderated state behavior. The same sentiment cannot be expressed with regard to the nonstate or terrorist organizations, which have demonstrated a desire to acquire and use BW capabilities ranging from deadly toxins to viruses and bacteria.[79]

Bioterror

According to Barton Gellman of the *Washington Post*, documents seized in Pakistan in March 2003 reveal that al-Qaeda has acquired the necessary materials for producing botulinum and salmonella toxins and the chemical agent cyanide—and is close to developing a workable plan for producing anthrax, a far more lethal agent. Even more worrisome is the possibility that al-Qaeda, perhaps working with Hezbollah or other terrorist groups, will recruit scientists with access to sophisticated nuclear or biological weapons programs, possibly, but not necessarily, ones run by the state.[80]

Introduction

When examining the question of whether a terrorist could develop a BW capability, the literature generally breaks down into two diametrically opposed camps. One school of thought makes the claim terrorists have the capability to develop and successfully use BW weapons. The second school of thought concludes terrorists do not have that capability and that there are too many hurdles to overcome for the terrorist to be able to execute all requisite steps to develop such a capability.

In summing the arguments supporting the first school of thought, a course at the University of Dayton on "Bioterrorism, Public Health and the Law" provides several short anecdotes to introduce the subject:

- Manufacturing a lethal bacterial disease agent requires little more than chicken soup, a flat whiskey bottle, and an available source of seed culture.
- Producing biological weapons was "about as complicated as manufacturing beer and less dangerous than refining heroin."
- In seminar presentations a few years ago, former CIA Director James Woolsey claimed that "a B-plus high school chemistry student" could produce biological agents. At a January 2000 meeting, he described producing biological agents as being "about as difficult as producing beer."
- A group of professors, graduate students, and pharmaceutical manufacturers concluded that several biologists with only $10,000 worth of equipment could produce a significant quantity of biological agent.[81]

It is useful to note that, while these introductory statements support the ease with which a terrorist is likely to be able to develop BW weapons, the course concludes that the effortlessness with which a terrorist could develop a BW capability seems to has been overstated.

Still it is useful to examine the arguments on both sides of the issue. It is also important to look at previous attempts by terrorists to develop BW weapons. For example, the Japanese cult Aum Shinrikyo failed to develop that capability with seemingly adequate resources and appropriate technical knowledge and capabilities. The Rajneessees were successful at the crude release of *E. coli* but were unable to develop more pathogenic BW capabilities. We also know that the anthrax used in the Amerithrax attacks were prepared in two different batches, with one being considerably less virulent due to having been "overcooked."

In a rapidly emerging center position, some analysts are taking the position that difficulties do exist for BW weapon development, but that advances in biotechnology are lowering these thresholds. These analyses take the position that the proliferation of biotechnology is increasing the ease of developing BW weapons, thus leading to an increased likelihood of a bioterror event. One such study that examines the likelihood, consequences, and risks for scenarios including biocrimes, state BW, and terrorism concludes the likelihood was low to very low for all state-sponsored attacks, based on historical precedent. For biocrimes involving a lone actor, the probability was assessed to be high, while for terrorism, the assessment was "low to moderate, but increasing." The rationale for this increase was specifically due to the increasing proliferation of dual-use technologies.[82]

A DOS briefing presented in July 2006 at a Naval Postgraduate School (NPS) conference on "Terrorism, Transnational Networks and WMD Proliferation: Indications and Warning in an Era of Globalization," concludes, "The international community faces a growing risk from extended networks of terrorists and facilitators seeking to acquire and use nuclear, chemical, biological and radiological (CBRN) weapons and devices." The brief lists four factors driving this increased risk: (1) diffusion of scientific and technical expertise, (2) growth in the illicit trafficking of certain materials, (3) persistent weaknesses in supply chain security for sensitive technologies and materials, and (4) widespread use of sensitive materials and legitimate dual-use technologies in the industry, medical, and agricultural sectors.[83]

Another noted expert, Bruce Hoffman, comments, "[M]any of the constraints (both self-imposed and technical) which previously limited terrorist use of WMD are eroding."[84] This concern is echoed by James Russell, from the Department of National Security Affairs at NPS in another brief from the NPS conference, "Framing Globalization, the Nexus, and WMD Proliferation." Russell concludes previous studies indicated that terrorists were not particularly interested in mass casualty attacks, but that changed in the 1990s, beginning with a series of high-profile attacks and actions.[85]

In considering the potential for terrorists' use of BW, another study in 1999 jointly conducted by the Center for Counterproliferation

Research at the National Defense University (NDU) and the Center for Nonproliferation Studies (CNS) at the Monterey Institute of International Studies (MIIS) assessed the likely impact of recent and anticipated advances in biotechnology on the ability of terrorists to acquire and use biological agents, as follows:

> It is the sense of the focus group that two types of bioterrorists are in the best position to apply the advanced techniques of biotechnology in research to enhance microorganisms for purposes of BW. The first type consists of states possessing BW programs and supporting international terrorist groups. Since these state programs can be assumed to be staffed with qualified technicians and scientists, well funded, and designed to operate for the long-term, they are best placed to undertake the type of risky R&D described above and to perform adequate field testing that would ascertain the newly developed agent's value for weapons use.
>
> The second type is the disgruntled or deranged scientist who works in a well-equipped clinical microbiology laboratory or academic laboratory involved in some aspect of microbiological research. This kind of person can be expected to have the knowledge, patience, and resources needed to undertake and complete the research he perceives is needed to accomplish his objectives and to do the testing necessary to ascertain the newly developed agent's value for weapons use.[86]

The study also identifies characteristics considered to be of value for a pathogen to be used in a terrorist attack. These characteristics include high virulence coupled with high host specificity, high degree of controllability, high degree of resistance to adverse environmental forces, lack of timely countermeasures to the attacked population, and ability to camouflage the BW agent with relative ease.[87] These will become important in considering the type of pathogen likely to be selected for the potential development of a terrorist BW weapon.

In turning to the argument supporting the second school of thought, Leitenberg arrives at the following conclusions as part of his work, "An Assessment of the Biological Weapons Threat to the United States": "(1) [It is] not just a matter of time before chem-bio terrorism occurs, (2) hoaxes and threats more likely than use, (3) chemical is more likely than biological substances, (4) small-scale more likely than large-scale attacks, (5) crude dispersal in enclosed area most likely mode of attack, and (6) CB [Chem-Bio] terrorism is not about to become the car bomb of the 1990s."[88]

Leitenberg, in the 2005 U.S. Army War College study, provides an even more negative assessment of the potential for a terrorist to develop BW weapons. Has the threat diminished between the 2001 and 2005 assessments? In reading these conclusions, one would have to believe something has occurred that would cause Leitenberg to believe even more strongly the bioterror threat has been overstated.

In pressing his case that the threat has been hyped, Leitenberg expresses concern that there is an opportunity cost associated with such a keen focus on biodefense, maintaining there are other more-pressing needs in the biotechnology and health fields requiring our attention, and that to focus on this single area is a disservice. The five conclusions of his 2005 study are listed in Figure 2–9.[89]

ASSESSING THE THREAT

1. Significance of the problem. "Bioterrorism" may or may not develop into a serious concern in the future, but it is not "one of the most pressing problems we have on the planet today."
2. The evolution of state biological weapons programs. The number of state BW programs has apparently been reduced by one-third or one-fourth in the past 15 years. The remaining number of countries appears to be stable; no compensating rise in offensive state BW programs has been identified.
3. The evolution of nonstate/terrorist biological weapon capabilities. The production and distribution of a dry powder anthrax product in the United States in 2001 is the most significant event. However, understanding to what degree that demonstration of competence is relevant to "traditional" terrorist groups is impossible until the perpetrator(s) of the anthrax events are identified. If it was done with assistance, materials, knowledge, access, etc., derived from U.S. biodefense program, the implications change entirely.
4. Framing "the threat" and setting the agenda of public perceptions and policy prescriptions. For the past decade the risk and immanence of the use of biological agents by nonstate actors/terrorist organizations— "bioterrorism"—has been systematically and deliberately exaggerated.
5. Costs of the U.S. biodefense program. On the grounds of "necessity," the U.S. biodefense research program appears to be drifting into violation of Article 1 of the BWC.

FIGURE 2–9 Assessing the Biological Weapons and Bioterrorism Threat

A 2000 Government Accountability Office (GAO) report supports the assessment that acquiring development of effective BW capabilities for a terrorist program is a nontrivial issue. The report concludes, "[T]errorists would have to overcome extraordinary technical and operational challenges to effectively and successfully weaponize and deliver a biological agent to cause mass casualities."[90] Of course, a significant qualifier contained in this assessment is that the goal of the terrorist would be to cause mass casualties. Looked at from the standpoint of what might be needed to cause fear and terror, one is likely to arrive at a far lower standard for the capabilities required.

The Gilmore Commission—an advisory panel established to assess domestic response capabilities for terrorism involving WMDs—also considered this issue. The commission released a series of five annual reports on the topic with the last release in December 2003. This panel also leaned more toward the assessment that a level of the complexity exists with respect to building an effective WMD capability, and that those suggesting an attack is "not only possible, but probable" are overstating the case. However, the commission did allow that a terrorist would "require sophisticated, though not exotic laboratory equipment" and, "a laboratory could be equipped for between $200,000 and $2 million."[91]

It is worth noting that both the GAO report and the first of the five annual reports of the Gilmore Commission were published prior to the Amerithrax attacks and therefore did not take into account this defining event, which provides a significant example of what a terrorist might be able to accomplish with the right tools and knowledge. It is interesting to note that by the fifth and final 2003 Gilmore Commission report, the sentiment expressed far less certainty, concluding, "a healthy respect for the uncertainties in both the current and potential future terrorist threat spectrum" is in order.[92] In the case of the GAO report, we must absolutely factor in that timing of the report. Much has been accomplished in biotechnology in the intervening decade.

Of course, the revelations in July 2008 that the Amerithrax attacks were likely perpetrated by a highly trained and experienced scientist from the U.S. Army Medical Research Institute of Infectious Diseases, Dr. Bruce Ivins, demonstrates both a potential proliferation pathway for acquiring the necessary material and that a high degree of knowledge is a prerequisite for developing an effective terrorist BW capacity.[93]

Deadly biological pathogens are readily available in the environment and contribute to human, animal, and plant disease regularly as part of normal daily life. The degree to which terrorists can use these natural pathogens in a coordinated way to have an intended effect is based on a number of factors, including the type of pathogen selected, the ability to weaponize and prepare it for delivery, and the scenario to be employed. The question therefore comes down to whether a terrorist has the technical capability and resources to acquire a BW capacity. On this question, we must reconcile the two diametrically opposed positions. So with the positions of the two camps established, an important next step is to examine what the record indicates with regard to terrorist activities concerning biological weapons.

What the Record Shows

One of the earliest uses of BW by terrorists was in 1910 by the Pancho Villa guerillas, a separatist group battling Mexican federal troops during the Mexican Revolution. The incident involved the use of cultured botulinum toxin, which was prepared and thrown at federal troops. There were no reports of any disease resulting from this incident.[94] This use of BW is interesting, but does little to provide a systemic overview of the history of modern BW use.

In 2003, the CNS at the MIIS conducted a study for the Department of Energy focusing on terrorist use of WMDs. For this analysis, chemical, biological, radiological, and nuclear incidents were considered. The findings were important in laying out the facts and arguments concerning this form of terrorism.[95] Perhaps the most interesting aspect of this effort concerns the total number of WMD and bioterrorist incidents during the period from 1900 to 2003. The data list only 383 incidents, of which only seventy-seven were biological. The data set does not include state-sponsored BW or hoaxes. The hoaxes, in particular, would include a large number of "incidents" because they tend to outnumber actual events by as much as one hundred to one.[96] Furthermore, the data reflect only known incidents. Most certainly, there have been other attempts made by individuals or terrorist groups to examine, experiment, or perhaps even weaponize biological material that have not been discovered. Still, even with this caveat, the data suggest that WMDs—and specifically bioterror—has not been a particularly central part of the terrorists' arsenal to date.[97] Several other important conclusions resulted from this study as well. The small number of incidents and the uniqueness of each limit the ability to draw definitive conclusions from the data. This lack of data is also limiting with regard to developing a predictive tool for assessing the likelihood of bioterrorist attacks. Instead, each event requires analysis individually to determine the key parameters and outcomes that defined the event and ultimately the success or failure of the attack. Worthy of note is that the MIIS database contains only four terrorist BW events since 1945 that have caused ten or more casualties. They are (1) Mitsuru Suzuki, 1964–66 (food borne—64 victims/0 deaths); (2) the Rajneeshees, 1984 (food borne—751 victims/0 deaths); (3) Diane Thompson, 1996 (food borne—12 victims/0 deaths); and (4) unknown (alleged to be Dr. Bruce Ivins), September/October 2001 (aerosol—22 victims/5 deaths). In fact, the history of bioterror is perhaps most noteworthy for the lack of information on the events and the groups that have perpetrated these BW attacks.

One study that examined the types of pathogens that terrorists have pursued concluded a severe mismatch in funds versus the potential threats has occurred. For example, no evidence exists that terrorists have attempted in the past thirty years to develop weaponized products from the causative agents of plague, tularemia, brucellosis, glanders, or melioidosis. Despite lack of evidence of a threat from these diseases, programs to counter these pathogens have received large investments since 2001 for research and other biodefense initiatives. The study did, however, conclude terrorists had demonstrated interest in pathogens including *Escherichia coli* (commonly *E. coli*), yellow fever, salmonella, malaria, typhoid, West Nile virus, and avian influenza virus. Furthermore, it concluded that availability was the primary factor in this interest, and not necessarily the potential for contagion or even efficacy as a bioweapon.[98]

Another particularly important source in examining the topic of bioterror is *Toxic Terror*, edited by Jonathan Tucker. The compendium examines twelve uses or attempted uses of terrorist BW and CW, providing information on the manner in which the weapons were acquired and the results of each effort. The case studies are summarized in Table 2–2.[99]

The analyses are highly informative: they describe the types of individuals or groups that have tried to acquire BW and chemical warfare (CW) capability and the inability of many of the perpetrators to come close to mounting an effective attack. In fact, in some cases the results of the efforts are almost laughable and certainly indicate an unrealistic conception of biological agents and potential attack scenarios. For example, in 1986 the CSA aimed to overthrow the U.S. government. They perpetrated an attack using potassium cyanide. Their attack was completely infeasible in terms of the means employed, the technical capabilities of the perpetrators, and the likely effect even if a "successful" attack had been conducted.

The two most instructive of the twelve scenarios are the Rajneeshee and Aum Shinrikyo efforts because they represented methodical plans in the Age of Modern Terrorism designed to develop BW capabilities. In the case of the Rajneeshees, they were able to successfully deploy a pathogen and cause disease in humans. However, to judge whether they had the intended effect requires examining their motivations. In this case, they failed, because they were not able to alter the outcome of elections in the town of The Dalles, Oregon, as they intended to do.

TABLE 2-2 Comparison of Case Studies Presented in *Toxic Terror*

CASE	MOTIVATION	AGENTS	OUTCOME
Avenging Israel's Blood (1946)	Mass killing of German citizens to avenge the Holocaust	Arsenic-containing mixture	Thousands sickened; number of fatalities unknown
Weather Underground (1970)	Temporarily incapacitate populations to demonstrate impotence of the U.S. government	Reportedly sought to obtain BW agents from Fort Detrick by blackmail of gay soldier	Informant reported planned attempt to blackmail soldier
R.I.S.E. (1972)	Kill off most of humanity to prevent destruction of nature, then start human race over with a select few	Microbial pathogens	Attack aborted when cultures were discovered. perpetrators fled to Cuba
Alphabet Bomber (1974)	Revenge against city of Los Angeles and the U.S. legal system for denying him a permit to open a dance hall	High explosive bombs, followed by an effort to produce nerve agents	Nerve agent was not actually produced or the threatened attack carried out; perpetrator was arrested
Baader-Meinhoff Gang (1975)	Release of imprisoned leaders of group	Containers of mustard gas	Probably a hoax based on reports of missing CW
Red Army Faction (1980)	Alleged biological attacks against West German officials or business leaders	A group member allegedly cultivated botulinum toxin in a Paris safe house	Probably an erroneous report, later denied by the German government authorities
Rajneeshees (1984)	Scheme to incapacitate voters to win local election, seize political control of the county	*Salmonella typhimurium*, a type of food poisoning bacteria	Plot was revealed when member turned informant following a successful attack
The Covenant, the Sword, and the Arm of the Lord (1986)	Carry out God's judgments, overthrow federal government, hasten return of the Messiah	Potassium cyanide	Group was penetrated by FBI informants and leaders were arrested
Minnesota Patriots Council (1991)	Cause damage to the federal government; obtain personal revenge	Ricin extracted from castor beans by mail order	Group was penetrated by FBI informants; four key members arrested
World Trade Center Bombers (1993)	Personal and political revenge for Arabs killed by the United States and Israel	Terrorists allegedly included cyanide in their urea nitrate bomb	Members of the group were arrested; the cyanide allegation is probably false
Aum Shinrikyo (1995)	Proof of prophecy, eliminate enemies and rivals, halt adverse court ruling, cause havoc, seize control of Japanese government	Biological agents (anthrax, botulinum toxin, Q-fever, Ebola virus) and chemical agents (sarin, VX, hydrogen cyanide)	Multiple chemical attacks (in Matsumoto, Tokyo, and assassination campaign) killed at least 20 people and injured more than a thousand
Larry Wayne Harris (1995, 1998)	Produce BW vaccines and antidotes for defensive purposes; alert Americans to the Iraqi BW threat	Obtained plague and anthrax (vaccine strain) and reportedly isolated several other bacteria	Arrested because he talked openly about BW terrorism and made threatening remarks to U.S. officials

Still, on balance, one would have to conclude this 1984 attack has many key elements that should serve as a cause for great concern. First, the group was able to obtain pathogens from legal sources for use in their experiments and subsequent attacks. Second, they were able to culture the necessary material in significant quantity for mounting a small-scale biological attack. The pathogens they used were not highly virulent, but their use certainly demonstrated a knowledge and basic capability to produce biological material suitable for use in an attack. The outcome would have been considerably different if a high pathogenic BW agent had been used instead of *Salmonella enterica*, which is the causative agent in salmonella and results in food poisoning. Third, the group was able to conduct their work with a minimal amount of expertise. Only the leader of the effort, who was trained as a nurse, and her "assistant," who was trained as a lab technician, had any medical training. Fourth, only modest amounts of equipment were required in order to develop a basic BW capability, serving to highlight that a BW capability, albeit rudimentary, can be achieved for a relatively modest investment. Fifth, the preparations for the attack and the actual attack went undetected. It was only after one of the cult's members was arrested a year later on an unrelated charge that the attack was uncovered, when one of the perpetrators confessed to the attack during questioning concerning an unrelated incident. Until then, the authorities assumed the illnesses had been caused by a bad batch of salad naturally tainted with salmonella.

In the case of Aum Shinrikyo, BW agents were released but had no effect: the attackers used nonlethal pathogens (i.e., a nonpathogenic variant of anthrax) and had difficulties in dispersing their agent. They were, however, "successful" in 1995 in a chemical attack with sarin gas on the crowded Tokyo subway. That attack killed at least twenty people and exposed thousands to the nerve agent.

The failed attempts by Aum Shinrikyo to acquire BW capabilities are puzzling. In some regards, too, they have served to reinforce the position of those who declare BW capabilities are difficult to develop and use, are beyond the capability of terrorists, and therefore the probability of such an attack is low. Aum Shinrikyo was a billion-dollar organization with a highly educated and even technically adept membership, including several people with medical experience. Still, their efforts fell short. Their difficulties included the use of a nonpathogenic form of anthrax for their weapon and the failure to get the particle size to be effective for dissemination of aerosol or inhalational anthrax. Additionally, the group experimented with other pathogens, including botulinum toxin, but were unable to weaponize this material, either.[100]

In looking past these historical examples, several vignettes may lead us closer to the question of the potential for terrorist development of BW capabilities in the future. In the United States, the BW program considered more than 675 strains of *Clostridium botulinum* prior to the program's termination in 1969 before it found one with the desired pathogenicity. Even experts have had difficulty in identifying the appropriate strains of pathogens. Dr. Jerzy Mierzejewski, the retired director of the Polish biological defense laboratories who spent his career working with *Clostridium botulinum*, lamented, "[O]ne culture cycle would produce toxin that was lethal and a few months later the next would not, and so on over the years."[101]

Another powerful vignette concerns a task William Patrick gave to a postdoctoral student. Patrick played a prominent role in the U.S. BW program until it was terminated in 1969. He served as the chief of the Product Development Program and is a recognized BW expert. He tasked this student to develop a mass casualty scenario using a pathogen that had been investigated in the pre-1969 U.S. program. The student was given a year to develop this scenario using the pathogen *Francisella tularensis*, the bacteria that causes the disease tularemia. At the end of the year, when the results were briefed, the student had made three fatal errors that would have doomed the effort and prevented a successful attack.[102] The student had failed to filter the product prior to use, leaving large particles which would plug up the spray nozzle. The atomizer specifications were not adequate for developing the required concentration. Finally, the student failed to consider the air handling capabilities of the building.

When six anthrax-filled letters were delivered to their addresses, at various addresses in the United States, real danger replaced theoretical "what ifs." Those letters demonstrated the potential for anthrax to be used as an effective terror weapon, even when simplistic delivery methods are employed. The amount of anthrax contained in all the letters combined was the approximate volume of a handful of crushed aspirin tablets. Leonard Cole writes, "During the fall 2001 scare, congressional sessions were suspended and the U.S. Supreme Court was evacuated. Infected mail disrupted television studios and newspaper offices. People everywhere were afraid to open mail."[103] Between October 4 and November 21, twenty-two people were diagnosed with cutaneous and inhalational anthrax. All eleven cutaneous victims recovered, while five of the eleven diagnosed with inhalational anthrax succumbed to the disease despite aggressive antibiotic treatment. The implications of this event can be best illustrated by the billions of dollars that have been spent on the clean-up and subsequent policies, procedures, and programs resulting from this attack. More on these biodefense preparations will be discussed later, in Chapter 3, but suffice it to say this was a defining event for the biodefense community.

The CNS at the MIIS provided another illuminating analysis, in addition to their study for the Department of Energy focusing on terrorist use of WMDs. The study traced attempts by al-Qaeda to acquire WMDs. What is startling about the information in the center's analysis is the alleged depth and breadth of al-Qaeda activities for acquiring biological capabilities. Pathogens investigated included anthrax, botulinum toxin, Ebola, and ricin. The documentation also includes some claims from government sources from the United States and its allies, including France and the United Kingdom, concerning alleged al-Qaeda BW activities. In all, the table data set contains more than thirty entries with information ranging from a single report such as, "Usama bin Ladin reportedly constructed 'crude' CBW [chemical-biological weapons] in laboratories in Khost and Jalalabad, Afghanistan, acquiring ingredients for CW and BW from former Soviet states" in June 1999 from "unspecified intelligence sources," to newspaper accounts such as, "Stephen Younger, director of the Defense Threat Reduction Agency, claims that al-Qaeda's [Qa'ida's] interest in BWs is focused mainly on anthrax."[104]

Several of the accounts also provide information on state sponsorship of terrorist BW activities. The general sponsorship falls into two categories: First is the proliferation of technologies through scientists and former weapons experts who are unemployed or underemployed as a result of the end of the Cold War. For example, a May 1998 entry from the data set contains a listing, "Bin Ladin's group reportedly purchases three CBW [chemical-biological weapons] factories in the former Yugoslavia and hires a number of Ukrainian chemists and biologists to train its members."[105] In fact, this concern has been recognized, and programs such as the Nunn-Lugar Threat Reduction Program are designed to close this proliferation window.

The second type of state sponsorship is the direct allegiance in which the state provides capabilities to terrorist organizations. An example would be the following alleged event: "Various reports describe Muhammad Atta, the leader of the September 11 hijackers, meeting in Prague with an Iraqi intelligence agent, who allegedly gave him a vial of anthrax."[106] Even in this case, it is difficult to unequivocally establish state sponsorship, because the agent may have been working for the government, but may not have been sponsored for this proliferation activity.

Another BW-related activity not normally captured in the data sources are hoaxes, which include a large number related to BW. In one report, the authors note, "in the midst of the turmoil [of the Amerithrax attacks] in late 2001, it largely escaped attention that more than 750 'hoax' letters claiming to contain anthrax were sent worldwide in October and November. More than 550 of these hoax letters were sent to abortion clinics in the United States by a single group called the Army of God."[107]

TABLE 2-3 Politics of Bioterrorism in America

YEAR	SYNOPSIS
1985	National Academy of Sciences reports that terrorist use of even low-level biological weapons against American civilians is a significant threat.
1992	Defection to the United States of Kanatjan Alibekov (later known as Ken Alibek). Alibek detailed significant Soviet advances and preparations in this area.
1992, 1993	Two reports from the OTA: (1) highlighting that BW might be more attractive than nuclear weapons to terrorists, and (2) statistics about the lethality of BW.
1992	U.S. Senators Nunn and Lugar develop legislation to stem the flow of WMD weapons and technologies from former Soviet Union.
1995	William Patrick speaks at the White house about the implications of the Aum Shinrikyo efforts.
1997	*Journal of the American Medical Association* dedicates an entire issue to the subject; Secretary of Defense William Cohen speaks passionately about the potential for a BW attack.
1996–1998	Two books and a television program feature BW prominently in their plots. *The Cobra Event* describes the release of a genetically engineered smallpox virus. Tom Clancy's novel, *Executive Order*, posits a bioterrorist attack with an aerosolized Ebola virus. An ABC *Primetime Live* airs a program called "Germ Warfare: Weapons of Terror."
1998	The IOM publishes a report that supports the notion that bioterrorism is a major threat to the United States.
1999	The Johns Hopkins Center for Civilian Biodefense Studies is established. Major features include exercises such as Dark Winter and Atlantic Storm, which become a major "resource" for supporting the need for more spending in this area.
2001	Amerithrax attacks occur in the United States.

In *Bracing for Armageddon*, William Clark examines what he calls the "politics of bioterrorism in America," tracing the evolution of thinking surrounding the bioterror threat in the United States. The results are summarized in Table 2–3.[108] Many of the events have largely been discussed previously within this book, but it is the collection of events along with the accompanying synopsis that makes the information noteworthy. After reviewing several milestone events from 1985 to 2001, Clark concludes rhetoric does not match the evidence and the funding for antibioterror far exceeds what would be reasonable, given the state of the threat today. Clark writes, "Taken together the technical realities, actual case histories and statistical records of terrorist behavior with chemical and biological substances undercut the rhetoric considerably and point not to catastrophic terrorism but to small attacks where a few, not thousands would be harmed."[109] In fact, Clark, a professor and Chair Emeritus of Immunology at the University of California, Los Angeles, continues with this theme. In the conclusions of this book, he rails against the wasteful spending on biodefense that has come at the expense of other more pressing medical needs such as HIV/AIDS.

In summarizing the potential for terrorist BW use and in particular acquisition of BW material, a government-sponsored CRS publication provides another outstanding synopsis, calling the information "contradictory and sketchy."[110] The reference notes many allegations of terrorist attempts to acquire these capabilities, but few that have been verified. Groups that fall into this category (besides al-Qaeda) include the Palestine Liberation Organization (PLO), the Red Army Faction, Hezbollah, the Kurdistan Workers' Party, German neo-Nazis, and Chechen separatists.[111]

Despite the Amerithrax attacks and the reports on al-Qaeda alleged activities, the overall data suggest BW—until now—has not been the weapon of choice for terrorists. This leads to some inevitable questions. If the history of terrorist BW is so limited over the past hundred years and the few recent incidents are so insignificant in terms of casualties and loss of property, why has the potential use of biological weapons by terrorists received such an increase in notoriety and—as we will see later—such an increase in funding? Have we overstated the case for terrorist BW?[112]

Building a Terrorist BW Program

In 2006, the *Washington Post* ran a series of articles that reported the findings of an investigative study designed to determine the ability to get access to the materials, equipment, and knowledge to develop a biological weapon. The series was clear and to the point. The capabilities for developing WMDs, particularly biological and chemical capabilities, are no longer the sole province of nation-states.

In considering the usefulness of the OTA proliferation pathway methodology discussed previously for state BW efforts, it simply does not account for small-scale efforts that could be undertaken by terrorists. Furthermore, that methodology does not have any relevance to a rogue actor who works in the field of biotechnology—say, in a laboratory environment—involved in drug research by day and building BW weapons using the same capabilities at night. To gain additional insights into the potential for a terrorist to develop a BW capability, we will now examine the steps that would be necessary.

The essential first step in the bioweapons development process is the acquisition of pathogens. Unlike with nuclear and even chemical weapon precursors, materials are readily available to provide the necessary seed stock for growing highly pathogenic biological products that would form the basis of a weaponized product. Given the nature of biological weapons, it follows that the acquisition of biological material from which to begin development is not a particularly limiting factor in readying for an attack.

A complicating issue in seeking to prevent biological proliferation is that material can be obtained from a variety of sources, some of which are commercially based. Sources of seed material include natural harvesting, theft from a research or commercial source, legal procurement of samples routinely available for commercial or research applications, and the creation (based on new techniques) of pathogens.

Because disease is part of life, the pathogens that cause disease are part of the readily available chain. Pathogens are found growing in nature. They can be found living within animals or humans that have been infected. Anthrax occurs naturally and can be harvested with relative ease, although it is more challenging to process and deploy effectively highly refined forms of anthrax using natural seed stock.[113] Likewise, hemorrhagic viruses such as Ebola and Marburg are naturally occurring, although not readily available, given the time between outbreaks and the normally remote areas in which these outbreaks occur. Other naturally occurring pathogens such as *Brucella suis* and *melitensis*—which cause brucellosis, a disease primarily of cattle, goats, and hogs—have been weaponized and would most likely be used against humans in an aerosol form to cause influenza-like symptoms.

If one is tracking disease through such online services as the Center for Infectious Disease Research and Policy (CIDRAP) at the University of Minnesota, one will find naturally occurring outbreaks—even daily outbreaks—of these disease-causing pathogens around the world.[114]

Another online service is provided by Program for Monitoring Emerging Diseases (ProMED), a global electronic reporting system sponsored by the International Society for Infectious Diseases (ISID).[115] One could continue, but suffice it to say it is possible to acquire at least some of these deadly pathogens by chasing naturally occurring outbreaks of disease in humans and animals. One must also remember that only a very small amount of material would be required initially, because quantities required for mounting a biological attack could be grown.

Other potential sources of biological material are the culture collections that are found within the governmental organizations responsible for health and veterinary issues, within academia for research, or within those commercial ventures dealing with product development, storage, and testing of biological material. The proliferation of biological material inadvertently or through theft is a real possibility. This proliferation must be closely guarded against. While export controls are in place to prevent the shipping of certain types of technologies and material, these are not 100 percent safe: an accidental release of this material to an unauthorized party remains a possibility. We must also be aware that while the United States has export controls, these measures are not uniform throughout the international community. The same is true for penalties for those organizations or companies not adhering to these measures. Thus, we must consider that proliferation from a legitimate source is a potentially real scenario. As an example, consider that in 1999 an Ohio man was able to purchase bubonic plaque cultures through the mail.[116] Some of the pathogenic material used in the Iraqi biowarfare program was also obtained from legitimate sources. The good news is that this source of proliferation and loss of control has been recognized and that procedures have been established to make it more difficult for this to occur.

Creating BW capabilities, as in the case of toxins, represents another source of BW material. Unlike bacteria and viruses that would require significant technical knowledge to develop, toxins including controlled substances such as botulinum toxin can be made easily in a lab. Using a simple formula, clostridial neurotoxin—the purified toxin from *Clostridium botulinum* organism—can be made using a liquid culture of 2 percent casein, 0.6 percent glucose, 0.05 percent thioglycolic acid, 0.25 percent Cerophyl, 0.25 percent yeast extract, at a pH of 7.4 placed in a solid medium of chopped meat and grown anaerobically at 37°C. The yield for this formula is approximately 50,000 human LDs per liter. *Clostridium botulinum* poisoning due to the botulinum neurotoxin constitutes one of the most lethal substances known to humankind and directly effects the respiratory system. Exposure would therefore require mechanical ventilation for all afflicted in order to prevent death. The symptoms have an extremely rapid onset and can last for months and even years. Death and even long-term sequelae such as neurological impairment are possible, depending on dose and treatment.[117]

Theft from a legitimate user of biological seed stock is another potential source of biological material. This is a proliferation window gaining considerably more attention, especially in light of the revelations about Dr. Ivins. In many respects, this should be cause for the greatest concern for the foreseeable future for pathogen acquisition. The idea of knowledgeable individuals using the proper equipment to develop these deadly capabilities and then providing them to a terrorist is a real possibility that has not been addressed appropriately to date.

We have already alluded to another method for acquiring biological material: the recombinant development of pathogens. The technology is evolving at such a rapid pace it is reasonable to assume the synthesis of artificially developed pathogens or the manipulation of naturally occurring pathogens will be possible in the future. As demonstrated by the work of Dr. Eckard Wimmer, the scientist who developed the artificial poliovirus, extraordinary progress has been achieved in this area. To date, the current scientific capabilities have only made the development of a simple virus such as poliovirus possible. With advances in genetic engineering and combinatorial chemistry that will allow for rapidly synthesizing peptides, polynucleotides, and other low-weight molecular material, however, the future is likely to see even greater capabilities in the synthetic development of biological material.

Unlike dealing with nuclear material, which has a yield that can be calculated with a high degree of certainty, biological agents are highly susceptible to changes in the environment, the growth medium, or the purity of the initial material. Therefore, predicting the yield from a particular growth of bacteria or virus would be less exact, making it more difficult to determine if a theft of a small amount of material had taken place.

Given the source material, the next step would involve preparing it for use. Previously, the equipment requirements for developing a state BW program were listed. They included, (1) for production, containment facilities with the appropriate barriers that protect workers, fermenters with a capacity of great than one hundred liters, centrifugal separators capable of processing five-liter batches, and cross-flow filtration equipment capable of processing twenty-liter batches; and (2) for stabilization, dissemination, and dispersion, freeze-drying equipment, aerosol inhalation chambers, delivery systems, and spray tanks to allow bomblet dissemination, warheads for missiles and development, and use of accurate short-term weather prediction.[118]

The question boils down to whether a small BW program could be developed using a subset of these capabilities, or using the same equipment with less capacity or perhaps even readily available substitutes in lieu of the actual equipment. For example, is a one hundred–liter fermenter necessary if one is only planning to produce one kilogram (approximately 2.2 pounds) of deployable agent? Could a household oven set at low temperature be used instead of commercial drying equipment?

In fact, smaller-scale efforts are possible and even have had some notable success. Consider the case of Dr. Steven Kurtz, an art professor from the SUNY at Buffalo.[119] In the spring of 2004, he woke one morning to find his wife had died in her sleep from cardiac arrest. He called 911 for help. When paramedics arrived, they were startled to find a fairly large laboratory including bacterial cultures, general biotechnology equipment, and even specialized equipment such as a mobile DNA-extracting machine used to test food for genetic contamination. They reported the odd configuration of equipment, and thus began an investigation by the Department of Justice and the FBI. Kurtz claimed to be using the equipment to incorporate biotechnology and transgenics into art. As a founding member of the Critical Arts Ensemble, he was using these materials to produce a theatrical production dealing with the subject of bioweapons production using a mock "anthrax" attack to elicit audience response. The material to be used was a BW simulant. This example provides valuable insights into the degree to which a nontechnical individual with open-source material can develop significant bioweapon techniques and capabilities. Kurtz was charged with Title 18, Part 1, Chapter 10, of the PATRIOT Act: prohibition with respect to biological weapons. Subsequently, the charges against Kurtz were dropped in April 2008.

The U.S. government has long since recognized the threat posed by the confluence of biotechnology, scientific knowledge, and the desire to acquire BW weapons. In 1999, long before the Kurtz incident, the DTRA commissioned an initiative codenamed Project *Bacchus* to determine the potential for a homegrown bioweapon. While we discussed the program previously with regard to the BWC, it is also instructive to consider it again in light of the ease of development of a small-scale BW capability. The *Washington Times* provided the following account:

> Operating out of a former barber shop and recreation hall without arousing any suspicion, the team purchased the necessary glassware, pip-

ing and filters from a local hardware store. It also ordered a 50-quart fermentation unit from Europe for growing the bacteria, high-ranking Pentagon officials said yesterday. The officials said the team purchased a milling machine capable of grinding dried material into fine powder from a store in the Midwest.

The team was not allowed to produce real stains of anthrax, but only biopesticides during two production tests in 1999 and 2000. Pentagon officials who studied the results of the test said the scientists, with anthrax spores, could have produced enough of the bacteria to have killed at least 10,000 people. The scientists succeeded in developing a lab capable of producing bacteria that could kill thousands of people, and did so on a budget of about $1.5 million.[120]

In returning to the questions of what type of equipment and how much throughput capacity would be required for a terrorist to develop a BW capability, consider that the letters in the Amerithrax attacks in 2001 each had about the volume of pathogen equal to that found in a sugar cube. The loss of life and economic losses from that small amount of pathogen certainly demonstrate that a little bit of BW in the hands of a terrorist can have a significant impact.

While developing biological material comes down to having the seed stock and being able to process it, weaponizing is a different skill set, requiring different equipment and large-scale testing for state BW programs. Testing would also be necessary—or at least highly desirable—for a terrorist BW program, which could be accomplished in a fairly compact space with a minimal signature. Given the proper precautions, the activity would likely be able to be conducted without being detected. Just as with other aspects of BW development, the differences between a state and a terrorist program come down to scale. For example, conducting tests of potential biological agents requires an aerosol chamber for releasing pathogens and determining their effectiveness when deployed. In all likelihood, animal storage facilities would be required for determining the effectiveness of the pathogens and the methods of employment. Therefore, for a terrorist program, perhaps a rudimentary air-tight enclosure could be developed and an animal model employed for the actual test.

Of course, the process of weaponizing a pathogen—that is, going from the "raw material" to the product that will be used in a weapon— is highly dependent on the type of delivery system to be used in the attack, the pathogen to be used, and the desired effects. Additionally, weaponizing the BW material introduces a degree of risk because it calls for increased handling and the accompanying potential for accidental release or exposure. However, given basic protections and the right motivation, weaponizing a BW pathogen appears to be within the reach of today's terrorists.

In the end, knowledge is the key component for developing a bioterror capability. As one expert lamented, "Our enemy now is not the Russians or Saddam. It's biotech itself. It's imagining what we can do to fight the technology."[121] While the proliferation of equipment, information, and capabilities can be regulated, it is fundamentally more difficult to regulate knowledge and basic research. Even if one were to try to do so, great arguments about the efficacy of such limitations would ensue. Some would argue that to place such limitations on basic research would limit the possibilities to further improve humankind, and some would argue that to do so in the 19th century would have infringed on the vaccine development undertaken by Louis Pasteur who founded the science of microbiology, proved the germ theory of disease, invented the process named after him—pasteurization—and developed vaccines for several diseases, including rabies. Today, the ethical debates concerning the use of stem cells falls into this category of potential advances running headlong into religious, ethical, moral, legal, and policy arguments. In fact, in the area of biology foundations have failed to keep up with science, and, therefore, much research and experimentation is being undertaken with few controls.

This lack of ethical, moral, legal, and policy standards is particularly troubling because biotechnology tends to be information intensive rather than capital intensive. That is, the cost in materials and equipment is generally quite low, and therefore, it is the intellectual property that is the limiting factor. The implications of this are critical, with regard to strategies for preventing proliferation of biological weapons and capabilities. Scientific knowledge must be placed at as least as high a premium as acquisition of seed stock from which potential weapons can be developed.

One report posted on the CIA's website, "Intelligence Support to the Life Science Community: Mitigating Threats from Bioterrorists," presents five incidents in which dual-use information was made publicly available with potentially serious proliferation implications. Several of these examples have been discussed in more detail previously. The first involved Australian efforts to genetically engineer mousepox, an effort which resulted in a more virulent form of the disease. The second was the publication of the details of the development of an infectious poliovirus from artificially engineered DNA sequences. The third case involved the identification of key proteins in smallpox that contribute to the virus's virulence and the discussion of how to synthesize the virulence gene through a genetic manipulation of vaccinia virus, a related yet less deadly cousin. The fourth case involved the development of a hybrid virus composed of an HIV core surrounded by the surface proteins of Ebola, which allowed for infection of lung tissue and which therefore might have had the potential for an aerosol attack. Finally, the fifth case involved the creation of a DNA-based system for reverse engineering the Ebola virus.[122]

The premise of this report is not that this sort of work should not be undertaken, but rather that the open publication of such material is a major step toward providing the capabilities necessary for "building" bioterror weapons. Furthermore, it is foolhardy to believe that in the future such cutting-edge technology and capabilities will not allow for greater access to the capabilities for developing these bioweapons. To go even further than the article in criticizing the life sciences community on these issues, one must ask whether such work with the Ebola and smallpox viruses should be undertaken at all. If so, the work should be restricted to only specialized facilities and to personnel with security clearances and a valid requirement to examine such issues.

Despite these anecdotal vignettes suggesting high potential for building a small-scale BW program, some experts remain convinced the complexities associated with acquisition, processing, weaponizing, and deploying these systems makes it highly unlikely it could be accomplished. According to Dr. William Clark, "It is almost inconceivable that any terrorist organization we know of in the world today, foreign or domestic, could on their own develop, from scratch, a bioweapon capable of causing mass casualties on American soil."[123] He does allow that the task would be made infinitely less difficult if a weapons-grade pathogen was provided to the terrorists or if the terrorists had help with some of the more challenging steps. Still, on this position Clark seems to have less company than with those who believe these capabilities are becoming available to terrorists and it is only a matter of time until there is a major BW attack on U.S. soil. This is especially true with the literature written in the aftermath of the Amerithrax attacks. In many respects, though, the issue comes down to one of degree. Clark's statement above has a number of caveats. He certainly sees the possibility of a attack. Where his analysis differs, though, is on the point of whether a terrorist can put all the steps together and launch a mass casualty, large-scale attack.

As a final exclamation point, one BW expert reports he was called to the White House as part of a team to provide a presentation to the vice president following the Amerithrax attacks. He had a vial of white powder about the size of his thumb that went through all the requisite screening without question. When the discussion concerning the ease of concealing BW material came up, he pulled out the vial and showed it to Vice President Dick Cheney, stating it contained 3 million doses of "simulant" lethal agent. Of course, these are theoretical doses and the act of dissemination with the associated losses through environmental degradation or even suboptimal deployment would limit actual casualties considerably, but the point was clearly made: it does not take much of a potent biological pathogen to have a large effect. This vignette also highlights the relative ease with which biological material can be concealed.[124]

Motivating Factors and Moderating Behavior

In 2003, one expert noted, although "terrorists have yet to employ successfully biological agents to carry out mass casualty attacks," those instances in which they have attempted to do so, have "involved readily available and easily deployed food-borne pathogens, resulting in relatively few casualties."[125] Is this because of a lack of capability or some sort of moderating influence that has limited terrorist behavior? Or is there an altogether different reason why bioterrorism has not resulted in spectacular mass casualty events to date?

A discussion of the likelihood of terrorist use of BW is not complete without examination of the motivating factors that could cause a terrorist group to develop and employ such capabilities, as well as of the moderating influences that could be used to deter and dissuade them from this activity. The excerpt below provides a headline from which to begin to understand the terrorists' potential motivations for use of WMDs. In a 2005 account concerning al-Qaeda's desire to obtain chemical and biological weapons, one article notes, "The international pursuit of Osama Bin Laden has not stopped his al-Qaeda network from seeking to build weapons of mass destruction, senior U.S. officials said last week. Recent intelligence indicates that the group is turning its attention to chemical and biological weapons. Despite severe technical obstacles to the launch of terrorist biowarfare, Washington believes Bin Laden has become convinced that only a WMD attack would be sufficient punishment for the U.S.-led invasions of Afghanistan and Iraq."[126] "The overwhelming bulk of the evidence we have is that their efforts are focused on biological and chemical weapons," says John Bolton, undersecretary of state for arms control.[127]

We have already discussed the technical and operational aspects of bioterrorism that make BW attractive from the standpoint of a terrorist.

However, other factors are also important in considering the potential for a bioterror attack. They include such issues as the psychological implications of employing these capabilities, the effect on the terrorists' ideological base, and the potential for eliciting an overwhelming response. These as well as several other issues fall into this category of motivating factors and moderating influences that will be extremely important in any assessment of the potential for a bioterror attack.

Psychological factors contribute to biological weapons having a degree of trepidation and intimidation that plays on people's fear of the unknown. It is not just a simple fear of disease, but also the uncertainty that would surround any bioattack. Christina Enemark notes, "People's ancient and deep-seated fear of infectious disease is compounded by the notion that someone would deliberately contaminate them and, if the biological agent is contagious, that they in turn might contaminate others. Moreover, a unique aspect of BW—uncertainty—would magnify that fear even further. Unlike in a conventional explosion where the casualty count is immediately apparent, no one would immediately know the source and nature of the BW attack or the number of victims."[128]

This statement is well supported by the evidence from the 2001 Amerithrax attacks. The amount of press coverage and the subsequent efforts to identify the perpetrator and prevent a repeat of this sort of attack in the future demonstrate the hysteria that surrounds BW. Additionally, in exercises conducted on BW scenarios, one of the factors inevitably discussed by hospitals is the projected numbers of "worried well" who will come to the hospital for treatment at the slightest sign of any influenza-like illness following report of an attack.[129]

The Amerithrax attacks serve as an instructive case for looking at terrorist motivations. The letters containing the anthrax warned recipients to seek medical treatment, indicating that the intent of the attacks was not to kill people, but rather to achieve some other purpose.[130] This reminds us that we may not always know or understand the motivations for a terrorist BW attack. Even now that the probable perpetrator of the Amerithrax attacks has been identified, the exact motivations continue to be elusive and may never be completely understood, at least in part because the key suspect committed suicide.

Much focus has been on the potential for large terrorist organizations to use BW capabilities. This was appropriate in the past because the magnitude of the threats posed by these organizations clearly warranted this attention. However, in a harbinger of the potential that technology is accreting to small organizations or even lone actors, Jessica Stern notes,

"Lone wolves are especially difficult for law enforcement authorities to stop, however. As technology continues to improve and spread, enabling what political scientist Joe Nye calls the 'privatization of war,' virtual networks and even lone-wolf avengers could become a major threat." This is now also becoming true in the area of BW where technologies are proliferating at a breakneck pace, placing more potentially catastrophic capabilities in the hands of smaller groups and even individuals. Stern also notes that dual-use nature of BW coupled with the proliferation of "methods for producing crude weapons of mass destruction are now widely available."[131]

While characteristics of BW make it attractive for causing terror and inflicting casualties, the indiscriminate use of BW against populations has a significant stigma likely to serve as a moderating influence. In one study, Christina Enemark makes the point, "terrorists seek to acquire and maintain some degree of influence over an identifiable audience."[132] The point is that terrorists have audiences with whom they must communicate to be effective. An indiscriminant use of BW that killed hundreds of thousands or even millions would likely cause the terrorists to lose support for the very cause they are trying to promote.

The use of a highly pathogenic agent that included human-to-human transmission would have several other pitfalls, including the potential that the weapons would affect civilian populations in close proximity. Therefore, as an example, the use of BW by Palestinians against Israel would likely have a negative effect on the Palestinians, as well as on the Israelis.

Another important psychological factor is the willingness of a society and the international community to "accept" a certain level of terrorism, while at higher levels of violence and number of attacks finding terrorism completely unacceptable and cause for an overwhelming response. The attacks of 9/11 provide a basis of this assertion. The world, including the United States, allowed bin Laden to operate and chose not to use overwhelming force for well over a decade in dealing with al-Qaeda. However, following 9/11 and the death of more than three thousand victims in the United States, the U.S. reaction was to attack Afghanistan and enter into direct combat against the Taliban. In taking the issue back to BW, Enemark makes her case: "[S]imply to convey a message to its human audience, mass casualties might not be necessary."[133]

Of course, not all agree that these moderating influences will continue to provide protection against catastrophic terrorist BW attacks. In *Toxic Terror*, edited by Jonathan Tucker, one contributing author notes, "Despite the disincentives to CBW (i.e., chem-bio warfare) use by politically motivated terrorists, several analysts argued that a 'new breed' of terrorists has appeared on the scene that may be more willing to employ mass violence for a variety of motives unrelated to clear political goals."[134]

In developing a risk analysis framework for examining the potential for terrorist use of BW, Jessica Stern develops several key themes that have great applicability for understanding the motivations and possible moderating behaviors that might influence a terrorist. She notes terrorist attacks threaten, "not just lives, but also political values, interests and institutions," as well as the government's legitimacy concerning the "state's monopoly over the use of force and protection of citizens."[135] The focus of these statements is the likely loss of confidence in the government that would ensue from a large-scale successful BW attack that sickened and killed thousands of citizens. Could the government survive such crisis in confidence? What would be the response of the people to a government that had failed to protect its citizens?

Stern also introduces the concept of "dreaded risks," a category of risk in which the fear of an act is disproportionate to the actual outcome. She identifies BW in this category as a means that causes fear, angst, and reactions disproportionate to the actual potential of these capabilities. To demonstrate this concept, she balances the statistic that each day in the United States more than one hundred people die in traffic accidents, yet people continue to engage in the act of driving as part of their daily lives. However, anthrax attacks, which killed five people in one incident, have elicited a response well beyond what seems reasonable, given the demonstrated threat. She maintains this overreaction is due to this concept of dreaded risk.[136]

Continuing with this line of reasoning, Stern identifies four aspects of dread that she labels as (1) disgust, (2) horror of the disease, (3) loss of faith in the ability of scientists to protect us, and (4) implications for risk analysis and policy. *Disgust* stems from the idea of involuntary exposure. *Horror of the disease* is based on the inherent fear of disease and possible contagion. The *loss of faith in the ability of scientists to protect us* pertains to both the idea of inevitability and the relatively new concept that science can be used for nefarious purposes, which diminishes our "technological optimism." Finally, in this construct, the conclusions have *implications for risk analysis and policy* that may have lasting negative or even unintended consequences that may on balance do more harm than good.[137]

Stern's framework should be both heartening and of some concern to those looking to prevent a terrorist BW attack. It serves to identify potential limits or thresholds on the use of BW as well as signify that, in some cases, the terrorist may find the use of BW to be an acceptable means for achieving an intended outcome.

In concluding this section, a CRS report provides a useful summation: "Historically, most terrorist groups have avoided using CBW [chemical-biological weapons], in part because they do not want to alienate their own constituencies, and in part because they have not had the technical expertise to turn them into effective weapons."[138] The same report ominously reports these weapons can have a "powerful psychological impact." Taken together, these statements indicate a tenuous balance for the terrorist between the desire to maintain support from constituents and the desire to achieve the intended strategic outcomes.

Some Models Considered

The discussion so far has examined the capabilities required for conducting a bioterror attack, several case studies that provide invaluable insights into the history of bioterrorism, and some influences that could contribute to or prevent such an attack. A useful next step is to examine these factors within the context of a system or model. This examination has both technical and psychological components that are essential and must be considered. The technical component examines the steps necessary to develop a BW program, including whether a terrorist has required knowledge, equipment, and material, while the psychological concerns examination of the conditions under which the terrorist would see it in his interest to develop these capabilities and potentially employ them in an attack.

Leitenberg provides a simple model that includes five steps. He identifies five essential requirements that must be mastered in order to produce biological agents:

1. One must obtain the appropriate strain of the disease pathogen.
2. One must know how to handle them correctly.
3. One must know how to grow them in a way that will produce the appropriate characteristics.
4. One must know how to store them, and to scale-up production properly.
5. One must know how to disperse them properly.[139]

Another source—an online article, or blog (i.e., a Web log)—provides another more-detailed model concerning the individual steps and specific handling of the pathogen to develop a BW capacity. The blog uses the 2001 Amerithrax attacks as a reference. It lists the five steps as

1. Germination—causing the seeds to develop into living germs.
2. Vegetation—growing sufficient anthrax germs to provide what is needed for the mailings.
3. Sporulation—causing the germs to create spores.
4. Separation—separating the spores from the dead "mother germs" and other debris.
5. Weaponization—turning the spores into a superfine powder.[140]

The blog goes on to discuss the capabilities required of the manufacturer. The conclusions, based on input from professors, were equally disturbing. The methods "are published," therefore processing "only requires standard skills" and no more than "graduate level training" would be necessary. The summation of the article quotes William Patrick, one of the United States' leading BW experts, as saying, "What concerns me are graduate students and professors in microbiology and chemical engineering who have a better appreciation of the finer points of detail. If they were to get disgruntled, I think they could, with a little trial and error, come up with a reasonably acceptable BW agent."[141]

Another terrorist BW model was presented in the DHS brief, "Leading Edge of Biodefense." The brief was presented by Lt. Col. George Korch, Deputy Director of the National Biodefense Analysis and Countermeasures Center (NBACC). The steps identified were "acquire, grow, modify, store, stabilize, package and disperse."[142] No supporting information was provided concerning the elements. Examination of the terminology, however, yields some interesting conclusions. First and foremost, the terms are scientific and seem unrelated to potential scenarios under which a terrorist might choose to employ such BW capabilities. Second, in some regards this listing seems similar to the OTA model for state programs, which also include many of the substeps of a robust state program that could likely be reduced, combined, or eliminated, depending on what the intended effect might be.

Another model Stern proposes focuses on the technical requirements for an attack, but also begins to suggest that employment of BW is a two-sided proposition whereby considerations must also extend to the target, and to examining such issues as desired effect, target characteristics, and susceptibility. She articulates a formula for successful terrorist employment of BW as follows: "The probability of infection for a given individual is the joint probability that a terrorist or terrorist group decides to use a biological agent; acquires an infectious agent in usable form; and disseminates it successfully in the vicinity of the person or, in the case of a contagious agent, in the vicinity of his contacts; and that the person is sensitive to the dosage received; medical countermeasures are not prescribed; or the medical countermeasures are not effective for that person."[143]

In this model, a number of vital, interrelated factors must be present to gain a desired effect. Even if the material is prepared appropriately and the attack launched successfully, the target might not be affected based on individual factors such as age, general health, and susceptibility. The example, perhaps a little absurd, supporting the necessity of understanding this concept would be a postulated anthrax attack against a U.S. military encampment when all the soldiers have been given the battery of anthrax vaccinations. In all likelihood, such an attack in which inflicting mass casualties was the objective would not be considered successful from the terrorist's perspective because the vaccinated population would not become infected.

Another interesting model that broadens the development of a bioterror capability to include the nontechnical requirements is provided by Dr. Jean Paul Zanders, director of the Chemical and Biological Warfare Project at the Stockholm International Peace Research Institute (SIPRI). Zanders's model was developed to examine both chemical and biological weapons development by a terrorist. It presents a system in which several important building blocks contribute to the success of the effort, including the material base, group leadership, and capabilities of the terrorists. For developing these basic building blocks for a BW attack, Zanders believes certain "material base" elements are necessary. The "physical base" subportion is related to the ability to acquire a suitable pathogen for use as a weapon. Components include where the development is conducted and financial abilities of the group. He asserts there is a benefit to developing these systems in a more advanced country and therefore increases the chance of successful development. The individual capabilities of the terrorists are also important. Zanders lists a number of capabilities, including educational level, technology base, and science base.

In Zanders' model, the collective abilities of the terrorist group are also reflected. The "organization culture" is key because it is from this aspect of the model that the organizational direction and cultural mores—which would either allow, encourage, or prevent a terrorist attack using these types of capabilities, in other words the motivating factors and moderating influences—which would allow the terrorist's effort to succeed.

The material base also relates to a requirement Zanders calls "import dependency." The more advanced the environment in which one is developing these capabilities, the less one will be dependent on imports for equipment and capabilities. Zanders's model also includes the concept of leadership, which encompasses the decisions that would need to be undertaken, such as decisions with regard to the type of pathogen and attack, intended effects, and the financing to be dedicated to the effort.

As these material base and leadership elements begin to come together, Zanders depicts an outflow resulting in the development of a chemical or biological weapon. The model is unique in that in many regards the focus is less on the science and more on the human factors involved in the development of a BW capability. This focus is in contrast to the earlier discussion concerning the required steps for developing biological weapons that focused on the technical aspects and steps required for gaining a BW capability.

Gary Ackerman and Kevin Moran, in their analysis "Bioterrorism and Threat Assessment," provide another model that identifies many of the subcomponents required for planning and executing a bioterror attack (Figure 2–10). In this analysis, the authors define the bioterrorism threat assessment as being a product of consequences of attack, and likelihood of an attack which are themselves products. The consequences of an attack is a product of the value of an asset, the bioagent hazard, and the vulnerability of the assert. The likelihood of an attack is a product of the intention and capability of the attacker.[144] In this way, the authors are able to create a

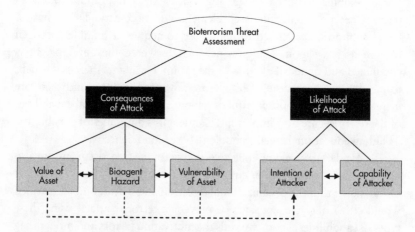

FIGURE 2-10 Ackerman-Moran Model for the Terrorist Acquisition of Chemical Biological Weapons

likelihood of an outcome using conditional probabilities to describe the three components of the attack as the value of the asset attacked, the type of pathogen selected, and the target's vulnerability to arrive at an overall probability for the consequences of an attack. The likelihood of an attack is the joint probability of the intention of the attacker and the capability of the attacker. Of note are the linkages between the elements as depicted by the dashed line in Figure 2–10. The equation to describe their bioterrorism threat assessment becomes

BIOTERROR THREAT ASSESSMENT =
(Consequences of an Attack) * (Likelihood of an Attack)
where
CONSEQUENCES OF AN ATTACK =
(Value of Asset) * (Bioagent Hazard) * (Vulnerability of Asset)
and
LIKELIHOOD OF AN ATTACK =
(Intention of Attacker) * (Capability of the Attacker)

This ensures that both the development of the BW capability and the desired scenario are represented as contributing to the overall bioterror threat assessment. The authors also discuss contributing factors such as organizational capabilities, financial resources, logistical resources, knowledge and skills, material and technology acquisition, weaponization and delivery, and state sponsorship, all of which contribute to the overall threat assessment.

In the same vein as Zanders, Ackerman and Moran discuss the motivational factors that may cause a terrorist group to employ or refrain from employing BW weapons. In this portion of the analysis, they examine the ideological, strategic, and tactical rationale that could serve as incentives or constraints concerning BW use. Table 2-4 summarizes the findings of this analysis. Of course, these incentives and constraints would be highly stylized to reflect the individual group, and it would not be possible to generalize in a meaningful way across all terrorist groups. Still, the incentives and constraints are descriptive of the types of issues likely to be considered in a strategic calculus done by a terrorist group prior to undertaking such a venture.

Los Alamos National Laboratory provides yet another methodology for examining the question of the process necessary for conducting a bioterror attack.[145] The model was part of a DHS-sponsored effort to better understand the threats posed by a bioterrorist attack. The study was

TABLE 2–4 Incentives and Constraints for Use of Terrorist BW

Motivations	Incentive	Constraint
Ideological	Achieves goals in an ideologically consistent manner Enhances status	Runs counter to group norms
Strategic	Causes specific outcomes Serves as a strong blackmail tool Helps build the organization	Perceived as counterproductive Opposed by state sponsors
Tactical	Exploits perceived target weaknesses Facilitates covert development and use Makes use of dual-use technologies Mimics previous attacks Meets idiosyncratic needs	Perceived challenges of development and use are high Unpredictability of the outcome Better conventional alternatives

completed in January 2006, with the results published in October 2006. Upon completion, the model became part of the DHS Bioterrorism Risk Assessment model. The analysis addresses twenty-eight bioagents and considers "fatality, illness and direct economic impact" resulting from an attack. The model begins by looking at the pairing of targets and biological agents as biological pathogens with discrete capabilities that must be factored into attack planning. The next step involves the production of the agent into a useable form for eventual release and subsequent dispersion. Because the model was used as a methodology for evaluating threat scenarios, the final steps involve analysis of scenario consequences and probabilities across a range of outcomes into a probabilistic distribution. Figure 2–11 depicts this methodology.

The objective of this analysis was an agent-by-agent analysis of potential scenarios related in terms of probabilities. The briefing states, "The principal product of the 2006 BTRA (Bioterrorism Risk Assessment) was the ranking of the risk of bioagents." Essentially, for each agent an event tree was developed that allowed for considering all possible outcomes. In all, the analysis considered 35 million total scenarios across all the different pathogens. The result was the development of a probabilistic set of data with a mean and confidence intervals describing the potential range of outcomes.

The event tree or network model that looked at possible outcomes consisted of a series of levels that considered different scenario parameters. The first level analysis identified six phases for analysis: (1) agent, target, and dissemination selection; (2) acquisition; (3) production and processing; (4) transport and storage; (5) attack; and (6) response. Within

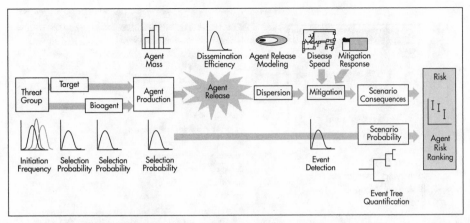

FIGURE 2–11 Los Alamos National Laboratory Model for examining terrorist BW

each of these phases, events were identified that further subdivided the phases into discrete activity categories. For example, in Phase 1 (agent, target, and dissemination selection), the activities included frequency of initiation by terrorist group, target selected, bioagents selected, and mode of dissemination. Across all six of the phases, seventeen events or activities were considered. Each of these can be further subdivided into subordinate activities, which is how the 35 million discrete scenarios were identified. It is important to note that not all these scenarios were deemed equally possible: in fact, some were deemed infeasible. Using this methodology, one can generate a large number of combinations for a single agent, each with a discrete probability of occurrence from 0 to 1.0, where 0 is no probability and 1.0 is absolute certainty. For *Bacillus anthracis* alone, 2.2 million scenarios were identified, of which 870,000 were assessed to have "nonzero" values—in other words, they have a probability greater than zero of occurring. Figure 2–12 provides an extract of the methodology for developing this event tree.

The methodology employs what are termed "basic consequence equations" to examine elements of an attack for generating such outcomes as effective mass release, number of illnesses, number of fatalities, and decontamination costs. All are measured in distributions or combined probabilities of occurrence derived from a number of contributing factors. As an example, the effective mass release scenario result can be obtained from the collective probability of the active fraction of pathogen after release, the respirable fraction, and the efficiency gained through the use of additives to improve the pathogen's stability.

Event	Event Heading	Branches
2	Target Selection	2.1 Large Open Building
		2.2 Small Enclosure
		2.3 Large "Divided" Building
		2.4 Large Outdoor Spaces
		2.5 Water Pathway
		2.6 Food Pathway
		2.7 Human Vectors
		2.8 Contact (letters)

FIGURE 2-12
Identifying Potential
Biological Weapons
Scenarios—
Los Alamos National
Laboratory

Event	Event Heading	Phase
1	Frequency of Initiation by Terrorist Group	
2	Target Selected	Agent/Target/ Dissemination Selection
3	Bioagent Selected	
4	Mode of Dissemination (also determines wet or dry dispersal form)	
5	Mode of Agent Acquisition	Acquisition
6	Interdiction during	
7	Location of Production and Processing	Production and Processing
8	Mode of Agent Production	
9	Preprocessing and Concentration	
10	Drying and Processing	
11	Additives	
12	Interdiction during Production and Processing	
13	Mode of Transport and Storage	Transport and Storage
14	Interdiction during Transport and Storage	
15	Interdiction during Attack	Attack
16	Potential for Multiple Attacks	
17	Event Detection	Response

When one combines the concept of the two schools of thought on bioterror—one that says the necessary steps are too difficult for the terrorist to accomplish and one that says that bioterror is imminent—with the probabilistic vulnerability and risk framework, it becomes clear neither of these polar statements is correct. Rather, they must be put on a continuum of possible outcomes that lie somewhere between these two absolutes.

In yet another model in the "Final Report and Commentary" of the Bioterrorism Threat Assessment and Risk Management Workshop hosted by Dr. Raymond Zilinskas, some additional insights into the development of a model for examining the potential for a bioterror event are provided. However, he also offers a cautionary concern: "This paucity of data suggests that the risk assessment would need to occur in two stages: a qualitative or semi quantitative vulnerability analysis stage, followed, depending on the data, followed by a more quantitative risk estimation stage with the latter involving four components: hazard characterization, hazard identification, exposure assessment, and risk characterization."[146] The two-stage methodology Zilinskas and the conference participants collaboratively developed assumes terrorists have made the decision to attack a target and therefore looks at the various scenarios and the likelihood of success of each.

The first component of the model entails problem formulation that links the terrorist's objectives and target into a scenario. The hazard characterization examines the vulnerabilities posed as a result of the selection of the target and the agent. This characterization allows the terrorists, in a sense, to gauge the potential outcome based on the target and the agent pairing. The closely related hazard identification examines the deployment capabilities and relates them to the ability of the terrorists to successfully deploy a BW capability. Finally, the risk characterization allows for development of probabilistic assessments concerning a specific attack scenario with a specific agent deployed in a specific manner.

The qualitative judgments from the first stage allow for assessments in the second stage of risk estimation that are more quantitative. The second stage of the analysis focuses on the risk associated with each of the potential scenarios under consideration. The vulnerability analysis must examine not only the potential scenarios, but also the propensity of a terrorist to engage in a bioterror event and the technical ability to undergo the necessary steps to achieve a biological weapons capability. This second stage looks more like the Los Alamos and Ackerman-Moran models, which would tend to result in a probabilistic assessment of outcomes.

Conclusions

In this chapter, the science of BW has been presented to provide an appreciation for the potential for a BW attack either by a state or nonstate actor. Additionally, we have focused on the capabilities required for mounting such an attack and the motivations or intentions that serve to make a BW attack more or less likely. In this regard, several conclusions are in order that will help us to frame the study's questions concerning the potential for a bioterror attack.

Many public pronouncements by experts have not been particularly helpful in developing an understanding of the actual threat we face from a bioterror attack. Some have great shock value and may even have contributed to higher funding levels, but should be cause for concern. The anecdote that comes to mind is the vial filled with anthrax simulant that was transported into the vice president's office that could have contained 3 million doses of anthrax. In reality, the potential for that vial was far less than stated when considering environmental losses and the difficulties associated with dispersing the agent in an "attack-useful" manner. Additionally, until a pathogen is paired with a dispersal method, it cannot be considered fully weaponized. Stated directly, a BW weapon includes both the material and delivery means.

BW, specifically bioterror, is most definitely a national security threat. Furthermore, the threat is increasing, tied to a variety of factors, including the explosive growth in biotechnology, an increasingly globalized world, greater sharing of information and proliferation of biotech capabilities, and a terrorist threat looking to conduct higher-casualty and more-spectacular attacks.

Additionally, BW presents the potential for very powerful attacks using a modest amount of biological material, especially compared with chemical weapons. The concern about BW is well founded in another regard: the source material is readily available in the environment. That is not to imply that all potential pathogens would be available, but rather that there are many pathogens that can cause diseases—anthrax, tularemia, glanders, noroviruses, and hantavirus to name a few—for which a potential bioterrorist would have a high probability of being able to acquire the material. Of course, other pathogens such as the virus that causes smallpox (a virus that no longer occurs naturally) or Ebola, which is highly infectious and would likely be difficult and even deadly for a terrorist to attempt to employ, would present greater challenges or even be infeasible for a bioterror attack.

We have indeed entered into a new era that some have called the Age of Biotechnology. In this new environment, we have seen great potential for improving the quality of human life, the elimination of diseases, and the potential for radically altering the way we think about biology. We have also seen the proliferation of the capabilities—including equipment, information, and knowledge—that could make BW capabilities more readily available to states and nonstate actors with potentially catastrophic outcomes.

At the same time, we have experienced a reduction in the number of states with BW programs. We should expect this trend to continue. These reductions are largely due to international policies that make state ownership of these capabilities a cause for the state to gain pariah status and that call into question the state's legitimacy.

The same calculus does not hold for nonstate or terrorist actors. While there has been no terrorist use of BW since the 2001 Amerithrax attacks, advances in the field of biotechnology have significantly lowered the thresholds for BW development. In many of the key technologies required for developing BW capabilities, we have seen a 400 percent increase per year.

While not attempting to trivialize the capabilities and knowledge necessary for BW development and use, much of the equipment is readily available. Alternatively, rudimentary substitutes could be fashioned, allowing for enhancement of pathogens. The Internet has become a ready source of information, and the scientific community has done little to moderate its behavior, especially with regard to scientific publications. If the terrorist wants to know what equipment is necessary, a simple Internet search will provide the information.

A question that continuously surfaces in the debates about terrorist BW capabilities is why a group such as Aum Shinrikyo, which was well financed and seemingly had staff with the necessary technical capabilities, failed to achieve success in their BW program and so turned to chemical weapons for their attack. Perhaps the more relevant question today is whether Aum Shinrikyo in 2009 (versus 1994) would have achieved a different outcome, given 400 percent annual increases in several important biotechnologies. The author believes that the likelihood—and in fact the probabilities—of success would be greatly increased by these technological advancements.

In fact, the Los Alamos model, which has become the basis for the DHS Biological Risk Assessment publication, uses a formula that considers factors including (1) ease of acquisition or synthesis, (2) environmental stability, (3) transmissibility person to person, (4) case fatality rate (untreated), (5) ease of dissemination (estimated), (6) frequency of serious sequelae (e.g., blindness or neurological disease) in survivors, (7) lack or unavailability of useful countermeasures or treatments and need for immediacy in diagnosis, and (8) treatment to ensure patient survival in developing probabilistic assessments of the potential for a successful bioterror attack.[147]

The biotechnology revolution has definitely affected factors (1) and (2) and potentially affected factors (3), (4), and (5) for any terrorist group that might have access to advanced biological capabilities. Of course, advances in biotechnology have also positively affected factors (7) and (8) concerning treatment potential. Therefore, if one were to consider the probability of a successful attack in 1994 versus 2009 (by which time there had been significant cumulative advances in biotechnology), the conclusion would be that the probability of a successful attack would have increased considerably.

We should expect these positive trends in biotechnology to continue, and therefore we should expect a complementary increase in the likelihood of success of an attempted bioterror attack. The real question then becomes, What will happen in 2010, 2020, and 2030?

Trends also suggest that, over time, the balance concerning the ability of a terrorist to develop and employ BW capabilities will be less about questions of capabilities and more about intentions. In turn, this implies our strategies will need to shift away from retarding or thwarting the technical capabilities and toward influencing terrorists' motivations.

In other words, the capabilities for developing BW will become more readily available based on our increasingly globalized world and advances in biotechnology. Therefore, in examining the question of the potential for a bioterror attack and how to influence outcomes, the motivations or intentions of the terrorist will become preeminent.

While historical precedents indicate previous efforts by terrorists to develop and employ biological weapons have not been highly successful, they do demonstrate (through actions and pronouncements) that some terrorists do have an interest in BW. The degree to which they will seek to acquire these capabilities will be based on their intentions. Those interested in increasing the level of violence and inflicting greater numbers of casualties will likely be drawn to WMDs, including biological weapons.

Overall, the motivating factors presented in this chapter lead to the conclusion that thresholds against biological weapons will continue to moderate terrorist behavior for many groups, but that it is not inconceivable that terrorists' rhetoric concerning BW will continue, as they attempt to gain notoriety and increase the visibility for their cause.

Dual-use issues will continue to complicate efforts to limit BW proliferation. We should not expect this to change. In fact, the issue will become more clouded as biotechnology continues to evolve and the field continues to expand. The Huxsoll explanation discussed earlier that compares the steps in vaccine development with those in weapons development underscores that the difference comes down to intentions.

Significant differences exist between the requirements for developing a state BW capability and a terrorist BW capability. Some of these differences are a matter of scale, and others are related to the question of what constitutes success. It is possible to conceive of an outcome from a bioterror attack that results in few casualties, yet gains significant media coverage, resulting in increased visibility for the terrorist's stated goals and objectives. This might constitute success from the terrorist's point of view. However, from a state's perspective, an attack that failed to have the intended battlefield effect would likely not be considered successful.

Before moving to the next chapter, an overall critique of the models is in order. A wide variety of models has been considered, from the highly formulaic quantitative approaches to the more subjective or qualitative approaches in order to examine the potential future terrorist BW threat. As we have seen, some tend to reduce the question to a technical formula: can the terrorist acquire the necessary material, prepare it for deployment, and then successfully launch an attack? In this way, one can examine the issue in a very mechanistic manner consisting of probabilities that form distributions over the range of outcomes. Doing this for a variety of pathogens and scenarios, the question can be condensed to a seemingly well-defined solution space represented by a probabilistic distribution.

Other models have been more qualitative, challenging the reader to consider a number of factors, but without a neat numerical outcome what is the environment in which the terrorist is attempting to develop these capabilities? Do they have the requisite knowledge?

Neither approach in isolation will be sufficient to examine this difficult issue. Rather, a combined methodology that examines the relevant factors and relates them to the terrorist's objectives must be used. This is particularly important in light of the low probability, high-consequence nature of the bioterror threat.

Furthermore, bioterrorism cannot simply be about capabilities, and must focus keenly on the intent of the actor. This is in many respects the more complex and interesting question. The behavioral considerations that would cause a terrorist to want to acquire and use BW capabilities or to refrain from such behavior will form the basis for our examination of the potential for a bioterror attack.

Finally, the author's criticism of many of the models is that they look at the world primarily through the eyes of the terrorist. What must the terrorist do to achieve a BW capability? What scenarios are available for employment of a BW weapon? What objectives do the terrorists desire to achieve? Only the Los Alamos model examines the concept of mitigation and consequences. This is an important distinction that will also form a basis for our examination of the potential for such an attack.

Continuing with this theme, a more interesting approach would be to look at the terrorist use of BW as a two-sided game with strategies, payoffs, and losses for each side. In this way, we can begin to construct a methodology that allows for actions and counteractions between the actors—in this case the potential bioterrorist and the U.S. government. We can also begin to understand the manner in which these actions and counteractions are related. This realization can become an important part of our nonproliferation, counterproliferation, and consequence management strategies in the future.

CHAPTER THREE

Homeland Security and Biodefense

Introduction

The concept of securing the homeland is not new, but it has received considerable attention in the post-9/11 world. In this chapter, the early roots of the current homeland security will be presented as an antecedent to our current system. This history will serve as a foundation and provide insights into the possibilities for protecting against a future bioterror event.

In a September 2006 DHS document, *Civil Defense and Homeland Security: A Short History of National Preparedness Efforts*, the concept of homeland security is reviewed in considerable detail. This review starts with the pre–Cold War period from 1916 to 1945 and ends in 2006. During the eighty-year period covered in this report, one can clearly see the significant extent to which the organizations, supporting legislation, and purposes evolved.

Early efforts were tied to protection from adversaries employing conventional weapons, such as those used in the first and second world wars. These initiatives included such bodies as the Council of National Defense, established in 1916 as a direct result of the observations of threats to Allied nations in World War I; the National Emergency Council (NEC), established by President Franklin Roosevelt in 1933 to examine a variety of issues, including civil defense; and the Office of Civilian Defense (OCD), established in 1940 as a mechanism to allow the states the capacity to better manage civil defense tasks.

The post–World War II period saw the emergence of preparations for protecting populations from radiological fallout caused by nuclear weapons. Terms such as "duck and cover" became household phrases during this period. The emergence of the Federal Emergency Management

Agency (FEMA) and the earlier efforts to provide states with capabilities for disaster recovery signal the official recognition of the government's role in disaster planning, mitigation, and relief. These initiatives included

- the abolishment in 1945 by the Truman administration of the OCD
- the establishment as part of the National Security Act of 1947 by the Truman administration of the National Security Resource Board (NSRB) and the Office of Civil Defense Planning (OCDP);
- the establishment in 1950 by Congress of the Federal Civil Defense Administration (FCDA), responsible for better supporting the states in their emerging civil defense missions;
- the dissolution in 1951 by Congress of the FCDA to make way for the Office of Civil and Defense Mobilization (OCDM);
- the bifurcation in 1961 by the Kennedy administration of the Office of Civilian Defense Mobilization (OCDM) into the Office of Emergency Planning (OEP) and the Office of Civil Defense (OCD);
- the replacement in 1970 by the Defense Civil Preparedness Agency (DCPA) of the OCD which was later moved under the DoD; and
- the establishment in 1979 by Executive Order under the Carter administration of the FEMA.[1]

In the later part of the pre-9/11 period there was general recognition of the need to protect against terrorist attacks, including those perpetrated using biological weapons. Early efforts included the National Defense Authorization Act for fiscal year 1994. This act required coordination and integration of all DoD chemical and biological defensive programs. The Oklahoma City bombing, which caused the deaths of 168 people, resulted in the issuing of the Presidential Decision Directive 39 (PDD-39). This directive, which provided a national strategy for combating terrorism, has three primary elements: "1. Reduce the vulnerabilities to terrorists' attacks and prevent and deter terrorist acts before they occur; 2. Respond to terrorist attacks that do occur—crisis management—and apprehend and punish terrorists; and 3. Manage the consequences of terrorist acts, including providing emergency relief and restoring capabilities to protect public health and safety and essential government services."[2]

Two other PDDs—PDD-62, which clarified the missions of agencies charged with defeating and defending against terrorism, and PDD-63, which called for security of national critical infrastructure—served to augment PDD-39.

The Nunn-Lugar-Domenici Act Domestic Preparedness Program, established in 1996, was instrumental in clarifying DoD as the lead federal agency for dealing with these types of events. It required mandatory coordination, with a variety of agencies and organizations from across the defense, law enforcement, health, and preparedness communities.

Also during this early post–Cold War period, some specific programs for dealing with the threat of BW were developed or expanded. Export controls have historically been an important part of our NSS. During the Cold War, control of militarily significant technologies such as computers, dual-use technologies, and weapons were expressly prohibited export to countries on the Commerce Control List (CCL). This included biological pathogens that could be used for developing a BW capability, and the equipment, technologies, and information that could be used in the development of BW capabilities.

The CDC also compiled a list of various pathogens of concern: "U.S. public health system and primary healthcare providers must be prepared to address various biological agents, including pathogens that are rarely seen in the United States."[3] The list is both prescriptive, in that the public health system must have the capability to deal with these pathogens, and descriptive, in that it is a list of the agents of most concern to the United States.

The Antiterrorism and Effective Death Penalty Act of 1996 required the regulation of select agents by the Department of Health and Human Services (HHS). The Select Agent Program (SAP) is yet another mechanism through which we have attempted to control the proliferation of biological material. According to the CDC website,

> The Centers for Disease Control and Prevention (CDC) regulates the possession, use, and transfer of select agents and toxins that have the potential to pose a severe threat to public health and safety. The CDC Select Agent Program oversees these activities and registers all laboratories and other entities in the United States of America that possess, use, or transfer a select agent or toxin.
>
> The U.S. Departments of Health and Human Services (HHS) and Agriculture (USDA) published final rules for the possession, use, and transfer of select agents and toxins (42 C.F.R. Part 73, 7 C.F.R. Part 331, and 9 C.F.R. Part 121) in the Federal Register on March 18, 2005. All provisions of these final rules supersede those contained in the interim final rules and became effective on April 18, 2005.

The term "select agent" can be used to apply to the pathogen, the amount of a particular pathogen, or even the genetic material of a pathogen. For example, some agents are considered to be select no matter what the quantity is, while others are only considered select above a certain level. To add to the confusion, the DNA from certain pathogens is considered select, while the actual organisms are not as they are naturally occurring and could not hope to be controlled in this manner.[4]

Biosafety and Biosecurity

Biosafety and biosecurity are two important areas in the discussion of BW and proliferation. Biosafety emanates from the combinations of laboratory practice and procedures, laboratory facilities, and safety equipment used when lab staff work with infectious microorganisms. The bible for dealing with biosafety issues is jointly authored by the CDC and the NIH in Biosafety in Microbiological and Biomedical Laboratories (BMBL).

The BMBL provide clear guidelines on laboratory procedures "to reduce or eliminate exposure of laboratory workers, other persons, and the outside environment to potentially hazardous agents for protecting workers from infection."[5] The operative term that best describes the biosafety program is "containment." This text is the key source document that describes safe methods for managing infectious materials in the laboratory environment.

At the heart of the program are the BSLs, rated between 1 and 4, based on "virulence, pathogenicity, antibiotic resistance patterns, vaccines and treatment availability."[6] These factors are considered in making a determination as to what level of protection will be required, ranging from simple barriers and precautions for BSL-1 microorganisms to triple-barrier, negative-pressure environments for BSL-4 highly pathogenic agents such as Ebola. In an example of unintended consequences, the biosafety program has exposed a new proliferation window.

In the aftermath of the Amerithrax attacks of 2001, there has been an increase in the number of BSL-3 and -4 containment facilities for conducting research into dangerous pathogens. This has come at some cost to the overall proliferation posture in several regards. First, the increase in these facilities makes the handling of these pathogens more commonplace: more scientists and even students are learning how to work in these dangerous environments. Second, it is allowing these pathogens to be stored in more locations around the country. Finally, in some cases the locations of the facilities are potentially exposing populations to these biological materials. For example, one such facility is at Boston University in the heart of Boston.

In a telling comment that may signal that the cure is worse than the disease, David Ozonoff, professor of environmental health at Boston University, said that the "dangers of bioterror research already outweigh the chance it will protect public health."[7]

In yet another article that examines the issue of the proliferation of these BSL facilities, Representative Bart Stupik is quoted as saying, "No one in the federal government even knows for sure how many of these labs there are in the U.S., much less what they are doing, or whether they are secure."[8] The article goes on to say that the range of BSL-3 labs varies from 277 to 600, depending on how the labs are counted and which data set is used in the analysis.

The proliferation of these facilities is one important concern. Another is the manner in which dangerous pathogens are handled. Significant biosafety lapses have been reported that call into question the degree to which these capabilities can be safely proliferated, even for use in research. In discussing problems at university labs in Texas and Wisconsin, Congressman John D. Dingell states, "It appears that there has been a surge in construction of biosafety labs over the past several years which has been financed, at least in part, with federal funds. While the research conducted at these labs is certainly valuable, we must make sure that it does not pose a risk to public health."[9] In an incident at Texas A&M University, several workers were exposed to *Brucella suis* and *Coxiella burnetii* in March 2006. Research at this facility was halted by the CDC until proper procedures and certifications had been established. A violation at the University of Wisconsin involved researchers making and manipulating copies of the Ebola virus genome in a BSL-3 lab when the work should have been done in a BSL-4 facility.

In yet another example of a biosafety lapse, a 2008 article on the CIDRAP website describes a "cross-contamination of clinical specimens in two Idaho hospital laboratories" while these labs were separately testing their ability to detect *Bacillus anthracis*. The event occurred in 2006 and was not made public until September 2008. The biosecurity lapses resulted in FBI and CDC investigations. In both cases, threat to the public was assessed to be negligible, although it served to underscore the necessity of proper lab practices.[10]

The proliferation of these facilities is not the only concern. Their general security is also in question. A GAO study published in September 2008 examined security at the five BSL-4 facilities in the United States.

Three of the facilities are owned and operated by academic institutions, and the other two are federal facilities. GAO's findings were shocking. The analysis considered all aspects of general security and concluded there was a lack of standardization across the facilities, due in large measure to a shortfall in published guidance and directives from the federal government. Concerning perimeter physical security, the assessment considered fifteen criteria, including requirements such as tiered perimeter security, blast standoff areas, loading docks located away from the main building, closed-circuit television monitoring, perimeter lighting, roving guards, and vehicle and visitor screening.[11]

Only one of the facilities met all fifteen criteria, and two others met fourteen and thirteen criteria, respectively. However, the other two facilities only met three and four of the criteria, respectively. Essentially, these biological containment facilities, home to the most dangerous biological material known to humankind, have inadequate and even dangerous physical security protections that place the U.S. population at risk and present a lucrative target to a potential thief or terrorist. In fact, two of the facilities did not even have command centers or response forces that would be essential to thwart a potential incursion. Simple issues such as a lack of back-up power were also an issue. This is of great concern because continuous and uninterrupted power is essential to maintaining the negative air pressure necessary for containing dangerous biological substances. One could certainly postulate a scenario where terrorists would breach the security system at a BSL-4 facility, gain access to the laboratories, and steal pathogens for use in a bioterror attack. Would we settle for this type of lax security at our nation's nuclear facilities?

While the discussion of biosafety has so far focused on U.S. programs, there is a strong international component to biosafety and the proliferation of dangerous pathogens that must be factored into the equation. Any biosafety system can only be as strong as its weakest link. Therefore, nations throughout the world must have similar programs and enforce similar standards. Many have, which is a step in the right direction, but this vigilance is not uniform and reflects the level of modernization and technology each country has achieved, among other things. One such international program is the Cartagena Protocol on Biosafety, adopted by more than 130 countries. This protocol limits exports of pathogens and provides a clearinghouse for information about living modified organisms.[12] Of note is that it focuses on biodiversity and agriculture biosecurity. This protocol is relevant to our discussion for two primary reasons. First, many of these same pathogens have the potential for spreading infection and disease in animals, plants, and humans. Second, the protocol can serve as a model for a similar document governing efforts in non–agriculture-related areas. Despite these efforts, lax standards and international inconsistencies have created a dangerous proliferation window that must be closed to prevent either the deliberate or inadvertent loss of control of potentially dangerous biological material.

Biosecurity is currently a less well-defined area, yet is a rapidly emerging field. A National Science Advisory Board for Biosecurity (NSABB) has been established to "provide advice to federal departments and agencies on ways to minimize the possibility that knowledge and technologies emanating from vitally important biological research will be misused to threaten public health or national security. The NSABB is a critical component of a set of federal initiatives to promote biosecurity in life science research." The board is charged specifically with guiding the development of

- a system of institutional and federal research review that allows for fulfillment of important research objectives, while addressing national security concerns;
- guidelines for the identification and conduct of research that may require special attention and security surveillance;
- professional codes of conduct for scientists and laboratory workers that can be adopted by professional organizations and institutions engaged in life science research;
- materials and resources to educate the research community about effective biosecurity; and
- strategies for fostering international collaboration for the effective oversight of dual-use biological research.[13]

A growing consensus is emerging that government has a key role to play in this area, in particular some responsibility for biosecurity policy and programs. However, some believe that the role should be modest, while others see a more aggressive role for government. The debate comes down to scientists, publishers, and industry that support self-governance, and to government's desire to impose regulations and establish an oversight regime. One thing is clear: individual scientists and biotechnology workers must have a code of ethics that governs their efforts. Systems must be in place for governing work and conducting compliance inspections. Nations must also report on potential issues that may arise to international organizations such as the WHO.

Another important aspect of biosecurity pertains to activities such as the transport and shipping of select pathogens. We have already seen several examples of lax practices in this area that have resulted in proliferation of dangerous pathogens to unauthorized individuals. The SAP provides provisions for appropriate handling of pathogens.

An important aspect of both biosecurity and biosafety is controlling access to information. In this regard, little has been done, and the "horse might be out of the barn." Vast amounts of information are readily available on the Internet. Genomic databases are available online, and articles have been published describing techniques for enhancing the virulence of pathogens by manipulating the genes of a pathogen. In one such article, the methodology was provided for modifying the *vaccinia* virus to change a protein to make it one hundred times as potent as the original version. This is irresponsible behavior on the part of the scientific community; that community must be appropriately policed. One noted expert, D. A. Henderson notes, "We have to get away from the ethos that knowledge is good, knowledge should be publicly available, that information will liberate us. . . . Information will kill us in the techno-terrorist age, and I think it's nuts to put that stuff on Web sites."[14]

While biosafety and biosecurity are important elements contributing to nonproliferation, by themselves they must be considered necessary but not sufficient, and must be placed within the context of the broader efforts to halt the flow of dangerous BW capabilities and equipment.

Building Biodefense Capabilities in the Post-9/11 World

The terrorist attacks of 9/11 and the Amerithrax attacks in October and November 2001 have driven the development of the homeland security structure, organizations, and processes in place in the United States today. In fact, if one looks for the homeland security "DNA" that has driven change, the most authoritative source for the recommendations and therefore the changes that have resulted is the National Commission on Terrorist Attacks upon the United States (Public Law [P.L.] 107–306, November 27, 2002). The product was the 9/11 Commission Report, published in July 2004, almost three years following the attacks. The result has been dramatically increased policy focus, programmatic changes, funding, training, and exercises to prevent another occurrence and better prepare the United States in the event of another attack.

The post-9/11 period has been an emotional one in American history. Since our founding as a nation in 1776, only one other time has the United

States suffered a large-scale attack: the strike on Pearl Harbor in December 1941. If one looks at the pace and magnitude of change in the national security structure throughout our history, the only other time such dramatic change occurred in the structure and processes of national security was in the aftermath of World War II with the National Security Act of 1947, as the United States emerged as a world power and the only nuclear nation on the planet.

The Homeland Security Act of 2002 was passed as a direct result of the 9/11 attacks. This legislation established the DHS with seven missions:

(1) prevent terrorist attacks within the United States; (2) reduce the vulnerability of the United States to terrorism; (3) minimize the damage, and assist in the recovery, from terrorist attacks that do occur within the United States; (4) carry out all functions of entities transferred to the Department, including by acting as a focal point regarding natural and manmade crises and emergency planning; (5) ensure that the functions of the agencies and subdivisions within the Department that are not related directly to securing the homeland are not diminished or neglected except by a specific explicit act of Congress; (6) ensure that the overall economic security of the United States is not diminished by efforts, activities, and programs aimed at securing the homeland; and (7) monitor connections between illegal drug trafficking and terrorism, coordinate efforts to sever such connections, and otherwise contribute to efforts to interdict illegal drug trafficking.[15]

The Homeland Security Act also established a Homeland Security Council (HSC), intended to be complementary to the National Security Council (NSC) established in the National Security Act of 1947. Many of the duties and organizational structures in the HSC parallel those of the NSC. In this regard, the function of the HSC is to advise the president on homeland security matters. The HSC membership consists of the president, vice president, secretary of DHS, attorney general, secretary of defense, and other individuals as may be designated by the president. With regard to composition, the difference between the NSC and HSC membership is that the secretary of state is in the NSC and the secretary of homeland security and the attorney general are in the HSC. The legislation allows for the convening of both the NSC and HSC simultaneously, at the prerogative of the president. In 2009, there was some merging of the NSC and HSC staffs to increase the synergy between them.

As a complement to the NSS that had been published in accordance with the Goldwater-Nichols National Defense Reform Act of 1986, a NSHS was also mandated. The first-ever publication of the NSHS includes significant discussion of the threats posed by WMDs and direction for strategies to prevent, protect, respond to, and recover from an incident of this sort. The second- and third-order effects and implied requirements have clearly highlighted the issue of WMD preparedness to include being prepared to respond to biological weapons.

The 2007 version of the NSHS document listed six objectives with regard to WMDs:

1. Determine terrorists' intentions, capabilities, and plans to develop or acquire WMDs.
2. Deny terrorists access to the material, expertise, and other enabling capabilities required to develop WMDs.
3. Deter terrorists from employing WMDs.
4. Detect and disrupt terrorists' attempted movement of WMD-related materials, weapons, and personnel.
5. Prevent and respond to a WMD-related terrorist attack.
6. Define the nature and source of a terrorist-employed WMD device.

The document goes on to state, "WMD in the hands of terrorists is one of the gravest threats we face, and we cannot permit the world's most dangerous terrorists to threaten us with the world's most destructive weapons."[16]

In fact, measures of the increasing importance of biodefense in the post-9/11 world can be seen clearly in the policy statements, programs, and budgets that have developed during this period. Most departments and agencies have established programs to address biodefense issues. Organizational modifications have frequently accompanied these programmatic changes. The HHS established a Bioterrorism Council and a strategic plan for addressing these issues based on the requirements contained in the Public Health Security and Bioterrorism Preparedness and Response Act of 2002. The strategic foci of this plan include preventing bioterrorism; enhancing state, local, and tribal preparedness for bioterrorism and other public health threats and emergencies; enhancing HHS preparedness for bioterrorism and other public health threats and emergencies; acquiring new knowledge relevant to bioterrorism and other public health threats and emergencies; and acquiring and deploying needed biodefense countermeasures.[17]

For each of the focus areas, subordinate objectives have been developed that provide guidance and direction to HHS, the public health and the medical communities, and first responders at state, local, and tribal levels for the types of capabilities to be developed. For example, the first strategic goal of "preventing terrorism" lists eight subordinate objectives, including the "safe and secure handling of potential bioterrorism agents." Some of the elements required for HHS's strategic plan also require some nontraditional programs such as "effective collaboration with counterterrorist initiatives of other agencies."[18] While not specifically stated in the document, this undoubtedly implies coordination between first responders, the medical community, law enforcement, and federal authorities that have counterterrorist roles, to name but a few.

The results of the legislation and the strategic plan can also be seen in hospitals throughout the United States, particularly those in areas believed to be at higher risk for a bioterror attack. Many hospitals have developed plans to deal with emergencies resulting from a mass casualty event, either natural or manufactured. Examples include the development in New Jersey of a public health network using 900 megahertz radios tuned to a specific response network for sharing information about potential health emergencies and response coordination. One of the hospitals in this network is preparing for treating patients with blast injuries and bioterror contamination.[19] In the Washington, DC, metropolitan area, hospitals are pooling resources and exchanging information to be prepared in the event of another attack like the Amerithrax attacks, as well as to be efficient in their preparations. Clearly, those localities that consider themselves on the frontline have taken measures to ready for a possible bioterror event.

A July 2006 *Washington Post* article concerning the establishment of the new NBACC at Fort Detrick, Maryland, provides useful metrics documenting this extraordinary growth in spending. In 2001, prior to the 9/11 attacks, the nonmilitary spending on biodefense was $418 million per year. After the attacks and by 2005, the annual spending had grown to $7.6 billion, representing an eighteen-fold growth in nonmilitary biodefense spending since 2001.[20] Within the total 2005 spending, the DHS portion of the $7.6 billion had grown to almost $3.0 billion. This growth is not without debate.

General concerns can be lumped into two categories. The first are concerns that the spending is at the perceived expense of other, "more-important" health and biological investigation programs such as cancer research. The second are concerns that the U.S. program would either violate the BWC or, as a minimum, be in a gray area. This concern is represented by the critics of programs undertaken by the government such as projects *Bacchus* and *Clear Vision*. One measure of the growth in attention focused on biodefense activities can be seen in the sheer number of new legislation and policy documents that have emerged since October 29, 2001. For example, twenty-three Homeland Security Presidential Directives (HSPDs) have been published, including several that directly relate to biodefense preparedness and response (Figure 3–1).[21]

HOMELAND SECURITY PRESIDENTIAL DIRECTIVES
• HSPD-4   National Strategy to Combat Weapons of Mass Destruction
• HSPD-5   Management of Domestic Incidents (National Response Plan)
• HSPD-8   National Preparedness
• HSPD-9   Defense of Agriculture and Food
• HSPD-10   Biodefense for the 21st Century
• HSPD-18   Medical Countermeasures Against Weapons of Mass Destruction
• HSPD-21   Public Health and Medical Preparedness

FIGURE 3–1 Relevant Biodefense Homeland Security Presidential Directives

A host of U.S. laws, executive orders, directives, and international treaties that pertain to biodefense have been enacted, signed, and ratified (Appendix E). Two, however are particularly important:

- HSPD-4, the National Strategy to Combat Weapons of Mass Destruction, published in December 2002, describes a strategy with three principal pillars: (1) counterproliferation to combat WMD use, (2) strengthened nonproliferation to combat WMD proliferation, and (3) consequence management to respond to WMD use.
- HSPD-21, which concerns biodefense preparedness and response, goes so far as to include specific programs for implementation, including biosurveillance, countermeasure stockpiling and distribution, mass casualty care, and community resilience. Each program contains additional details and directions on required biodefense programs as well as target dates for implementing the directive.[22]

Additionally, legislation enacted in December 2004 required establishment of a National Counterproliferation Center (NCPC) for the purpose of "taking into account all appropriate government tools to prevent and halt the proliferation of weapons of mass destruction, their delivery systems, and related materials and technologies."[23] This center has a sister organization, the NCTC, which has cross-cutting missions to fight terrorism in the same way that the NCPC has a requirement to fight proliferation.

As further evidence of the growth in BW issues in April 2005, DHS also published fifteen scenarios in *National Planning Scenarios*.[24] Of these fifteen scenarios, five deal directly with a potential biological attack on people, the nation's food supply, or livestock. The scenarios are used to guide training and exercises as well as to drive resource expenditures, and therefore have a high degree of relevance to the preparations and policies being developed.

The concept of risk management has received a great deal of scrutiny from DHS. Absolute protection is not possible and certainly not affordable. Therefore, a way to manage risks must be established. In this regard, a CRS report describes the DHS risk formula (which is the same as that from the Los Alamos National Laboratory discussed in the previous chapter) where

$$RISK = Threat * Vulnerability * Consequences[25]$$

While the basic formula remains the same, the idea that risk can be both asset- and geographically based yields some interesting conclusions. Asset-based risk pertains to the strategic threat estimates made by the IC on which assets would be most vulnerable to the methods most likely to be used. The asset-based risk assessment is particularly interesting in considering the potential for a terrorist BW attack because it directly relates to the motivation and potential for constraints that may drive a terrorist to use these capabilities. In contrast, geographic-based risk relates to the characteristics associated with the location to be protected. In this regard, Figure 3–2 provides a useful elaboration of the components that contribute to this overall concept of risk. The methodology relates consequences, vulnerability, and threat, which then can be examined in terms of probabilities. The methodology also provides an important capability for understanding the subcomponents for these three areas. Developing relationships between potential targets and the threat provides great insights into both the capabilities and intentions of the potential attacker and the defender.

In January 2008, the National Response Framework (NRF), which replaces the National Response Plan (NRP), was released. The framework incorporates the lessons that were learned during the Hurricane Katrina response as well as lessons learned since the first plan was published in

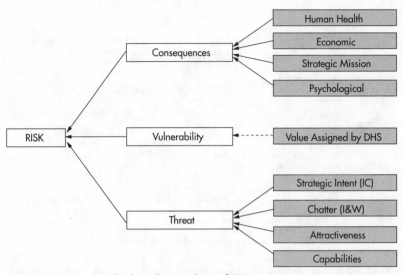

FIGURE 3-2 Asset-Based Risk Analysis Attributes of DHS

2004. While a description of the entire emergency management system is well beyond the scope of this analysis, an overview of the linkages between the federal, state, and local levels is appropriate to the discussion of changes to the strategies, programs, and policies that undergird changes that directly reflect and contribute to biodefense preparedness and response. Figure 3–3 provides a graphic representation of this highly complex and inter-related system.

U.S. biodefense preparedness and response begins from the perspective that local responders are the first to arrive and that local authorities must be trained and ready to execute their assigned missions in the event of an incident. The difficulty in this position is that local authorities generally lack resources to support biological incident response for prolonged periods, and therefore must have relief and additional support when requested. The states are key to the response; the governors have significant powers in this regard. To this end, under the Stafford Act, the governor has the responsibility to "(1) Assess the damage, (2) Request the Emergency Management Assistance Compact (EMAC) or other mutual aid, and (3) Request Presidential declaration."[26] One can imagine that for a significant BW incident, a state's capabilities would also be overwhelmed quickly and federal capabilities requested almost immediately. This is especially true with regard to the Strategic National Stockpile (SNS) in which drugs and treatments have been stockpiled for deployment and distribution in the event of such a biological incident, either natural or manufactured. The

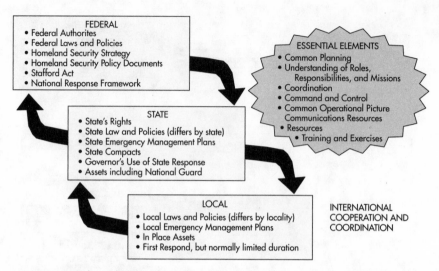

FIGURE 3-3 Linkages between the Federal, State, and Local Systems for Preparedness and Response. Note: This figure was developed by the author to depict key linkages between the various levels of government.

SNS includes, among other essentials, antibiotics, antivirals, and personal protective equipment (PPE).

In considering a national level response, a state governor has the authority to invite the federal authorities into the state. (This was an area of great debate during Hurricane Katrina because the Louisiana governor and her staff failed to request federal assistance and the federal government did not want to infringe on the state's rights.) Once federal assistance has been requested, FEMA's regional office evaluates the situation and makes a recommendation to the president. However, general agreement now exists that for major WMD events, including nuclear, chemical, or biological events, a federal response would be warranted immediately due to the specialized nature of the response and recovery effort. The state governors have at their disposal National Guard capabilities, including the Weapons of Mass Destruction–Civil Support Teams (WMD-CST) as well as state and local first responders now trained on WMD preparedness and response. However, these capabilities would most likely need to be augmented almost immediately after such an attack.

Other major lessons learned as a result of 9/11 includes the need for better capabilities for coordination between first responders, and the development of standardized plans and procedures. The Amerithrax attacks also highlighted the lack of preparedness for mobile decontamination and testing. These deficiencies must be addressed through various policy documents designed to enhance coordination and the procurement of capabilities for biodefense, including those within the BioSense, BioWatch, and BioShield programs. BioSense focuses on biosurveillance techniques. BioWatch focuses on sensors and monitoring stations deployed around the country to monitor key locations judged to be susceptible to biological attack. BioShield focuses on stockpiling drugs and treatments such as antibiotics and antivirals for dissemination in the event of a biological attack. While these programs have been established, much needs to be done to bring them to maturity.

From the Amerithrax attacks of 2001 to 2009, the United States has spent more than $56 billion addressing the issue of biodefense. Given this expenditure, a reasonable question is whether this spending has improved our capabilities in the area of biodefense. Dr. William Clark, in *Bracing for Armageddon?: The Science and Politics of Bioterrorism in America*, provides an assessment of six pathogens or categories of pathogens considered to have potential for use in a bioterror attack.[27]

If one is to believe his assessments, then the threat of BW and, in particular, the threat of terrorist use of BW, is minimal and even manageable largely based on programs implemented during this period. His analysis depicts that in all categories of pathogens considered, the threat level (as measured from 1 to 10, where 10 is the most severe) have fallen or remained the same from 2001 to 2008. In the 2008 assessment, Clark considers that no pathogens are rated higher than a "4," and most, including anthrax, are rated only a "2." His analysis specifically provides the following ratings:

1. Smallpox, rating changed from 8 to 3, because there are adequate vaccines and drugs for treatment in the pipeline.
2. Anthrax, rating changed from 5 to 2, given the increased stocks of antibiotics.
3. Plague, rating changed from 6 to 2, based on vaccines in the pipeline.
4. Botulism remains at 4, with no rationale for the rating provided.
5. Tularemia remains at 3, because it should be manageable with antibiotics.
6. Hemorrhagic fever, rating changed from 4 to 2, based on vaccines in the pipeline.
7. Genetically modified pathogens, rating changed from 3 to 2, given Clark's assessment that the technology is beyond the terrorists' capabilities.

By way of an assessment, many of Clark's arguments seem to be prematurely dismissive, as in the case of hemorrhagic fevers, where he notes that vaccines are in the pipeline. While work has been done on some of these pathogens, the vaccines—for Ebola and Marburg, for example— are far from ready to be used widely on human subjects.

While Clark's cautions about the overstatement of the threat and his consistent theme about the inadvisability of shifting funding away from more-important priorities provides an interesting analysis, in some regards it is an outlier within the biodefense community. We must remember that Clark's assessment reflects a single unclassified analysis and not necessarily an agreed national position on the bioterror threat that we face. Clark provides little information on how these assessments were developed.

Despite this optimistic picture, the consensus from the other BW experts is that we must not be lulled into a false sense of security, and that there is still cause for significant concern. Consider that genetic modifications of the smallpox virus during the processing phase could render the current vaccine ineffective. To do such an assessment cannot be accomplished sufficiently without linking the use of BW to a scenario and desired terrorist outcome for an attack. For example, if the goal of a terrorist BW attack is to gain publicity, cause additional expenditure of resources, and even lead to a loss of government credibility, then even a marginally effective use of BW could be a credible threat. The resources expended to care for the victims and to decontaminate rooms and buildings, and the fear that a bioterror attack would cause must be factored into any calculus of the threat that we currently face from a terrorist use of BW.

Prudent reasoning indicates that we should be somewhat circumspect in considering our ability to detect and respond to a BW attack. Many pathogens have a long prodromal or incubation period during which the bacteria or virus could spread unbeknownst to public health officials and unsuspecting populations. Even detecting *E. coli* outbreaks demonstrates the complexity and magnitude of the problem we face. Two examples provide evidence of the issue: the scare in the summer of 2008 which initially was attributed to tomatoes but eventually was traced to jalapeño peppers, and the swine influenza pandemic beginning in March 2009 that was not discovered until April 2009, more than a month later.

Another reason to not underestimate the potential for a bioattack is that the ramifications of such an event are enormous. Even though a vaccine is available for smallpox, 30 percent of those who get the disease will die with or without medical care or the vaccine. One exercise, Atlantic Storm, estimated that more than 600,000 people would be infected prior to the determination that an attack had been perpetrated. This means that approximately 180,000 people would perish as a result of this smallpox attack from just the initial wave of infected people.

While considerable attention has been focused on preparing for a bioterror attack through sensors, planning, and stockpiling of medicines, some signs suggest that identifying a biological event, either natural or manufactured, would fall to the public health and medical community in the United States, which for some very good reasons may lack the experience and even the capacity to initially isolate the pathogen and respond effectively. In *The American Plague*, which describes the yellow fever outbreak in Memphis in the 1870s, Molly Caldwell Crosby comments on the ability of the medical community today to rapidly assess that an outbreak is occurring: "[In] America, these diseases are so rare that doctors would doubtfully even recognize the symptoms in twenty-four hours."[28] In fact, diseases such as plague and dengue fever are so uncommon today that when victims report to clinics, emergency rooms, and health-care providers, initial misdiagnoses frequently occur. An analogy describing this issue is that when doctors hear hoofbeats, they have been trained to think horses, not zebras. In this globalized world in which naturally occurring disease can travel around the world with great speed and terrorists have demonstrated the desire if not necessarily the expertise to acquire and employ biological weapons, doctors as the first line of defense must broaden their repertoire to include both horses and zebras.

In *The Ghost Map*, Steven Johnson describes the chase to identify the culprit of the spread of cholera in London in the 1850s. While the science of disease has changed considerably since these early days of "modern" biotechnology, the parallels are striking. In the case of London, it took decades to settle the question of the source of cholera as the runoff from the early sewerage system as the source of contamination of the locals wells. The development of the now-famous map created by Dr. John Snow was a key step in eventually convincing local authorities that the source of the disease was the water supply from the Broad Street well. However, this realization would take almost two decades to become widely accepted. Today, with the potential for the spread of new and exotic diseases introduced either naturally or intentionally, we can ill afford such a lengthy period of discovery.[29]

For modern examples of the importance of biosurveillance, we can observe the criticality associated with unraveling the mysteries of modern outbreaks and epidemics. The SARS epidemic of 2003 and the swine influenza pandemic of 2009 demonstrate the forensic type of effort that has been essential to understanding the origins of the disease, the manner in which it spreads, and, ultimately, the best practices for halting the spread of the diseases. The modern-day mystery search for "Patient 0" was important to understanding this novel strain of influenza.

Despite the importance of these types of analysis, today our health-care system continues to be largely based on anecdotal medicine that relies on the expertise of the individual doctor or practitioner rather than on the collective competencies of the system. In other words, medicine is more *art* than *science*. The medical profession has been taught to rely on the art of medicine for presumptive diagnosis of disease and treatment of individuals, and, only if this fails, to bring in the science.

While this assertion is largely subjective, a person who has been to an emergency room during influenza season with headache, fever, and malaise has likely experienced that in lieu of any other more unique symptoms, the presumptive diagnosis will be seasonal influenza with the course of treatment prescribed a "cold pack" with further instructions that if the symptoms do not get better in a couple of days, the patient should return. For maladies such as seasonal influenza, definitive testing is not the normal course of diagnosis. The result is that, in many cases, a presentation of influenza-like symptoms does not result in a definitive diagnosis. This has significant consequences for the detection and treatment of biowarfare-induced outbreaks.

Several major studies have been conducted concerning the ability to detect outbreaks of disease. In the two Dato studies (which took place in 2001 and 2004 focusing on outbreak detection and characterization), the findings were that, of the forty-three outbreaks considered, 53 percent were detected by health departments, 28 percent by an "astute" clinician, and 19 percent by laboratory networks using "advanced testing and fingerprinting of specimens."[30] This means that in 72 percent of the cases, the patient left the treatment facility without the outbreak being detected. This statistic should be of great concern, especially if one postulates a BW attack using a contagious pathogen with a short prodromal period and a low LD in which the population and the individual would benefit from a rapid definitive diagnosis so that preventive measures can be taken immediately.

In the Ashford study (which took place in 2003 and focusing on outbreak detection and characterization), of the 1,099 outbreaks considered, 36 percent were recognized either by health-care providers or infection-control practitioners, 31 percent by health departments, 5 percent by surveillance systems, 2.7 percent by ministries of health, 2 percent by nongovernmental organizations, 1.5 percent by the WHO, 1.1 percent by the Indian Health Service, and 4.5 percent by clinics, laboratories, or private citizens. These statistics indicate that only in about one-third of the cases was the patient accurately diagnosed at the time of initial presentation. The study also concluded that, in some of the cases, the outbreaks were never discovered. In describing the state of biosurveillance, the study noted, "The time delay from the first case to recognition of the existence of an outbreak ranged from zero to twenty-six days. This study is also interesting because it analyzed 44 outbreaks caused by biological agents with high potential for use by terrorists."[31]

These two studies are cause for considerable alarm. First and foremost is that two of the three studies were conducted after the Amerithrax attacks in October and November 2001. One would have expected a higher level of capability and sensitivity in the post-Amerithrax attack period.

The length of time to determine that an outbreak had occurred is also disconcerting. Outbreaks identified in the later part of the range data (i.e., approaching twenty-six days) implies care by the medical system was either presumptive and successful, presumptive and not successful, or the disease was subclinical. In the case of the presumptive and not successful, the implication is that the disease naturally reached the final stage of the clinical disease model, "recovery, disability, or death" without appropriate intervention by the medical community.[32] In fact, the swine influenza time-lines for recognition of a new strain of virus took more than thirty days.

The response to cases in the Amerithrax attacks also indicates a system not prepared to deal with the sorts of agents, symptoms, and outcomes likely to result from a BW attack or of the type we would expect a competent biosurveillance system to address. Four of the victims of the attacks were sent home from the hospital with incorrect initial diagnoses.[33] Several of these individuals later died. While there is no attempt to place blame for these deaths on the initial treatment they received, one can certainly see how a failure to make a timely, accurate, and definitive diagnosis may have contributed to these negative outcomes.

The anecdotal nature of medicine can be seen clearly in looking at several of the individual cases of the Amerithrax attacks. In the case of Bob Stevens, the first victim to die, the entire sequence of events is known:

- September 28—first symptoms were noted
- September 30—first trip to the hospital, where he received the diagnosis of meningitis
- October 4—following the four-day lag in time for the definitive diagnosis of inhalational anthrax to be made
- October 5—death

This sequence clearly demonstrates the implications associated with failing to receive a correct diagnosis. The diagnostic gymnastics following his initial admission to the hospital on September 30 to October 4 when the definitive diagnosis was made should serve as a cautionary anecdote that highlights the need for a rapid and definitive biosurveillance capability with an equally rapid and definitive medical system.

Bob Stevens was the first casualty of the anthrax attacks, but he was not the first victim. On September 18, an assistant to Tom Brokaw, the NBC anchorman, handled a letter that contained white power. She later noticed an edema where the powder had come in contact with the skin. Days later, a black eschar, characteristic of cutaneous anthrax, formed in this same area of exposure. By October 1, she had been diagnosed with cutaneous anthrax. A similar course of events occurred with the seven-month-old son of an ABC producer who was also exposed to anthrax and who later developed the cutaneous form of the disease. The linkages between these events took days and weeks to form despite the extreme rarity of anthrax exposure in this country, coupled with the improbability that either of these victims would be exposed naturally to such a pathogen.

The nature of the health-care system and the rising cost of care makes gaining 100 percent definitive diagnosis virtually impossible. However, raising the percentage of diagnoses from the presumptive to definitive should be a goal of the health-care industry. In other words, we must try to reduce the percent of cases where presumptive diagnoses are used for treatment in favor of achieving a greater percentage of definitive cases. This is also important as we work to reduce antibiotic and antiviral resistance, because one significant reason for such resistance is overprescription of these products when they are not appropriate for treatment. Increased capability in this area includes developing Food and Drug Administration– (FDA) approved tests and kits readily available for rapid confirmatory testing, and in some cases elimination of other potential diagnoses. It can be just as important to determine that an individual *has* seasonal influenza as it is to establish the individual *has not been exposed* to anthrax.

The health-care system's contributions to biosurveillance are also hindered by a significant number of seams that greatly complicate the ability to develop and maintain a coherent biological common operational picture (COP). To be effective in this regard, there must be recognition through both comprehension and action that health care is a system that must function on multiple levels, and that what happens on each of these levels plays an important role in the efficacy of the entire system.

For example, the biosurveillance system must function and com-municate at the international and national levels. Outbreaks of avian influenza (H5N1), the swine influenza (H1N1), and even more exotic diseases such as tularemia and Ebola in far-off lands *do* matter to the U.S. health-care system. For each reported case, the CDC and WHO track the course of the disease and the transgenic shift that has occurred, assess the stage the disease is in (i.e., to determine whether human-to-human transmission is occurring), and determine which treatments and prevention techniques have been and will be most effective. Indications are that international openness with regard to health affairs and outbreaks remains problematic. The government of China has had and continues to have great reluctance sharing information on SARS even now, several years after the outbreak.[34] Likewise, in the case of avian influenza, many foreign governments have not always been forthcoming with regard to providing samples to the CDC for analysis.[35]

The health-care system, to include biosurveillance, must also function and communicate at the national, regional, state, and local levels. Disease and illness do not respect artificial boundaries such as borders. In times of crisis or attack, the development of coherent responses will be essential. Consider a line release anthrax attack in the District of Columbia using an aerosol formulation. If the prevailing winds are five miles an hour from the northeast, the affected area will likely include the Washington, DC, metropolitan area, including suburban Maryland and Virginia. Certainly, the response required will be local, state, regional, and federal because first responders from all localities would undoubtedly be involved.

Seams also exist between government and nongovernmental organizations, and between military and civilian authorities. This is especially true in a metropolitan area such as the Washington, DC, area where there are more than twenty different law enforcement jurisdictions, three states (Delaware, Maryland, and Virginia), and the District all in close proximity, as well as a mix of public and private medical facilities all overlaid in a relatively compact area.

Another seam is between the health-care field and traditional national security entities. Health care and biodefense have not typically been considered national security issues. However, some progress toward recognition of the linkage has recently been made. The planning scenarios that the DHS has developed and is using for planning for a broad range of possibilities certainly help to make the case for health and biodefense as a national security issue because one-third of the scenarios are based directly on terrorist-caused and natural outbreaks of disease.[36]

These changes will require both cultural adaptations and information-sharing enhancements. Nontraditional partners must learn to cooperate and information systems will need to be modified, developed, or shared to allow for the flow of vital biosurveillance data. Some progress has already been made. The National Retail Data Monitor (NRDM) is a tool that allows for sharing of information about sales of over-the-counter medicines from nationwide retailers. The Global Public Health Intelligence Network (GPHIN) allows for monitoring global media and websites for information about outbreaks and other issues of health concern. The ProMED and other public health–related websites provide another source of push and pull data for public health communities.[37]

Information sharing through common architectures and databases remains a weak part of the national biosurveillance system. Any "man-in-the-loop" interfaces are ripe for inefficiencies and inaccuracies. The current system lacks a national system for collecting the information, compiling it, and then disseminating it for use in making real-time diagnoses.

Data sharing would undoubtedly result in sensitivities that will need to be addressed. Local authorities would likely be sensitive to providing data to higher levels because they would be concerned with how the data are to be used and the uncomfortable position of having "higher headquarters" looking at, judging, and perhaps even directing local actions. National authorities such as the CDC and DHS would need to demonstrate the value added of collecting, managing, and making available potentially sensitive public health data. It would not be reasonable to expect local health departments to provide information unless they receive a significant return on their investment.

Indeed, the sheer number of organizations that have a role to play in the biosurveillance system and the manner in which these groups will work cooperatively to achieve common goals are considered keys to developing a global system that is both effective and efficient.

Another significant issue with regard to response and recovery centers on the lack of capacity within the medical system. In some regards, the system has been optimized to ensure facilities and personnel are occupied at as close to 100 percent as possible without exceeding this threshold. On a daily basis, historical averages and algorithms help generate staffing targets, hospital requirements, equipment densities, and work flow. From these calculations, we know that we need a certain average capacity, and that this is the level supported by the hospital. But what happens if a terrorist attack has just destroyed a major U.S. city or launched an anthrax attack?

A significant deviation from the anticipated targets through natural, terrorist, or accidental actions changes the requirements, and unfortunately the system no longer has a surge capacity to handle these increases. Even given the recent pressures of achieving a higher degree of preparedness, the fiscal challenges have taken priority with hospitals motivated to move patients through as rapidly as possible with little time to look for the sorts of low-probability diseases likely to be seen in a biological attack. In fact, the data indicate that the trends in national emergency room capacity are actually worsening. In one study conducted in the late 1990s, emergency room capacity decreased by more than 8 percent during the five-year period considered.[38]

While it is not possible to provide an "average" for emergency room capacity across the country, evidence of overcrowding and long wait times has become common. A 2005 article on emergency room preparedness indicates a planned increase in capacity not for surge, but to reduce extreme wait times for an already overcrowded hospital in California. The article discusses the Inland Valley Medical Center's plans to double the size of its emergency room by the end of 2006 in a move that was expected to help relieve overcrowding and long wait times at Southwest Riverside County hospitals. The article noted that the bed capacity was to be increased from fourteen to twenty-seven, making it the largest of the county's three hospitals and increasing the county's capacity from thirty-three to forty-six emergency beds. Despite this increase, shortfalls are likely to continue because the population has grown by more than 50 percent. The additional capacity was programmed to reduce excessive waiting times in hospital emergency rooms in the county.[39] The increases would do little to alleviate the crush of patients that would be reporting to emergency rooms following a bioterror attack. One can certainly imagine how the hospital described in this article would be rapidly overwhelmed in the event of a mass casualty event resulting from a terrorist BW attack. Even the normal daily flow of patients stresses current capacity.

Concerns about the medical system capacity extend beyond the emergency room. Equipment shortages are also prevalent. In the case of a pandemic influenza, we know the 700,000 respirators across the United States would be in use within the first two weeks of the outbreak. That means that unless someone dies or recovers to the point she no longer needs a respirator, we would not be able to assist any other patients with mechanical ventilation. A CDC brief concerning the potential for a pandemic similar to the 1918 disease that swept the globe is projected to have devastating effects (Table 3–1). The table indicates the potentially

TABLE 3-1 A 1918 Pandemic Today Would Exact a Horrible Toll

SEVERE PANDEMIC (1918-LIKE)	
Illness	90 million
Outpatient medical care	45 million
Hospitalization	9,900,000
ICU care	1,485,000
Mechanical ventilation	745,500
Deaths	1,903,000

dire outcomes should a highly pathogenic strain of the avian influenza (H5N1) achieve a Phase-6 condition capable of "increased and sustained spread in general human population."[40]

The implications for biosurveillance are equally clear. Our just-in-time system is designed for throughput and cost efficiency and does not react well to changes in the environment. The same system optimized to maintain close to 100 percent capacity without exceeding this threshold also maintains only the necessary testing equipment such as PCR test kits and culture growth media as can be used effectively and efficiently within an established period. This system is known as the economic order quantity. It correlates the supply and demand requirements looking at the most economically affordable quantity to maintain coupled with the seasonal historical demand for the item allowing for modest surge requirements. In a managed system such as this, a penalty for overbuying or hoarding excess capacity exists. Adding expensive "zebra" testing kits or testing everyone to provide definitive testing would undoubtedly be met with concern by the accountants. Who would pay for this excess cost? And is it necessary?

In concluding this section, it is useful to summarize the threat as follows. Generally, most experts see the threat as continuing to emerge with the potential for naturally occurring and genetically altered pathogens as a real concern that will only continue to expand as the dual-use technologies continue to proliferate. In response, much recent activity has been undertaken in the form of regulations, legislation, and programs to address the perceived threat from terrorist use of BW. However, we also know that major shortfalls exist within the capabilities of the medical community with regard to surveillance, detection, and capacity. National efforts are ongoing with the BioSense, BioWatch, and BioShield programs as the spearhead of the effort, coupled with intense training and education efforts at the federal, state, and local levels. Over $56 billion has been spent since the Amerithrax attacks. Some progress has been made, but it is clear that these efforts must continue.

Proliferation and Terrorist BW Programs

The U.S. government has a number of key tools that can be brought to bear in the fight against proliferation. However, it would be foolhardy to believe that the same tools discussed previously in the subsection "Attempts to Moderate Behavior" in Chapter 2, will be successful against a nonstate or terrorist threat. The BWC was established as a treaty between sovereign nations and is most relevant in dealing with state proliferation. Even then, its efficacy is questionable. The minimal requirements and the lack of an overt signature associated with BW also complicate N/CP efforts.

In addressing the topic of denying WMDs to rogue states and terrorists, the "National Strategy for Combating Terrorism" identifies WMD in the hands of terrorists as one of the gravest threats we face. The "Strategy" also highlights the need to take aggressive measures to restrict terrorists' access to the materials, equipment, and expertise. Particularly noteworthy is the identification of the various key actors, which includes all levels of government, the private sectors, and foreign partners.[41]

The *Strategy* lists six objectives for this comprehensive approach that pertain to all WMDs, including nuclear, chemical, and biological weapons and capabilities. Abbreviated versions of the objectives are found in Figure 3–4. Each objective has many N/CP tasks associated with it.

SIX OBJECTIVES FOR COMBATING WMDs

- Determine terrorists' intentions, capabilities, and plans to develop or acquire WMDs.
- Deny terrorists access to materials, expertise, and other enabling capabilities required to develop WMDs.
- Deter terrorists from employing WMDs.
- Detect and disrupt terrorists' attempted movement of WMD-related materials, weapons, and personnel.
- Prevent and respond to a WMD-related terrorist attack.
- Define the nature and source of a terrorist-employed WMD device.

FIGURE 3–4 The Six Objectives from "National Strategy on Combating Terrorism," September 2006

Denying WMD to terrorists will require restraints on access to knowledge about developing these systems, the necessary source material, and the equipment necessary to process biological weapons. For BW systems, this is particularly difficult because the pathogens to be used in developing the weapons are naturally occurring and nearly impossible to limit. The issue is further complicated by the minimal requirements for an area to process the pathogen and the relatively small amount of agent that can have a significant effect.

In a critical review of the five years following 9/11, the White House published *9/11: Five Years Later: Successes and Challenges.*[42] The progress noted can be measured in dollars invested and programs designed to prevent proliferation of all WMDs. In a special section, "Promoting Biosecurity and Biodefense," the document addresses efforts related specifically to biological weapons. These efforts highlight the BioSense, BioWatch, and BioShield programs, but emphasizes little in relation to the proliferation of dual-use technologies and availability of the pathogens. This is in contrast to the detailed discussion associated with nuclear proliferation. However, we must realize that this is due not to an act of omission, but rather to the difficulties associated with placing restrictions on naturally occurring living organisms and technologies related to a sector of the U.S. economy that accounts for almost 20 percent of the gross domestic product (GDP)—the health-care industry.

In thinking about technology that can be used to limit the ability of either a state actor or a terrorist from successfully employing BW weapons, "Militarily Critical Technologies List Part II: Weapons of Mass Destruction Technologies," provides interesting insights. Table 3–2 lists the detection, warning, and identification technology parameters; and the biological defense systems available or in development.[43] The source document was prepared in 1998, so one can expect that the state of development will have progressed significantly. For example, light detection and ranging (LIDAR) detection has already been deployed around key facilities such as the Pentagon in Washington, DC.

Perhaps the strongest message that can be drawn from this listing is that, just as technologies for developing BW weapons are maturing, so too are the capabilities that will be necessary to counter these threats. To some extent, we are in a battle to ensure that the defensive mechanisms will provide the options necessary to counter the emerging terrorist BW capabilities gained from the development of improved development technologies, enhanced pathogens and delivery mechanisms. Fielding

TABLE 3–2 Technologies for Detection, Warning, and Identification and Biological Defense

PURPOSE	TECHNOLOGY	DESCRIPTION
Detection, warning, and identification technology parameters	Immuno-based detectors	Capable of detecting organisms of AG agents
	Gene-based probe	Capable of detecting organisms of AG agents
	Molecular recognition (e.g., antigens, antibodies, enzymes, nucleic acids, oligomers, lectins, whole cells, receptors, organelles)	Capable of detecting organisms of AG agents. Can recognize weapons grade agent, by-products of its preparation or manufacturing signatures; does not recognize normally occurring environmental materials.
	Mass spectrometry	Capable of scanning samples of 10,000 daltons or less in 30 minutes or less
	IMS (ion mobility spectrometry)	Detects hundreds of organisms
	Scattering LIDAR	Detects agent (liquids and aerosols) at any distance
	Transducers (e.g., optical, electrochemical, acoustic, piezoelectric, calorimetric, Surface Acoustic Wave ([SAW]; fiber-optic wave guide)	Converts recognition of agents to an optical or electrical signal; low hysteresis; optical/electronic component processing within 30 minutes
	Sample collection (e.g., air, liquid, dust, soil sampling)	Collects and concentrates <10 mm particles into liquid medium
	Sample processing (e.g., cell disruption, concentration, purification, or stabilization)	Completion within 30 minutes
	Development and use of sensor models	Specific performance of military sensors

of these capabilities would provide a real capacity for both defense and deterrence if the defensive systems can be matured more rapidly.

Many of the technologies listed in the table have been incorporated in the suite of sensors currently deployed in more than thirty cities across the United States at more than five hundred sites. In addition to LIDAR, capabilities such as the immunoassays that form the backbone of the BioWatch system provide definitive testing capabilities at selected laboratories across the country. The same is true for the BioShield program, which is stockpiling key equipment, drugs, and vaccines.

In 2008, the future of biodefense was once again in the public eye. The commission on the Prevention of Weapons of Mass Destruction

TABLE 3-2 Continued

PURPOSE	TECHNOLOGY	DESCRIPTION
Biological defense systems	Production and design technology for protective masks	Communications (microphone pass through); respiration (air management); eye protection; composite eye lens retention system; anthropometrics; performance degradation; ability to consume fluids
	Production and design technology for collective protection	Affordable; deployable; adaptable to structure
	Decontamination	Volume of agent; time required; adaptability to unknown agents; environmentally sound; identification of what needs to be decontaminated; identification of decrease of toxicity to allowable level
	Vaccines	Efficacy of vaccine; efficacy of prophylaxis; pre- vs. postexposure treatment
	BRMs (Biological Response Modifiers)	Efficacy of prophylaxis; pre- vs. postexposure treatment
	Regenerative collective protection—membrane filtration	Removes particles having average diameter of 0.1–15 mm, and allows rapid flow of air
	Regenerative collective protection—plasma destruction	Production of lightweight plasma generators (e.g., ozone that is bactericidal or inactivates viruses)
	Encapsulation; liposomes; polymer entrapment; micelles; emulsions; immobilization of biopolymers	Ensure release of prophylaxis and therapeutics shortly after contact with plant, animal, or human tissues
	Antibiotics	Inhibit cysteine proteases or cellular transport

Proliferation and Terrorism brought it back to the forefront. This six-month, congressionally sponsored study was released in December 2008. The commission decided to concentrate its efforts on the biological and nuclear aspects of WMDs and forgo an extensive examination of the chemical or radiological components.

The commission concluded, "[U]nless the world community acts decisively and with great urgency, it is more likely than not that a weapon of mass destruction will be used in a terrorist attack somewhere in the world by the end of 2013." Furthermore, the commission found that terrorists are more likely to be able to obtain and use a biological weapon than a nuclear weapon, and suggested that the U.S. government needed to move more aggressively to limit the proliferation of biological weapons and reduce the prospect of a bioterror attack.[44]

Intentionally written at a high level, the report offers few details concerning the nature of an attack using WMDs or, more specifically, biological weapons, nor do they speculate on the number of likely casualties or the pathogen to be used. Despite these omissions, the commission correctly identifies a significant vulnerability that presents both national and global threats. In addition to urging the federal government to act "more aggressively to limit" the chances for an attack, the commission also provides two recommendations for managing future bioterror threats (Figure 3–5).

COMMISSION RECOMMENDATIONS

RECOMMENDATION 1: The United States should undertake a series of mutually reinforcing domestic measures to prevent bioterrorism: (1) conduct a comprehensive review of the domestic program to secure dangerous pathogens, (2) develop a national strategy for advancing bioforensic capabilities, (3) tighten government oversight of high-containment laboratories, (4) promote a culture of security awareness in the life sciences community, and (5) enhance the nation's capabilities for rapid response to prevent biological attacks from inflicting mass casualties.

RECOMMENDATION 2: The United States should undertake a series of mutually reinforcing measures at the international level to prevent biological weapons proliferation and terrorism: (1) press for an international conference of countries with major biotechnology industries to promote biosecurity, (2) conduct a global assessment of biosecurity risks, (3) strengthen global disease surveillance networks, and (4) propose a new action plan for achieving universal adherence to and effective national implementation of the Biological Weapons Convention, for adoption at the next review conference in 2011.

FIGURE 3–5 Commission on the Prevention of Weapons of Mass Destruction Proliferation and Terrorism Bioterror Recommendations

Despite the strengths of the commission report concerning bioterror, some inherent flaws are evident. First, the study focuses keenly on the security and safety of pathogens in labs today, highlighting the lack of vigilance in protecting this biological material. Obviously, this is a major proliferation window. However, the study recommendations do little to recognize the major proliferation window that exists based on the natural occurrence of these deadly pathogens. Second, the recommendations provide actions that can be undertaken by governments to improve biosecurity. By themselves, however, these actions are necessary but not sufficient to protect us from the threat that we face from bioterror now and in the future. Third, the report makes the point that prevention is the key to dealing with the bioterror issue. While not attempting to foreshadow the next chapter in which we will examine the potential for a bioterror attack, the commission report does not discuss in detail the components of prevention and therefore fails to account for the increasing likelihood of a terrorist being able to acquire, process, and weaponize a deadly pathogen based on trends in globalization, terrorism, and biotechnology.

Despite these criticisms, the report recommendations with regard to response and surveillance are crucial for managing a potential bioterror attack. Just as was discussed previously with regard to these topics, we remain only marginally prepared for a bioterror attack. Biosurveillance continues to be more art than science, leading to potentially lengthy periods between initial exposure and definitive diagnosis. Likewise, our first responders and medical infrastructure lack the training, equipment, and capacity for handling a bioterror attack. While the training has improved the most, more must be done in this regard. The preparedness of the medical and public health system is now and will remain a significant cause for concern.

Returning to the policy for biodefense and looking to the future as part of the policy work for the Obama-Biden transition in late 2008 and early 2009, the transition team developed a four-point strategy for preventing bioterror and mitigating the consequences should prevention not be successful:

1. Prevent bioterror attacks. Strengthen U.S. intelligence collection overseas to identify and interdict would-be bioterrorists before they strike.
2. Build capacity to mitigate the consequences of bioterror attacks. Ensure decision makers have the information and communication tools they need to manage disease outbreaks by linking health-care providers, hospitals, and public health agencies. A well-planned, well-rehearsed, and rapidly executed epidemic response can dramatically diminish the consequences of biological attacks.
3. Accelerate the development of new medicines, vaccines, and production capabilities. Build on America's unparalleled talent to create new drugs, vaccines, and diagnostic tests and to manufacture them more quickly and efficiently.

4. Lead an international effort to diminish the impact of major infectious disease epidemics. Promote international efforts to develop new diagnostics, vaccines, and medicines that will be available and affordable in all parts of the world.[45]

The provisions of the strategy were aimed at the important issues in biodefense today and designed to build on the BioWatch, BioSense, and BioShield programs implemented by the George W. Bush administration. Undoubtedly, they will form an important foundation for future biodefense efforts. Perhaps the question is whether they go far enough, given the potential threats we face from bioterror. This issue will be discussed in greater detail in Chapter 4.

Biological Terrorism Exercises

With the emerging emphasis on bioterrorism and more generally biodefense, we have witnessed unprecedented growth in the number of exercises related to these topics. Previously, we introduced the fifteen DHS planning scenarios with five related to these issues. A natural progression from planning is to test or validate these efforts using tabletop exercises, functional exercises, and full-scale events that examine either portions of a plan or the full plan. We also previously introduced exercise Dark Winter, which examined the release of a smallpox weapon by terrorists. Given the high level of resources that go into these exercises, it makes sense to delve more deeply into what we have learned through these opportunities. Table 3–3 provides a listing of the major international bioterrorism exercises that have been conducted. Each entry reflects a major commitment of resources for the development of the exercises as well as the commitment of senior leader participation. Of note is that the table does not include other exercises dealing with naturally occurring disease outbreaks, such as the avian influenza (H5N1) that has received so much press since 2004. Additionally, it does not include the hundreds of lower-level exercises held at the federal, regional, and local levels, as well as the many smaller exercises that have been held internationally.[46]

It should come as little surprise that many scenarios considered in these international exercises would postulate the deliberate release of contagious pathogens such as smallpox and plague because these represent the greatest challenges. While anthrax gets a good bit of press as a potential weapon, a deliberate release of this pathogen would be more like the release of a chemical weapon, in that it would be geographically limited, unlike a contagious pathogen that would ride the globalization pathways discussed

TABLE 3-3 Major International Bioterrorism Exercises

EVENT	SCENARIO	PARTICIPANTS
Global Mercury (2003)	Smallpox	Senior health ministry officials from eight countries, plus European Union (EU) and WHO
Silent Twilight (2004)	Smallpox	Eurasian state, plus Switzerland, Turkey, United States, EU, NATO, Organization for Security and Cooperation in Europe, WHO
Atlantic Storm (2005)	Smallpox	Former senior officials from nine countries, plus EU and WHO
TOPOFF 3 (2005)	Plague, mustard gas	First-responder organizations in Canada, the United Kingdom, and the United States
Black ICE (2006)	Smallpox	Five organizations from the UN system and seven independent organizations
Black Death (2007)	Plague	Senior law enforcement officials from nine countries and five international organizations

earlier. In a microcosm of what a deliberate release might look like, the incidence of SARS in 2003 provided evidence of how quickly a highly contagious pathogen can spread and become a pandemic.

Atlantic Storm is another informative exercise with regard to the global preparations for a bioterror attack. In addition, it illuminates some of the key decisions that would be required. A synopsis of the exercise results is provided online.[47] Conducted in January 2005, Atlantic Storm was organized by the Center for Biosecurity of the University of Pittsburg Medical Center (UPMC), the Center for Transatlantic Relations of Johns Hopkins University (JHU), and the Transatlantic Biosecurity Network. The cautionary disclaimer that introduces the exercise states that it is not intended to be a predictive model, but rather a possible scenario that examines how international senior leaders might respond and the decisions that would be required in the event of such an attack.

The exercise documentation makes the point that this scenario does not constitute a worst-case scenario, because there are more than 700 million doses of smallpox vaccination available worldwide, and we have experience with eradication of this disease. In the scenario, the terrorists made use of one of the elements of globalization, our international transportation network. The planning assumptions included deliberate release at six international locations—Istanbul, Frankfurt, Rotterdam, Warsaw, Los Angeles, and New York—between January 1 and January 4. The sites targeted were primarily major transportation hubs such as Penn Station in New York and the Frankfurt Airport. The exception was Istanbul, in which the Grand Bazaar was targeted. At each location, between 8,000 and 24,000 victims were assumed to have been infected. Assumptions on the spread of the pathogen were also not a worst-case scenario. A 25 percent mortality rate was assumed, with a person-to-person spread in the first generation of cases of 1:3 in all nations within the exercise scenario. A seven-day incubation period was assumed.

During one poignant point in the proceedings, Madeline Albright—who role played the president of the United States—was faced with the dilemma of whether to release part of the SNS for use by international partners in the hope of successfully conducting ring vaccinations such as was done in the eradication of smallpox in the late 1970s. One can see the complexity with making such a decision. If the president releases part of the SNS, there is less vaccine available for Americans. Conversely, not releasing part of the SNS could perhaps allow infections to reach the United States, which puts us at greater risk.

Another instructive moment in the exercise was related to discussions about the manner in which the spread of the disease should be contained. One camp argued for mass vaccinations, while the other argued for the ring vaccination technique. Trade-offs between the two methodologies had to be considered in making the decision. Listening to participants discussing these issues was both informative and somewhat disconcerting. Did they have enough knowledge to make the decision? Did they understand the science behind the decisions they were making? Were the decisions being made to ensure the best international outcomes or the best national outcomes?

The range of decisions required was also startling: they ranged from the scientific to the political. Should NATO (North Atlantic Treaty Organization) invoke the mutual defense clause (Article V) that an attack against one is an attack against all? What role should multinational organizations play in this response effort?

The overarching lessons learned and conclusions drawn include the following:

1. Preparation matters.
2. Increased knowledge and awareness are essential.
3. Homeland security must look ahead.
4. The WHO's authority must be aligned with expectations.
5. Effective communication among nations and with the public is critical.
6. Adequate medical countermeasures must be developed.
7. Biosecurity is one of the great global security challenges of the 21st century.

Perhaps the lesson learned that will require the most political will to implement and even lead to a potential loss of some national sovereignty is the fourth lesson, concerning aligning the WHO's authority with expectations. This is a veiled way to increase the role of the WHO by supporting budgetary, political, and organizational adaptations to make it more capable of fulfilling an international role in biosecurity. Would we be ready to turn over such an important public health policy question to an international organization such as the WHO?

Exercises such as Atlantic Storm are being conducted at all levels of governments to examine the difficult issues associated with biodefense resulting from either a naturally occurring event such as a pandemic influenza or a terrorist release of a deadly biological pathogen. The lessons learned will be applicable no matter the source of the infection. Issues such as isolation and quarantine will test our capacity as a nation and perhaps call into question the delicate balance between public protection and individual rights. The conclusions from the Atlantic Storm exercise are strikingly similar to those of a Hillsborough County, Florida, exercise in April 2006 that examined the effects of a pandemic influenza outbreak.[48] Perhaps these similarities can be exploited in a more deliberate manner in order to prepare at all levels for a potential public health emergency from either a naturally occurring pandemic or a terrorist attack. In short, what these exercises tell us is that the issues we will face in the event of either scenario are difficult, and require a different kind of thinking and a different kind of response.

A Practical Assessment of Our Readiness

Much has been accomplished in the area of biodefense preparations in the United States, beginning with the Rajneeshee incident in 1984. In 2001, during the Amerithrax attacks, these preparations were put into hyperdrive, bringing an awareness and urgency that can be seen in funding streams, public pronouncements, and in exercises at all levels of the government and within private industry, domestically and internationally. Policies, strategies, and programs have been established for the expressed purpose of protecting the American people from BW threats. The question we face today is whether all the preparations have resulted in a more safe and secure United States.

In September 2008, at a press conference in Washington, DC, the Partnership for a Secure America (PSA) released its report on the federal government's progress toward preventing terrorist attacks with WMDs.[49] The cochairs of the PSA were Lee Hamilton, a former Democratic

TABLE 3–4 PSA's Bioterror Preparations Assessment

CATEGORY	GRADE	ASSESSMENT
Denial of access to bioterror agents	B	Funding for global threat reduction is strong for most programs, but they still account for less than 2 percent of the total biodefense budget. Multinational cooperation, particularly with the former Soviet Union, has been weakened by U.S. disengagement from the BWC. Although biosecurity efforts have been strengthened with Asia and the Middle East, the measures have not addressed large parts of the world, particularly Sub-Saharan Africa.
Detection of plans for biological attacks	C–	U.S. labs that work with bioterror agents are poorly monitored and global efforts to track work on and movement of bioterror agents are lacking.
Interdiction by law enforcement	B–	Federal policies to strengthen laws and promote cooperation among law enforcement groups are helpful, but need a more comprehensive strategy and better resources. The U.S. government is part of a security initiative, along with eighty other nations, to intercept WMD materials, but the focus is mainly on nuclear materials.
Confidence building to distinguish dual-use research	D+	Accusations and mistrust over the six-year weakening of the BWC have undermined international cooperation and security. Also, the U.S. government has strongly opposed the creation of a global organization to oversee and coordinate bioterrorism prevention policies. However, DOS is aware of the concerns, and efforts are under way to promote new detection technology and assess how scientific advances related to bioterror threats could influence treaty requirements.
Developing resilience by stockpiling and developing new countermeasures	C–	Project BioShield has supported the acquisition and stockpiling of medical countermeasures, but concerns have been raised about decision making and coordination within the program. Regarding the development of new countermeasures, there has been little coordination with the EU and other developed countries. Mechanisms for the oversight of dual-use research have been developed in the United States, but internationally are more limited.
Mitigation through public health preparedness and response	B	Between 2004 and 2006, the U.S. government spent $84 million on key programs to improve international surveillance and detection capacity. However, plans to improve global cooperation are moving slowly, and planning for a biological attack has lacked a focus on multidimensional threats, such as a repeated attack that would drain response resources.

representative from Indiana, and Warren Rudman, a former Republican senator from New Hampshire. The PSA assessment was that preparations to prevent a terrorist attack were a C effort, and preparations to prevent a bioterror attack were a C–.

In this regard, one of the key findings was, "U.S. disengagement from the Biological Weapons Convention (BWC) has undercut the confidence necessary for effective multilateral cooperation." The study also provided assessments with respect to bioterror in six categories (Table 3–4).

The PSA report findings provide a concise yet mixed assessment of the preparations for bioterror since the 9/11 Commission report was published. The PSA report also serves to highlight areas of great complexity that require multilateral efforts, the cooperation of the scientific community, and targeted initiatives to mitigate the threats and vulnerabilities in these areas. The conclusions about U.S. policy concerning the BWC are both noteworthy and problematic, in that they conclude that the BWC detracts from the overall goals and objectives of preventing a bioterror attack.

The PSA report represents a useful point of departure from which to begin the conclusion for the chapter on homeland security and biodefense, highlighting what has been accomplished yet also how much still needs to be done. With the establishment of the DHS and the reorganization of a significant portion of the U.S. government, many of the law enforcement and response and recovery capabilities have been reshuffled. This has been disruptive, although necessary to better consolidate and support U.S. homeland security efforts.

Exercises at all levels have also been important to increasing the capabilities of public health and first responders. Still, evidence suggests that in many ways our public health system remains unprepared for a large-scale bioterror event. Biosurveillance capabilites represent a significant shortfall. Consider the length of time required for determining that the source of the *E. coli* outbreak in 2008 was caused by jalapeño peppers, or that the salmonella outbreak caused by peanut butter and discovered in late 2008 and early 2009 had been ongoing, undetected for several years.

Exercises also suggest the lack of preparedness by key decision makers concerning difficult issues such as the distribution of the SNS or when to quarantine. They also highlight the interconnectedness of the international and national public health and response systems. With regard to naturally occurring or bioterror events, our globalized world mandates that we have data sharing that is real time, complete, and accurate. Failure to have that data sharing could put at risk millions of people around the world, including within the United States.

While the SNS represents an important capability, the author does not share optimistic assessments such as those espoused by Dr. William Clark. Small genetic manipulations to pathogens could limit the effectiveness of the drugs that we have stockpiled or even render these preparations irrelevant.

While we have focused efforts on halting proliferation through denial of access to biological agents, we have largely failed to put in place effective regulations for scientists, laboratories, and academicians. This represents a serious proliferation window. Additionally, our national policy positions on the BWC have effectively eroded the treaty at a time when we should be looking to strengthen it. In this regard, a more systemic approach to biotechnology proliferation and bioterror would be useful. To artificially decouple these two areas exposes a potentially dangerous seam.

It is interesting that the PSA assessment provides one of the highest grades in the area of biosurveillance. The author's judgment is that this is a system that requires a considerable overhaul. Through technology, we have the capacity to input real-time data for all people being treated at clinics, doctors' offices, and hospitals. Yet for a variety of reasons, we have failed to mandate these systems in the United States. Additionally, the use and distribution of sensors leaves key facilities sparsely protected and in some cases even unprotected. Our current family of sensors lacks the real-time qualities necessary for detect-to-warn systems. We have settled for detect-to-treat when this might be a catastrophic decision for combating a highly pathogenic, contagious disease.

Conclusions

Just as in biotechnology, in homeland security and biodefense we are in a race against time. Eventually, we are likely to have more-robust sensor systems and even a "zebra chip" for managing challenges to our immune systems. But this is in the future. Until these capabilities are widely available, a bioterror threat will continue to present a significant challenge.

We would also do well to develop key systems that have applicability across both scenarios of naturally occurring disease and bioterror. We are far more likely to experience an influenza pandemic that kills 2 million U.S. citizens (as projected in CDC estimates should a 1918-like influenza occur) than to suffer the same number of casualties due to a bioterror event. This does not mean that we should disregard a bioterror threat, but rather that, whenever possible, we should try to have "dual-use" capabilities that would be beneficial in either case. Furthermore, in our preparedness we must be mindful to examine both the probability of an event and the potential magnitude of the threat we face.

Earlier, in Figure 3–4, the six WMD-related objectives from the "National Strategy on Combating Terrorism" were presented as an introduction to our policy on the subject. The objectives address all WMD, and are not specific to nuclear, chemical, or biological agents. One can clearly see, however, that areas such as denying terrorists access to materials has significantly different implications for nuclear versus biological weapons. We must recognize these differences and modify our strategy accordingly. For example, in the case of biological weapons, attempting to keep the material out of the hands of terrorists, given that these pathogens are living organisms that occur in nature, seems unreasonable.

As we consider the totality of U.S. biodefense preparations, on balance, the efforts to date have established a baseline of capability from which to grow, but the shortfalls in the public health and medical preparedness coupled with the the lack of real-time detection capability must be juxtaposed against the advances in biotechnology that are seeing ever-more increasing capabilities for devleoping BW in the hands of a greater percent of the population. This creates a window of vulnerability that must be closed with the utmost urgency. In short, the 400 percent annual growth in key technologies is outpacing our biodefense capabilities where progress has been consistent, yet at a considerably more moderate pace.

If this gap between our homeland security and biodefense capabilities, compared to the proliferation of biotechnology, continues to to expand at the current pace, a potentially dangerous situation could result. Terrorists, motivated for increasingly bolder and lethal attacks, enabled by ever-more readily available biotechnology capabilities, are likely to begin to see BW as an important emerging capability for use in promoting their causes. Given the properties of BW, the most effective means to employ against them will be enhancements in our biodefense posture to deter and dissaude them from employing BW capabilities.

CHAPTER FOUR

Examination of the Potential for a Bioterror Attack

The distance between the capacity of a terrorist group to conduct a biological attack and the nation's preparedness for such an attack is widening. . . . [There is a] growing complacency in national security circles, the government, and the public mind . . . and the exponential growth of emerging, dual-use technology in biological and medical science is making the situation much more dangerous than in the past. There are reasons to believe terrorists plan to conduct an attack on the United States.

Margaret Hamburg, Former Assistant Secretary for
Planning and Evaluation at the HHS speaking at the
Center for National Policy[1]

Overview

The potential for a bioterror attack relates directly to the critical nexus we have identified between globalization, terrorism, and biotechnology. As a result of these relationships, we find a world in which all indicators individually and collectively point to the increased capacity for terrorists to develop and use biological weapons in support of their objectives. As described in earlier chapters, prolific writings and discussion on these topics have resulted in little universal agreement as to what the future holds. Some see globalization as inevitable and a benefit to humankind. Others see globalization, or at least portions of it, as a negative force. Still others postulate a retrenchment away from globalization as a possible global outcome as they recognize the downsides of a globalized world on their insular nations, societies, and cultures.

Biotechnology is most often seen as improving the quality of life around the world, yet there is a dark side here as well on which many experts report and over which they express grave concerns. A significant tension exists between medical professionals looking to advance biotechnology for the sake of humankind and those saying that these advances represent a form of dangerous proliferation that must be controlled. However, even those that support controlling the proliferation of these capabilities recognize, in the same breath, the challenges associated with such a position. What does the future hold for a field experiencing 400 percent annual increases in capacity? Is that growth rate sustainable? Will the rate increase even further? What about the potential for the introduction of nanobiotechnology?

Terrorism continues to be perceived as one of the most important issues facing America today, yet we cannot even agree to a definition, either nationally or internationally. It remains a highly emotional subject, with some calling terrorists murderous thugs and others rationalizing their actions. The literature tells us that where one stands on this issue is highly correlated to the target attacked and one's personal sympathies. With such a lack of clarity in understanding terrorism, attempting to address the issue becomes that much more problematic.

Turning to bioterrorism, one sees a similar lack of clarity. Many symptoms combine to make this issue perhaps one of the most difficult national security challenges we face. Even understanding the history of the issue presents challenges because previous incidents provide few definitive insights. Likewise, even with regard to the science, widespread disagreement exists concerning the potential for a bioterror attack, with some claiming the science is trivial and others claiming it is far too complex for all but the most highly trained scientists. As we begin this examination, three concerns are worthy of mention.

First, the nature of reporting on bioterror has made getting to the "truth" highly problematic. After the Amerithrax attacks, it seems as though the floodgates opened: the proliferation of articles and information about BW and, in particular, terrorist BW, has occurred at a rampant pace. However, much of this information reflects circular reporting. In other words, when one goes to the literature from books to articles to blogs, the information generally comes from a handful of key sources. The effect has been volumes of information that lead to more reporting, all based on information from just a few sources. In some cases, the sources are unconfirmed assertions. Perhaps of even greater concern is that national policy is being set based on such information. Examples can be found in of the reporting about al-Qaeda's alleged efforts to acquire WMDs that were in a listing of article compiled by CNS.[2] Several of the notes indicate that many of these allegations have not been proven. Still, they were reported and have collectively formed some of the foundations on which we have based U.S. policy.

Second, the proliferation of technical capabilities and knowledge has likely made bioterror an inevitable part of the security landscape of the future. Scientific journals, information available on the Web, and the general information available through educational sources reflect only a subset of the potential resources available concerning biological topics, some of which would facilitate terrorists developing the capability to launch a BW attack. If you want to know what gene is thought to make the Ebola virus transparent to the immune system, you can find it in a scientific article posted on the Web. If you want to understand how to make anthrax more stable in the environment, there is a blog that can help you.

Finally, even with all the potential for proliferation of BW capabilities, the experts remain divided, with some believing a large-scale bioterror attack could be imminent, and others believing the threat is exaggerated and massive funding for biodefense detracts from other, more-pressing public health issues. Even gaining agreement on the ease with which a terrorist could develop and use BW weapons has remained a subject of intense debate. How can opinions on such a technical issue be so divergent? Which camp do we believe? And what if the camp you follow is wrong?

It is within this somewhat confused framework that we examine the nexus between globalization, terrorism, and biotechnology to gain an understanding of the potential for bioterrorist attack. We also want to understand the parameters under which a bioterror attack could become a reality. Therefore, in this chapter, we will examine four fundamental questions:

1. Will biotechnology developments make BW more readily available for terrorists in the future?
2. Have terrorists demonstrated the intent to acquire, weaponize, and use biological weapons?
3. Are the international N/CP regimes adequate to deter, dissuade, and thwart terrorists from gaining biological weapons capabilities?
4. What level of capabilities will be required to prevent and protect against terrorist BW proliferation and attack?

Before examining these complex issues, we must delve into what is meant by a bioterror attack. For this analysis, we will consider this type of attack to be one executed by a terrorist, perpetrated using biological material as the means. Additionally, we must delineate the attack into a small-scale or large-scale attack. As we will see as part of this analysis, differences exist in requirements for perpetrating an attack based on the scale. These differences will figure prominently in our conclusions.

The author has selected the threshold of one thousand casualties with a mix of mortality and morbidity as the delineation between the two categories. Any event with 999 or fewer casualties would thus be considered a small-scale attack. However, we must realize that several important factors will go into categorizing an attack in such a way. The number "one thousand" was set above the level of the largest known modern use of BW weapons: the Rajneeshees' attack in 1984. However, the number is also set well below the 9/11 casualties that resulted in approximately three thousand deaths. In comparing the two events, the author argues that the Rajneeshee attack—with no deaths, approximately 750 sickened (with no long-term effects), using a low-pathogenic agent—would be considered a small-scale attack, while the 9/11 terrorist attacks (although they did not involve BW) with more than three thousand killed, thousands more injured, and economic losses approaching $1 trillion, would be considered a large-scale attack.

Of course, outcomes matter. The Rajneeshee attack, if it had used dried Ebola virus sprinkled on the salad bars and had affected the same 750 people, would have resulted in 90 percent primary casualties and perhaps secondary casualties of family members and health-care workers who treated the victims. The attack would thus likely have approached or perhaps even exceeded the one thousand threshold. The numbers coupled with the horrific nature of the disease would undoubtedly move this categorization into the large-scale classification, even if the threshold had not been exceeded.

The delineation of large scale versus small scale would also be based on other factors, including economic and policy implications. Incorporating these factors, a case could be made that the Amerithrax attacks had a significant effect on the United States, specifically on biodefense policy and funding, so that it should be categorized as a large-scale attack. While the policy and funding impacts are real, setting the threshold so low with fewer than ten deaths and disease in fewer than twenty-five people overstates the impact in an unhelpful way. Thus, while the economic and policy implications have been significant, they do not raise the Amerithrax attacks to the large-scale category.

Picking thresholds will always be difficult. Some will argue that any deaths due to bioterror are unacceptable. Others may argue that the numbers to date are so low they represent an acceptable loss. Placed in the context of naturally occurring disease, with 6 million casualties per year globally to the combination of tuberculosis, malaria, and HIV/AIDS, the number "one thousand" seems almost inconsequential. However, we must balance this opinion with the concept that Jessica Stern calls "dreaded risks," which she defines as a category of risk in which the fear of an act is disproportionate to the actual outcome. She identifies BW in this category, as a means that causes fear, angst, and reactions disproportionate to the actual potential of these capabilities. The loss of confidence in government institutions were it to fail to protect the American people from BW attacks that killed one thousand would be unacceptable and intolerable.

Another delineation that will undoubtedly figure into the question of scale will be the geographic effects of the attack. BW attacks that would be geographically contained, such as those from a small amount of a noncontagious pathogen, are more likely to be categorized as small scale, assuming the number of casualties is below the threshold. However, even a relatively small release of a contagious pathogen has the potential to grow into a large-scale event if the outbreak is not identified and contained quickly. Therefore, in this case, even if the number of casualties may not reach the threshold of one thousand, it could still be considered large scale based on the greater potential of a contagious pathogen, especially if it were highly pathogenic.

This discussion implies that the delineation of a large-scale versus a small-scale attack has an element of art and cannot be reduced to a neat scientific equation. Still, the threshold of one thousand seems an appropriate dividing line from which to begin a more definitive assessment on a case-by-case basis.

The Impact of Biotechnology on Availability of BW Capabilities

This section will examine the proliferation of biological capabilities. Three components will be analyzed: (1) the steps necessary for developing a terrorist BW capability, (2) the trends in biotechnology development, and (3) the historical precedents or lack thereof concerning the use of WMDs, in particular biological weapons.

Much has been written about the threats humankind faces from terrorists' use of WMDs, with a growing body of experts claiming biological terror is becoming the most dangerous threat we face. The basic logic goes something like this: nuclear weapons, while extremely dangerous, are difficult to manufacture due to significant processing requirements, the lack of readily available fissile material, and the signature that a nuclear program produces which makes it susceptible to discovery and elimination. Chemical weapons, while producing a fairly predictable effect and being relatively straightforward to develop, are highly inefficient due to the significant quantities of material required to achieve a large-scale outcome. Biological weapons, conversely, can be extremely potent, easily concealable, made from readily available source material and dual-use equipment, and elicit a strong psychological response among governments and victims. The detractors caution that working with biological material is not trivial and that the technical capabilities required go well beyond those of most terrorist organizations.

Required Steps for Developing a Terrorist BW Capability

We have already discussed in some detail many of the required steps for a terrorist BW program. In the subsection "Building a Terrorist BW Program" in Chapter 2, we introduced several models developed to analyze the requirements for developing a bioterror weapon. We also alluded to the inadequacy of the current models, particularly with regard to understanding terrorists' motivations. Our goal in this section, therefore, will be to develop a model that accounts for the range of capabilities and intentions that must be considered in developing a terrorist BW capability.

The OTA assessment for a state BW developmental effort provides a useful departure point for this analysis. To be useful for examining requirements for a terrorist BW program, however, it must also be adjusted for the reduced rigor and scale inherent in such an effort. So what are some of the differences?

A state planning process to incorporate a BW capability into its arsenal would have a developmental course whereby the doctrine for employment would be established determining such issues as how such a capability would fit into overall military capabilities and under what conditions such a system would be deployed. Thorough research, development, testing, and evaluation would be undertaken as well. A state would want to understand the operational parameters under which such a capability would be most effective. A logistical network would also be developed and a rotation plan established to ensure the viability of the BW material. All these steps for a state would contribute to the "fielding" a BW the capability that could be used for tasks ranging from deterrence to combat.

Additionally, the OTA includes steps and requirements that would not be relevant to a bioterrorist. The proliferation pathway described in the Congress's 1993 OTA report (see Chapter 2, this volume) articulates a formal acquisition process that exceeds the basic entry-level requirements for a small BW program. Many of the component elements such as "develop and pilot-test production process" within the first step—R&D—have greater applicability for large-scale weapons programs. The same can be said of the "acquire individual and collective BW defense, including vaccines" in the fourth step—delivery systems acquisition. These requirements would go well beyond what might be necessary for developing and deploying a basic terrorist WMD capability.

The OTA proliferation pathway makes no attempt to address the minimum steps necessary for developing a rudimentary yet effective "terror" weapon. Just as the hijackers on 9/11 were only concerned with taking flying lessons to learn how to operate the flight controls, but expressed little interest in learning how to land the aircraft, so too could a terrorist only incorporate certain key steps of the acquisition process into his BW program.

Furthermore, while difficult to generalize the motivations of all terrorists, previous attacks have tended toward targets of opportunity designed to gain notoriety for specific causes. While some attacks have resulted in significant mass casualties such as the Africa embassy bombings and 9/11, in some regards the "battlefield" effects were less important than the psychological outcomes. This same philosophy would likely apply to deployment at a terrorist BW program where the actual capabilities would matter less than they would for a state deploying such a capability, which implies a lesser requirement for testing and even efficacy.

Finally, a terrorist BW program does not require extensive production and storage facilities. The amount of biological material necessary for use in an attack means that facility requirements are modest. One can certainly envision a scenario whereby the weaponized material would go directly from preparation to deployment, with no storage requirement. Additionally, terrorists have not demonstrated a desire to develop an arsenal system for storing these types of capabilities.

While terrorists have a "doctrine" of sorts, it tends to focus on achieving success in single tactical engagements. For example, al-Qaeda documents recovered from Afghanistan had material on conducting attacks and the development of BW capabilities, but did not include operational- and strategic-level doctrine for combining all their capabilities over the course of a lengthy campaign plan.[3] All these factors point toward a less stringent requirement for development of a terrorist BW program.

Given these limitations of the OTA proliferation pathway for considering terrorist BW developmental capabilities—which amounts to the overdesign of the proliferation process from the perspective of the terrorist or substate actor—one can identify several subcomponents constituting the minimum essential steps for a BW program.

Beginning with the OTA framework and eliminating those steps beyond what a terrorist would find necessary to develop a BW capability yields a streamlined requirement consisting of five major steps (Figure 4–1). The steps account for both the capabilities and intentions that would go into preparing and executing an attack, and would include acquisition, processing, weaponizing, planning, and deployment. It is important to note each step in the model contains elements of both capabilities and intentions. For example, in the first step of acquiring the pathogen, there is the technical capability associated with gaining access to the material, growing it to acquire the necessary amount for an attack, enhancing or preparing it to have desirable characteristics, and even in knowing it will cause disease. This last bit of information is very important in dealing with biological material because even small genetic variations can yield vast differences in outcomes, as the Aum Shinrikyo cult discovered with regard to their efforts to develop an anthrax weapon.

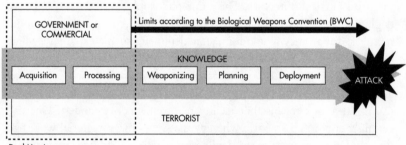

Dual-Use Area

A terrorist's ability to employ biological weapons can be represented as an engineering process with discrete components. It follows that interdicting a bioterrorist attack can be examined within the context of achieving success in any of the six phases from acquisition to attack; if the terrorist is not able to successfully execute any one of the phases, then the attack will not succeed. Throughout the process, knowledge is essential to gain appropriate materials, process and weaponize them, and finally plan and conduct an attack.

FIGURE 4–1 Steps for Developing a Terrorist's BW Capability

Figure 4–1 displays the components of a generic terrorist BW program as a systems engineering process. This is both deliberate and necessary to understanding not only how the process functions, but also what can be done to decrease the chance of a successful bioattack. To carry the systems engineering analogy to the next logical step, a successful attack is based on having the requisite knowledge and achieving success in each of the component areas or five steps. Failure across any one of the components will result in an overall system failure. This becomes essential in understanding how to structure the U.S. homeland security doctrine to prevent, protect, respond, and recover from a BW attack. Figure 4–1 also alludes to the BWC. More on the effectiveness or lack thereof of the BWC will be discussed in a later chapter. Suffice it to say, the BWC with its inherent limitations for moderating state behavior would have even less effect on moderating terrorist behavior.

The acquisition step also relates directly to the intentions of the terrorist. The type of pathogen selected becomes essential to the type of possible attack. Using anthrax would allow for an attack against a specific target that could cause mass casualties over a defined geographic region. The area may be large and casualties high, depending on factors such as deployment method, virulence of the biological material, concentration to the weapon, weather conditions, and susceptibility of the population, but it would be contained within a predictable footprint. In fact, deployment in this manner would yield results more in keeping with what one would expect in a chemical attack. Casualties could measure in the hundreds of thousands or even millions, according to some studies, such as the 1993 OTA report cited above. However, anthrax would not be effective for a doomsday scenario. Such an attack would need to use a highly contagious pathogen such as smallpox. Even smallpox, unless genetically altered to make it impervious to the current vaccine, would not result in an "end of the world" scenario and likely would be controlled by using similar techniques as applied in the previous eradication campaign.

While not meaning to trivialize this first step, one begins from the premise that material suitable for developing a BW capability is naturally occurring and can be found in a variety of laboratories and storage facilities around the world, such as the ATCC in the United States. While many of the loopholes associated with unauthorized personnel gaining access to ATCC stocks have been closed in the United States, the same cannot be said for all nations or commercial entities that work with these pathogens. We also know from a recent GAO report that theft is another potential proliferation window. Additionally, some the BW material can be produced easily in a laboratory. *Clostridium botulinum*, the organism that causes botulism poisoning, can be created in a laboratory using commonly found material and limited technical knowledge, as discussed earlier in Chapter 2. The same is true for many other biological toxins that can be derived from naturally occurring and readily available biological sources.

We know that attempts by terrorists to acquire such exotic pathogens such as Ebola have failed in the past. However, the availability of these pathogens around the globe can be seen daily in monitoring such websites as CIDRAP from the University of Minnesota, or the ProMED, a global electronic reporting system sponsored by the ISID. Both of these websites provide daily updates on infectious human and zoonotic diseases around the world.

At this point, a cautionary note is in order. The evidence certainly indicates a terrorist organization could gain access to pathogenic biological material. However, this does not imply a terrorist could gain access to all types of pathogenic material. Clearly, limitations would prevent access to certain pathogens. Smallpox has been eradicated as a naturally occurring pathogen, with the only known stocks held by the United States and Russia. Chasing diseases around the world, such as al-Qaeda attempted with Ebola, may make obtaining those diseases that occur episodically difficult as well. Obtaining the right type of a certain pathogen could also prove challenging. However, the evidence suggests that acquiring pathogenic source material for use in an attack is well within the reach of a determined terrorist organization. Consider that both the hantavirus and *Francisella tularensis* responsible for HPS and tularemia, respectively, are endemic to the United States and together cause several hundred casualties per year due to natural sources of infection. They are also considered potential BW agents.

The next two steps in the engineering process are closely related: processing and weaponizing the acquired seed material into refined pathogens with the characteristics desired for employment in an attack. The literature concerning developing these capabilities indicates increasing availability of the resources required for these steps, including the knowledge necessary to perform this preparation. In short, advances in biotechnology suggest these steps are becoming technically less challenging.

A basic kit for the processing of seed stock into the quantities required for taking to the next step of weaponizing of the bacteria or virus is not particularly sophisticated. Such a kit can be approximated using common equipment found at a home improvement store. The list of dual-use equipment for export control provides an initial shopping list for a terrorist program and includes fermenters (capacity equal to or greater than one hundred liters), centrifugal separators (capable of flow of one hundred liters per hour and steam sterilization), cross-flow filtration equipment (equal to greater than five meters), and freeze-drying equipment. In addition, some sort of PPE would be required, although it could likely be improvised and still be effective against most bacteria and viral agents, given careful handling.

This brings us face to face with the dual-use issue. While perhaps not seemingly related at first blush, similarities exist between the development of bioweapon material and such industrial processes as beer making. Both are biologic procedures in which a fermenter is used to drive a fermentation process in which microorganisms are grown. While home brewing kits would be highly inefficient, commercially available systems such as those used by microbreweries could easily serve the purpose of developing biological weapons.

Separating the agent from the byproducts could be easily accomplished using a standard centrifuge. While not particularly efficient for large-scale production, the use of a centrifuge or even several centrifuges would be adequate to produce a sufficient quantity for terror attacks with more limited aims. If even a fraction of the potential noted earlier in Chapter 2 from some of the assessments from the WHO, CRS, or the U.S. government's experiments (such as the anthrax-filled light bulb deployed in the subway that scientists estimated could have infected up to a million passengers) were to be achieved, a very small amount of material would have a significant effect.

Likewise, a simple drying system could be configured. The key to drying is establishing an area with low humidity and a source of medium heat so as not to harm the material while removing the moisture. Experts have also indicated the ease with which this part of the process can be managed using a lyopholizer or freeze-drying equipment, which would allow for quickly converting wet germ cultures into dried agent. However, more crude methods could also be used.

In laying out the case against Dr. Bruce Ivins, the now-deceased scientist accused of perpetrating the Amerithrax attacks in 2001, speculation is that he used these more rudimentary drying methods. An article concerning the investigation provides a cautionary note indicating the drying step could have been carried out with equipment no more complicated than a kitchen oven. Of this technique, Sergei Popov, a former Soviet bioweapons scientist who now specializes in biodefense at George Mason University, in Fairfax, Virginia, relates the relative ease with which the basic procedure could be accomplished. At the same time, he notes it would be difficult to reproduce the results. Popov also notes that going too fast in the drying process yields "sand," and therefore the potential bioterrorist would need to be cautious in this technique. In fact, he attributes the variance between the first and second batches from the Amerithrax attacks to this learning curve, noting that the product was greatly improved in the second batch.[4] All of this illustrates the propagation of information concerning the development of these capabilities is proliferating in a dangerous manner, and that the capabilities required can be quite modest.

Turning the dried material into a fine power could also be accomplished using easily obtainable equipment. For example, one solution, although makeshift, could entail using a sealed canister such as a coffee can with marbles inside into which one could place the dried material. Then, either manually or mechanically, one could begin the milling process until the desired size agent is achieved. While the solution may lack elegance, it certainly could be effective in preparing the agent for dissemination.

Weaponizing a pathogen—going from the "raw material" to the product to be used in a weapon—is related to the type of delivery system to be used in the attack, the pathogen to be employed, and the desired effects to be achieved. Additionally, weaponizing the BW material introduces a degree of risk because it calls for increased handling and the accompanying potential for accidental release or exposure. However, given basic protections and the right motivation, the thresholds for weaponizing a BW pathogen are continuing to be lowered and will soon be well within the reach of today's terrorists.

Also important to the question of whether a terrorist could achieve a BW capability are the facility requirements. We have already alluded to these rather modest requirements, but they are worth reviewing. Several pieces of equipment have been identified as required or at least desirable for building a BW weapon. The term "desirable" was used to signify that field-expedient capabilities could be used in lieu of the actual piece of equipment, should it prove too difficult to obtain. However, even with the list provided, all necessary components could fit inside a ten-foot by ten-foot area, with limited facility requirements for power. The only specialized facility requirement would be the capability to ventilate the room to protect the workers. Additionally, the signature would be very small, almost negligible, throughout most of the process. The only significant signature would occur if there was a release during the process that was ventilated to the outside where it might be identified using a sensor, perhaps from the BioWatch program. Therefore, searching for an illicit BW lab is truly looking for the proverbial "needle in a haystack."

Regardless of the pathogen to be used, terrorists likely would want their bioweapon to be highly virulent, to remain so during dispersal, and to retain those properties in storage and during deployment. Techniques are available to increase the stability and encapsulate the material to make it more resistant to environmental degradation. As discussed throughout this volume, literature on these techniques is readily available. The advances in biotechnology that included stability and encapsulation are continuing to advance at 400 percent per year.

Another important development in considering the ability of a terrorist to develop a BW capability is the increasing number of knowledgeable individuals with the skills either to engineer pathogens to increase virulence or to develop designer pathogens. As the field of biotechnology matures, more people are gaining access to the knowledge and capabilities necessary to make these genetic modifications. Events such as the following serve as cautionary anecdotes concerning this proliferation potential:

- Dr. Eckert Wimmer synthesizing a live poliovirus
- Dr. Mark Butler manipulating the mousepox virus based on a published article and inadvertently creating a more virulent strain of the virus
- Project *Bacchus*, sponsored by the U.S. government, developing a small lab for a modest investment
- an untrained individual experimenting with BW simulants in the "Kurtz case"
- the lack of restraint on the part of the scientific community with respect to the publication of potentially dangerous, dual-use information
- the general explosion of the biotechnology field

The next step in the process is planning the attack. The effectiveness of a BW event will ultimately be directly related to the planning. As in the case of the highly publicized use of a radiological "dirty bomb" that would use low-level radioactive material and conventional explosives, it is certainly possible to launch a BW attack using crude weapons and delivery methods. Historical examples include but are not limited to

1. the Mongols catapulting corpses contaminated with plague into Genoese fortifications, causing that population to flee (1346);
2. the British providing smallpox-infested blankets to the Indians in colonial America (1767);
3. the documented use by the Japanese of a variety of agents and employment methods against the Chinese in Manchuria (1932–45);
4. the Rajneeshee religious cult's crude introduction of salmonella bacteria into local restaurants in Oregon (1984);
5. the Aum Shinrikyo cult's attempted release on anthrax from the roofs of buildings in Tokyo (1994); and

6. members of a Minnesota militia known as the Patriots Council who intended to use ricin in an attack against law enforcement officers (1995).

While the "state-sponsored" BW attacks by the Mongols, British, and Japanese were somewhat effective, other terrorist organizations attempting to employ these weapons have not been particularly successful. This does not imply the threat of BW terrorism is not cause for concern, but rather that to date we have likely not seen the full potential of a bioterrorist BW attack based on a well-conceived and well-planned BW attack using appropriate biological material and dispersal equipment.

In considering potential bioterror scenarios, we must conclude the number and types of scenarios are virtually unlimited. The Los Alamos model, which considered more than 35 million scenarios for twenty-two different agents, provides some indication of the variety of possible attacks. Each pathogen has different characteristics that must be considered and that could result in different diseases. Biological agents can be spread by aerosol sprays, explosives, vectors such as mosquitos, contact through the contamination of food and water supplies, or even by using humans as BW weapons. Since BW weapons use living organisms, the attack profile has a significant impact on the overall effectiveness of the attack. Ultraviolet light, wind speed and direction, and atmospheric stability certainly affect outcomes. In fact, attack profiles vary greatly even within the same family of pathogen. Consider an attack using anthrax as the pathogen: three very different attacks are possible with three equally different outcomes.[5] By way of an example, we will consider the differences for three different types of anthrax exposures: inhalation, gastrointestinal, and cutaneous.

Inhalational anthrax requires the most refinement to ensure the particulates are of the appropriate size. If they are too small, they will be exhaled and not infect the host. If they are too large, they will not be suspended in an aerosol form and therefore will not be subject to inhalation. At the right size, one to five microns, the spores will both suspend in the air in an aerosol form and, once inhaled, remain in the lungs and eventually attach to the epithelial cells within the aveolis in the lungs. There the spores will germinate and the disease will begin to run its course. The course of the disease includes an incubation period of one to thirteen days, followed by twenty-four to forty-eight hours of fever, chills, cough, malaise, and chest tightness. A dose of ten thousand spores (but possibly as few as one hundred) may be sufficient to cause lethal infection. Left untreated, the disease will progress to respiratory distress, sepsis, and eventually death.

Another form of the disease is gastrointestinal anthrax. The incubation period is three to five days and the initial symptoms include twenty-four to forty-eight hours of fever, nausea, vomiting, and anorexia. The disease rapidly progresses to vomiting of blood, rectal bleeding, acute symptoms of the abdomen, and potentially severe pulmonary symptoms. Without prompt and proper treatment, death is inevitable. The size of the spores is less important for an attack by this route because even larger spores could be ingested and absorbed within the gastrointestinal tract.

The third form of the disease, cutaneous anthrax, has an incubation period of one to six days. It results in ulcerated skin where the contact occurred. The disease causes a blackened area of dead tissue of about two to three centimeters over a two- to five-day period. This variant of anthrax generally affects hands, forearms, head, and neck, but may also affect chest, eyes, and mouth. In about 20 percent of the cases, the patient succumbs to the disease. The spore size is much less important for cutaneous anthrax.

None of the three forms anthrax has documented human-to-human transfer. Additionally, the spores are highly sensitive to disinfectants—the recommended disinfectant is a 10 percent hypochlorite solution. In all forms, infection is based on contact with the pathogen, through either inhalation or contact. Treatment options, mainly consisting of antibiotics and supportive care, have a high degree of success if administered early in the course of the disease. Reports of resistant strains of anthrax have surfaced, but the use of broad-spectrum antibiotics would still likely have a positive effect.[6]

The point of this detailed anthrax discussion is to establish that the planning and scenario development for employment of the pathogen is critical. One can see that, given these very different forms of the disease, equally distinct forms of attacks (in terms of delivery method, desired effect, and potential for causing mortality and morbidity) would need to be contemplated. The use of larger spores for either cutaneous or gastrointestinal anthrax might be suitable for a small-point target. One could easily envision larger spores being used in an attack in a cafeteria in a government building or sent through the mail and distribution system in a manner similar to the 2001 Amerithrax attacks. Casualties would be expected to be fairly low and restricted to those having direct contact with the spores, but an attack in this manner would be possible.

If an inhalational attack were to be conducted, the refined spores could be deployed in the form of an aerosol blanketing an area. All initially exposed and potentially those involved in the clean-up, who might cause the spores to become airborne again in a secondary aerosol during the decontamination process, would need to receive vaccine and antibiotic treatments. Given the wide area and the time elapsed between the launch of the attack and the beginning of treatment, casualties would vary greatly. The deadly potential of a highly refined inhalational form of anthrax can be seen in reports of the Sverdlovsk accidental release in 1979 that killed 66 of 96 people infected and continued causing symptoms over sixty days after the inadvertent release, and the Amerithrax attacks in which five of the eleven victims with the inhalational form of the disease died.

Unfortunately, given the complexity associated with the acquisition, development, weaponization, and planning of an attack, the deployment of the weapon to the point of attack and conducting an attack are not the most technically difficult steps within the engineering process described. Just as 9/11 reinforced, attacks can be launched creatively using capabilities solely intended for peaceful purposes—such as civilian airliners—and have devastating consequences. We should be prepared for this same creativity from bioterrorists in the execution of their attacks. The Amerithrax attacks in 2001 are yet another demonstration of how systems designed for peaceful purposes, such as the U.S. Postal Service, could be hijacked by terrorists for their attacks.

Given the relatively compact nature of BW weapons and the lack of telltale signs, such as in the case of nuclear weapons that would result in an explosion and a radiological signature, a BW attack would be very difficult to detect. In all likelihood, with some careful planning the terrorists would be able to deploy their biological weapon and be gone long before the effects of such an attack became evident. In fact, initial cases would probably not be detected as originating from a bioterrorist attack because people presenting at emergency rooms would likely have influenza-like symptoms and not begin to cause suspicion until the numbers grew to well beyond expected norms. A biological weapon deployed during the normal influenza season would probably take even longer to isolate to establish definitively an attack had occurred.

Throughout the discussion of the five steps for developing a terrorist BW capacity, an implicit assumption has been that knowledge would be necessary to achieve each of the steps individually and then to combine them collectively into an attack scenario. This is where globalization—advances in communication, transportation, and information technologies—has worked against our ability to keep these processes and capabilities out of the hands of those not requiring them for legitimate research and medical requirements.

The global proliferation of knowledge in all areas has greatly reduced the threshold for developing BW. The Internet is a virtual market where goods and services are bought and sold or even left "lying around" for anyone to find them. If you want to know how to process a particular pathogen, you will likely find helpful information on the Web. If you want the genomic sequence of a pathogen, another website is easily accessed that lists a wide variety of pathogens, including CDC-controlled Category A, B, and C material (see Appendix C). If you want to buy a fermenter or freeze-drying machine, you can order one from the comfort of your home. Even information available from sanctioned research is available on the Web. If you have an interest in anthrax weaponization and deployment, there are numerous journal articles that describe techniques that are useful in controlling pathogenity.

The articles concerning the Amerithrax attacks and the alleged perpetrator provide but one example of this tension between our desire to know what happened and our need to protect the methods used in developing the weaponized anthrax. An astute terrorist would certainly be able to learn quite a lot concerning anthrax development by examining the published material concerning the attack in the days and weeks following the suicide death of Dr. Ivins.

Given these concerns, it is prudent to secure information in the same ways we have chosen to secure the pathogens and biological precursor material. In fact, it is irresponsible to release controlled information that could potentially contribute to the development of bioweapons. Unfortunately, the proliferation of knowledge today continues with little more than the discretion of the scientific community as the final arbiter. We know, for example, that open source material was used to support the Iraqi biological weapons program, including information made available by the SIPRI.[7] Additionally, little government oversight exists with regard to education and basic research. It makes great sense to increase government visibility, encourage responsible behavior (such as ensuring trade journals control what they publish), and increase international cooperation.

As ever-increasing numbers of foreign students are educated in U.S. schools, "proliferation" will undoubtedly increase as well. Of course, this is a double-edged sword. On the one hand, there must be concern with the proliferation of these technologies. On the other hand, the potential for foreign students to learn Western standards of biosafety and biosecurity and then take these procedures back to their home countries assists in countering proliferation.

While this section has presented the five-step process for development of a bioterror capability, the next section will deal more directly with the technical capabilities required primarily in the processing, weaponization, and deployment steps articulated previously. As we will see in the next section, these technical capabilities are becoming less of an obstacle, given the meteoric advancements in biotechnology.

Trends in Biotechnology

Given the previous discussion concerning the steps necessary for developing a terrorist BW program, a reasonable question concerns how general trends in biotechnology will affect the ability of terrorists to develop a BW capability. "Militarily Critical Technologies List Part II: Weapons of Mass Destruction Technologies" from the DoD provides a useful point of departure.

Important trends and insights can also be gleaned by examining the health industry and public health in our society. In the United States today, the health-care industry comprises a $2.5 trillion industry out of a $13 trillion GDP. This reflects a market share of almost 20 percent of the total GDP, a staggering percentage. Any attempts to place limits on these types of activities likely would be cause for industry concern, and adversely impact potential advances that could benefit humankind.

Today, we are seeing advances in medicine resulting from R&D, refinement of medical procedures, and emerging technologies challenging traditional values, concepts, and beliefs. Legal systems and control measures have not kept up with theses advances, with the industry largely on autopilot. The work done as part of the manipulation of the genomes of living organisms is but one example of such groundbreaking work that has and will continue to alter our lives in dramatic ways. Ray Kurzweil's assertion that human life could be extended to 150 years and perhaps longer dramatically underscores these advances.

The military critical technologies graphic presented in Figure 2–1 depicts the relative change over time in several key technologies required for BW weapons development. The changes depicted were linear, showing how biotechnology fields have evolved in the period 1940–2000. Another way to examine the data is to analyze the percent change over time. In this way, one gets a better sense of the magnitude of the change the field is undergoing. The point is not just that capabilities in these technologies are doubling every six months, but that capabilities in these areas are increasing at an almost unfathomable rate.

Consider the field of the Human Genome Project, which is listed as doubling every six months since its inception in 1989. In the eleven-year period from 1989 to 2000, this area has seen an incredible growth of more than 4 million times more capability—of course, that is to be expected with a doubling in the field every six months or a 400 percent annual growth rate. With this sort of compounding, the increases in biotechnology will undoubtedly reach levels leading to extraordinary breakthroughs in the medical, scientific, and health fields, as well as to expose a critical BW proliferation window.

While the leading-edge science is continuing to see unprecedented growth, the "center of mass" of these fields is also changing dramatically. The example used in Chapter 2 was PCR, discovered in 1983. PCR is now a common analytical technique used for a variety of applications from sensors to DNA fingerprinting to gene therapy research. In other words, these technologies have gone from cutting edge to ordinary in a relatively short period. As these technologies become mainstream, access to them will increase. Just as we have observed with other technological advancements, the likelihood that they will be misused will also increase as terrorists may see them as a positive way to further their causes.

Imagine a terrorist with the scientific knowledge to engineer pathogens to make certain genes express themselves, thus increasing the virulence of a pathogen by an order of magnitude or being able to encapsulate the pathogen to make it more stable in the environment. Consider a scenario whereby a terrorist was able to manipulate the bacteria *Francisella tularensis*, which causes the disease tularemia. Perhaps as a result of the manipulation, instead of requiring ten to fifty organisms to cause infection, the dosage is reduced to require only one to five bacteria. Alternatively, perhaps the terrorist altered the virulence so the bacteria was antibiotic resistant and the mortality raised from 35 percent if left untreated to 95 percent if left untreated, or even to 35 percent if treated.[8] These would be frightening outcomes for society and the public health community.

An even more frightening development would be the synthesis of the smallpox virus, now eradicated, using these advanced biotechnology knowledge, techniques, and equipment. Some might argue this is a technological schism no terrorist group will be able to cross. As several key events demonstrate, however, this may not be a valid assertion. Dr. Eckert Wimmer demonstrated the technology for creating a live poliovirus using synthetic material. The poliovirus is a Class-4 RNA virus from the *Picoraviridae* family that typically has seven thousand to eight thousand base pairs as part of its genomic sequence. In contrast, smallpox is a Class-1

DNA virus from the *Poxviridae* family. It has approximately 200,000 base pairs and approximately two hundred genes.[9] In comparison to the poliovirus, smallpox has greater complexity in both size and structure. Still, the genomic sequences for both these viruses are readily available—on the Internet, in fact. So while there are differences between the two in scale and complexity, to be sure, with biotechnology maturing at 400 percent increase per year, it seems only a matter of time before we are able to synthesize smallpox using these same recombinant technologies. If we are able to do so, when will we reach this level of sophistication and be able to accomplish this feat—2010, 2020, 2030?

As we contemplate this question, we must consider that the proliferation of advanced equipment and techniques is rapidly lowering the threshold for gaining access to many of these technologies and capabilities. Recombinant technology to build biological capabilities is no longer the province only of those working at the cutting edge. Gene synthesizers are commonplace in labs, pharmaceutical companies, and even in many universities. This equipment can make genes for use as primers in PCR analysis that is important for testing and sensors. However, if one knows the genomic sequence—which, as stated before, is readily available—it is possible to synthesize biological material.

The Amerithrax attacks have also had an interesting yet ominous effect on the proliferation of these types of capabilities, as well as on the number of facilities available for handling the most highly pathogenic biological material. In fact, both are beginning to proliferate, in some cases leading to even a greater threat. Since these attacks, the number of BSL-3 and -4 laboratories—those able to work with CDC Category A and B agents—has dramatically expanded, which has led to a complementary proliferation of knowledge and capabilities, as well as to an increase in the storage of these dangerous pathogens in more areas around the country. In fact, as discussed earlier, we are not even clear about the actual numbers of these facilities.

This discussion is not intended to imply that BW will become as readily available and used as often as an AK-47 assault rifle or C-4 explosives, but rather that the thresholds for developing biological weapons have been considerably lowered through the biotechnology revolution. Given the continued expansion of the biotechnology field and the economic incentives to do so, it is highly likely these trends will continue and the technical thresholds will be lowered even further.

Even if the biotechnical capabilities necessary to develop BW remain too sophisticated for a terrorist to master, the proliferation of these technologies leads one to possible scenarios whereby a terrorist organization could seek to obtain some of these pathogens through blackmail, theft, or even from a sympathizer with knowledge of biotechnology who might be willing to serve as a supplier. Building on one of these scenarios, if a knowledgeable terrorist trained in basic laboratory skills were able to obtain viable weapons-grade BW material, it is entirely possible to project he would be able to grow enough material for use in an attack or even alter a pathogen to make it antibiotic resistant, and then conduct a successful large-scale attack.

The Amerithrax attacks should serve as a final reminder that these advanced capabilities have allegedly already been used in a successful terrorist attack. While much of the information concerning the attack remains within law enforcement channels, by all accounts the material used had been successfully processed and weaponized. Of course, today we believe the material was produced in a U.S. facility and therefore developed using laboratory-quality facilities, highlighting this potential proliferation window from a legitimate source.

What History Has Taught Us

Fortunately, the history of terrorist use of biological weapons is limited. Therefore, few case studies are available from which to obtain useful information. Most of this history concerns hoaxes and pronouncements, with only a handful of actual programs or attacks to study and on which one can base conclusions. Another large percentage of previous BW programs include attempts to poison specific targeted individuals using such pathogens as ricin, and would be more in keeping with criminal activity than with a terror plot.

However, three cases in particular are worthy of examination in attempting to understand the potential for a bioterrorist attack in the future: the Rajneeshees, Aum Shinrikyo, and the Amerithrax attacks. A useful depiction of the significance of these three cases to the overall examination of the potential for a terrorist BW attack is provided in Figure 4–2. The figure also establishes the relationship between capabilities, intentions, and knowledge, and the potential for an attack in the future. It clearly depicts that increases in biotechnological capability and requisite knowledge coupled with the increased desire for more violent and spectacular terrorist attacks are leading to a complementary increase in the probability of a viable bioterrorist attack.

The x-axis depicts a sixty-year time horizon, with 2009 in the center. The y-axis depicts the probability of a terrorist conducting a viable attack.[10]

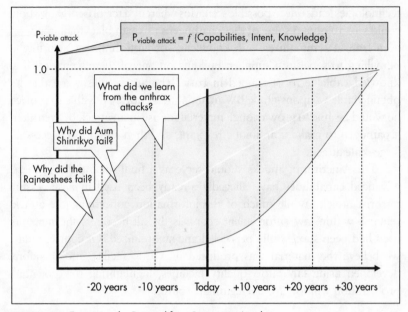

FIGURE 4–2 Examining the Potential for a Bioterrorist Attack

The boxes in the figure ask three basic questions about the attacks to be examined in this section. The elliptical polygon in the diagram depicts the probability of a terrorist conducting a viable attack in the future. The solution space, depicted by the polygon, shows that the probability of a viable attack is increasing and will likely approach 100 percent at some point in the future based on both the proliferation of biotechnology knowledge and capabilities and general globalization trends that provide a greater availability of means for perpetrating a BW attack for those terrorists with the intent to do so. Of course, without the intent to employ BW in an attack, the conditional probability of a viable attack is reduced to the lower part of the polygon.

By way of an example, in considering the potential for a BW attack in 2030—approximately twenty years in the future—the probability of a viable attack would vary from approximately 50 percent to 95 percent, based on the likely technical capabilities at the time and the desire of the terrorist to engage in this sort of attack. Just as with the other models considered, the variance can be explained by such factors as (1) technical prowess, including biotechnology capabilities, (2) the technology base of the location in which the development of the pathogen occurs, (3) the education level of the terrorists, and (4) the intentions and motivations of the terrorist including decision making: normative constraints, constituent constraints, state sponsor constraints, religious constraints, and internal politics within the group. Over time, as the technical capabilities continue to proliferate, the viability of conducting an attack would be related more to the intentions and motivations of the terrorists. Thus, the overall probability increases toward 100 percent for those groups desiring to engage in this type of attack.

In looking at the Rajneeshee incident, some might take issue with the categorization of this effort as a failure. The author has chosen to do so because the scenario and attack were not sufficient to achieve the desired outcome (i.e., the changing of the electoral balance in a local election). This is true although, when the attack was conducted, the motives were more about being a nuisance or retaliating than for any greater purpose. Additionally, the final target selection indicates a "target of opportunity" rather than a carefully considered attack with realistic goals and objectives.

While the attack sickened more than 750 people, the crude methods of development of the material and the crude attack itself indicated a significant lack of technical capability. In fact, had the perpetrators been working with a highly pathogenic agent, they would likely have sickened themselves based on their sloppy lab techniques and failure to use PPE. Still, the attack demonstrated that a determined group could obtain source material from a legitimate source (although their loophole has now been closed), our food supply was extremely vulnerable, and epidemiological capabilities resident in the small city of The Dalles, Oregon, and more generally nationwide, were not sufficient to rapidly identify an ongoing BW attack.

Aum Shinrikyo presents an interesting dilemma. The group was extremely well funded and had biological and laboratory expertise within its ranks. They experimented with several pathogens including anthrax, botulinum toxin, Q-fever, and Ebola virus, but were unable to successfully develop BW weapons before deciding to conduct a chemical attack using sarin gas. That attack was successful.

In examining the Aum Shinrikyo case, one clear assessment is that the means available were completely inconsistent with their stated goals because their methods could not possibly have led to accomplishing the strategic outcomes they desired of ending the world. None of the pathogens in which they had previously expressed interest would have applicability for use in a catastrophic doomsday scenario. Their techniques demonstrated an inability to successfully use the five steps in the BW development process:

- They attempted to use variants of the pathogens that were not pathogenic to humans.
- Their attempt to release anthrax as documented in the picture of the plume of material emanating from the top of a Tokyo building indicates the processing of the material was inadequate and certainly not to the proper size for a successful inhalational anthrax attack.
- There is no evidence they attempted to manipulate the pathogens using advanced biotechnology to increase stability, virulence and ultimately their chance of success.

Furthermore, the crude deployment methods called into question their ability to understand how to deploy either CW or BW. In the case of the subway attack, they placed the liquid sarin in plastic bags. At the time of the attack, they poked holes in the bags, resulting in a release of the agent. In the case of the oft-ridiculed anthrax operation, one can see in the picture of the attack a thick plume emanating from an aerosol device on the top of a Japanese building using particles far too large to be used in such an attack. Furthermore, they used a form of anthrax that was not pathogenic to humans.

The Amerithrax attacks in 2001 provide ample evidence of the potential for a terrorist BW attack using a mix of capabilities. The pathogen appears to have been well prepared to the appropriate specifications in terms of size and pathogenity. First-hand accounts discuss the material floating in the air and the ease of re-aerosolization just by moving close to the material as it was sitting on a countertop. The deployment methods, however, were simplistic. Placing the anthrax in envelopes and mailing the material along with threatening letters was relatively unsophisticated. Still, on balance, the attacks were successful, although even now the motivation remains a mystery. The most important aspect of the Amerithrax attacks was the reminder of a significant proliferation window with the potential for theft from a legitimate source that would go undetected until after an attack and require significant forensics work to trace the material back to the source.

Two other incidents are also worthy of consideration for considering the potential for developing BW capabilities. The U.S. government's investigation into the potential for developing a BW weapon as part of Project *Bacchus* certainly demonstrated that the development of these capabilities is not particularly complex or costly. In this case, the DTRA sponsored a study to determine if a group of scientists could develop an "anthrax" weapon. The group used a simulant, *Bacillas globigii*, for their work to avoid violating the BWC, but concluded that it was indeed possible to develop such a capability using modest means, equipment, and facilities. The second incident is the Kurtz case mentioned above, in which a non-technical individual was able to acquire and weaponize a BW simulant for use as part of his performance art. This incident provides valuable insights into the degree to which a nontechnical individual with open-source material can develop significant bioweapon techniques and capabilities.

Two notes of caution are in order. First, while capabilities will continue to proliferate and the potential for large-scale attack will continue to increase, biological weapons are living organisms and will continue to be sensitive to their environments. They can easily be destroyed if not handled appropriately. Given these limitations, some pathogens may prove elusive for incorporation in a terrorist's BW repertoire. Second, just as when one goes fishing, the type of fish caught depends on where one casts the line. So, too, with biological weapons: not all pathogens will be available for a terrorist to use in a BW weapon. Therefore, a secondary conclusion is that some pathogens will likely be too technically challenging to employ or else will not be physically available.

Overall, however, we must assess that thresholds for acquiring a BW capability and conducting a successful attack have been significantly lowered through a combination of the proliferation of the scientific knowledge, increasing biotechnical capabilities, and the growing trends in globalization placing more powerful capabilities in the hands of potential terrorists. The dual-use nature of BW makes this finding even more certain. Simply stated, the evidence strongly suggests it is possible now and will be more possible in the future for terrorists to develop and deploy BW capabilities. The issue with regard to the potential for a bioterror event in the future will come down to the question of motivation and intent.

Understanding Terrorist Intent with Regard to Biological Weapons

Understanding terrorist capabilities and intent are crucial when assessing the likelihood of an attack. As many of the models considered previously indicate, examining technical capabilities is clearly less complex than assessing intent. Furthermore, given the increasing availability of BW capabilities and the conclusions presented above, it becomes all the more critical to understand the intentions of the terrorist. Judging their intent will always be difficult, however. One must understand the motivations of the terrorist to assess the conditions under which certain actions or weapons might be used. This is especially true with regard to WMDs, where international norms strongly argue against their use under any conditions. In cases where state actors have employed WMDs, the international outcry has been significant. For example, Saddam Hussein gassing the Kurds certainly contributed to the 2003 United States–led invasion to oust him from power.

In understanding the potential for terrorist use of BW, several emerging trends are useful as harbingers of what the future might hold. First, the data suggest thresholds associated with level of violence as measured in terrorism fatalities have been altered with the U.S. embassy bombings in Tanzania and Kenya in 1998. Before those events, the number of fatalities was approximately 250 per year, on average. The Africa bombings, 9/11 attacks in the United States, and bombings in London, Madrid, and Bali indicate a trend toward larger, more deadly events against purely civilian targets.

Second, continuing globalization has created the perfect environment for fomenting discontent and airing grievances on the world stage. The twenty-four–hour news cycle and nature of reporting provides both a cause for and a means of getting one's message out. If one wants to get on the evening news, a suicide bomb that kills three people including the bomber will likely get only a mention, if that. However, a bombing that kills hundreds, such as the bombing of embassies in Africa, will make news for weeks, months, or even years to come.

Third, the databases and literature all indicate that several major terrorist groups and some loner actors have expressed an interest in biological weapons. A number of hoaxes also signify terrorist interest in biological weapons, if only for the purpose of inciting fear. Clearly, al-Qaeda has signaled an interest in at least examining these weapons, although it is unclear from the literature whether they want to use them or simply talk about their use by way of a threat in order to gain notoriety. For instance, as recent evidence from actions in Iraq by AQI demonstrate that when violence was excessive or directed toward the civilian population, the support of the populace diminished. The nature of BW suggests that, in almost any scenario, civilian casualties would be very likely.

Fourth, in considering the potential for terrorists developing BW capabilities, we must consider the full range of motivations that could cause them to seek to acquire these systems. Some terrorists may want to develop these capabilities for use in an attack. Others may simply want them for status or to use as a deterrent. The degree to which terrorists find BW interesting will be related to their motivations. Terrorists groups such as the Irish Republican Army (IRA) that are moving toward becoming political entities are unlikely to be interested in developing BW capabilities. They would likely see developing these capabilities as contrary to gaining acceptance and promoting their cause. Groups such as al-Qaeda, which are actively fighting and who rely on the support of the populace for financial and ideological support, may also approach large-scale use of BW with caution. This caution may come in the form of carefully selecting those targets to attack with BW to ensure they are "military" objectives or perhaps only threatening BW use versus actually conducting an attack. Apocalyptical groups such as Aum Shinrikyo will likely be more inclined to employ BW capabilities in large-scale attacks. Another subset of terrorists that has used BW in the past is the lone actor using a substance such as ricin to target specific individuals. We should expect this use to continue.

Fifth, strong international norms that argue against use of these weapons will prove to be a moderating factor for some. However, many terrorist organizations, especially those involved in active fighting, will believe, as bin Laden says, "acquiring weapons for the defense of Muslims [is] a religious duty. . . . It would be a sin for Muslims not to try and possess the [unconventional] weapons that would prevent the infidels from inflicting harm on Muslims."[11] However, we must also exercise some caution in looking at the statements such as those of bin Laden and understand that some of this rhetoric is likely for internal consumption and may not be a statement of intended policy.

Sixth, the technology associated with developing a BW capability will likely limit development of these capabilities to global terrorist networks or those within more-modern nations. A national terrorist group in an underdeveloped nation is far less likely to pursue these capabilities. If it does, it will need to rely on external support such as state sponsorship or theft to obtain them. The technological hurdles and danger posed by working with many of these pathogens, particularly those that are contagious or for which there are no treatments or vaccines, will effectively limit the population of agents terrorists will pursue, at least in the near term.

Despite the norms against such activity, the evidence suggests BW remains an interesting capability for the terrorists to investigate, develop, and perhaps even use. However, the decision to use BW will be based on individual preferences rather than on a generalization that would be uniformly adopted by all groups. The motivations and the sense of needing to mount increasingly more violent and extreme attacks will likely drive some terrorists toward developing a BW capability in the future.

Considered in its entirety, the issue comes down to this: Only a small subset of terrorist organizations will be able to muster the resources, capabilities, intentions, and support structure to engage in BW proliferation in the near future. Even fewer would be able to mount a large-scale bioterror attack.[12] This is not to imply that the threat of bioterror is not credible or we should not prepare for it, but rather that we should understand the complexities associated with this threat make it a relatively low-probability yet high-consequence event.

The Adequacy of Current Nonproliferation and Counterproliferation Regimes with Regard to Terrorist BW

Nonproliferation and counterproliferation are two closely related activities designed to prevent the use and proliferation of dangerous WMD capabilities and technologies. Nonproliferation activities include dissuading or impeding access to or distribution of sensitive technologies, material, and expertise through diplomacy, arms control, multilateral agreements, threat reduction assistance, and export controls activities. Counterproliferation includes detection and monitoring, offensive operations, active defense, and passive defense taken to defeat the threat or use of WMDs. The two activities are designed to be used together, individually, and even sequentially, depending on the nature of the threat.

A cornerstone of the U.S. nonproliferation strategy includes the BWC. Unfortunately, the inadequacy of the BWC has long been recognized and contributes to a significant gap in our BW nonproliferation architecture. Several important issues combine to render the BWC largely ineffective for both state and nonstate actors. The lack of a verification regime in the BWC was in a sense the original sin. With no way to determine through an official verification regime if states were violating the provisions of the treaty, enforcement was virtually impossible. This shortfall has been well documented, and attempts have been made to strengthen the treaty provisions in this area. Despite these attempts, the treaty remains without any viable verification mechanisms.

If the lack of a verification regime was not enough to render the BWC ineffective, the fact the BWC is a treaty signed and enforced by nation-states at a time when the threat from state BW is decreasing while the terrorist BW threat is increasing provides further evidence the BWC in its current form is both ineffective and obsolete. The dual-use nature of BW weapons and the proliferation of biotechnology capabilities have more recently left the BWC all but irrelevant for anything other than an official declaration by a state as to whether it is a signatory and whether it is in compliance. Dual-use issues have seriously complicated any attempts to strengthen the BWC for state programs. This was illustrated at a 1997 United Nations

Educational, Scientific and Cultural Organization (UNESCO)–hosted conference on the "Possible Consequences of the Misuse of Biological Sciences." The conference's conclusions included the following:

> Dual-use technologies, materials and equipment have spread throughout the globe as biotechnology and pharmaceutical industries have grown. The widespread presence of dual-use technologies, equipment and materials in countries around the globe makes monitoring of the biological weapon proliferation very difficult. Tell-tale signs of a covert biological weapons programme are scarce and even discrete signs of a covert weapons programme can be hidden if a government is willing to pursue germ warfare in antiquated facilities without modern safety precautions, such as specialized containment facilities and worker vaccination.[13]

Furthermore, as we have seen with the U.S. Project *Bacchus*, even compliance is a matter of interpretation and is not necessarily an enforceable standard. However, evidence suggests fewer states are attempting to acquire BW capabilities. The international norms against use of BW capabilities, especially given the ever-increasing conventional capabilities available, remain extremely high and even may render these weapons obsolete, from a state's perspective.

Perhaps this dire assessment of our nonproliferation and counterproliferation capabilities as they pertain to BW is an overstatement? Surely, the means to process biological material into highly pathogenic substances must involve specialized equipment, carefully designed facilities, and highly controlled growing conditions? Unfortunately, this is not the case. We must also ask how far commercial dual-use capabilities have proliferated since 1997. The activities by groups such as the AG and the PSI have certainly been useful in raising the visibility of the issue. However, they are facing an uphill battle in attempting to stem the flow of dual-use equipment, technologies, and knowledge.

Because experts assess the inadequacy of the BWC for state programs and the lesser requirements associated with a terrorist BW program, it stands to reason the BWC will be even less effective in dealing with nonstate BW proliferation issues. In fact, Project *Bacchus* highlights the difficulties associated with attempting to detect small BW weapons programs. While a state program would have a modest signature assuming capabilities for storage and loading of the munitions were part of the program, the footprint for a small program such as one for a terrorist actor could be as small as a ten-foot-by-ten-foot room stocked with a modest amount of readily available equipment. As the Kurtz case demonstrates, viable BW programs can be established in innocuous and modest surroundings, even in one's house. Because of the lack of a signature and the small facility requirement for a BW program, the counterproliferation issue becomes quite a challenge, at least for conducting offensive operations to eliminate terrorist BW capabilities.

Overlaying the N/CP activities with the doctrine for homeland security of "prevent, protect, respond, and recover," we see these activities pertain only to the "prevent" and "protect" areas of the doctrine. Prevention and protection are activities to anticipate, preempt, detect, and deter threats. Response and recovery are coordinated, comprehensive federal responses and the mounting of a swift and effective recovery effort.

To get a sense of overall preparedness and the difficulties associated with attempting to deal with the emerging terrorist BW threat, one can look systematically at the ability to interact across all five of the proliferation steps within each of the homeland security doctrinal areas. A graphical depiction of this analysis is provided in Figure 4–3. The matrix within the figure has been coded to reflect the ability we have to impact outcomes corresponding to "virtually no ability to affect," "some," and "significant," and "not applicable," respectively.

Given the nonproliferation issues discussed above, we assess "virtually no ability to affect" the *acquisition, processing,* and *weaponization* of BW material into weapons-grade material suitable for use in an attack for the *prevent* category, although we do assess

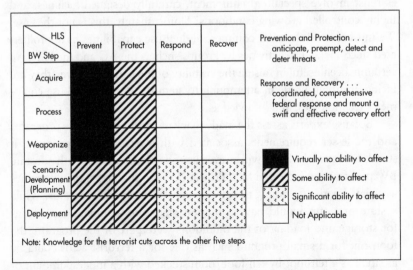

FIGURE 4–3 Two-Sided Analysis for Examining the Ability to Limit Terrorist BW

"some ability to affect" in the *protect* category. This rationale is based on the minimal requirements for BW development and the availability of naturally occurring pathogens. Concerning the *protect* category, some actions such as vaccinating populations against a certain pathogen can make use of this agent unattractive and therefore provide a degree of preventive measure. While these conclusions are supported by the evidence, they may not be universally accepted by some who still believe these BW development steps are considerably more technically challenging. However, given the increased knowledge available and proliferation of equipment, developing BW capabilities will prove to be less challenging in the future. This does not mean, as we discussed previously, all pathogens will be available: some may prove too difficult to handle or obtain, even once recombinant technologies become more readily available. This assessment is not to imply nonproliferation efforts should be totally abandoned, but rather that the thresholds for terrorists to obtain BW have been lowered; a fact we must recognize.

Examining the ability to *prevent* and *protect* terrorists from *planning* and *deploying* BW weapons, we clearly have "some ability to affect" moving toward "significant ability to affect" in the *protect* category. Effective measures will include (1) anticipating where the threats are likely to be greatest and taking countermeasures, (2) determining which pathogens are most likely to be employed and employing preventive measures, (3) deterring the threat through a variety of active and passive measures, (4) preempting the threat prior to deployment of a BW weapon, and (5) detecting the release of BW to allow for rapid identification of pathogens and clearing of the area under attack and treatment of victims. Certainly other actions could also be used. This list is representative, not all encompassing.

Other specific measures in the *protect* column of the figure for *planning* and *deployment* include increased use of sensors, red teaming to assess the likelihood of potential scenarios, and employment of passive defense counterproliferation measures.[14] Additionally, some nonproliferation activities will contribute to a more robust posture and therefore decrease the likelihood of a successful attack. We are continuing to see advanced biotechnology employed to improve sensor performance, improve protection from various pathogens that have the greatest likelihood of use, and increase awareness by governments and the public with respect to these issues. Success in the area of *protection* will be based on being able to provide more protective measures for which we have a greater degree of control, including:

- outside sensors for covering targets considered to be high value,
- greater stand-off distances between potential targets and access approaches,
- improved air-handling capabilities in buildings,
- inside sensors that detect anomalies in air quality and allow for rapidly activated low-regret options to be implemented, and
- enhanced vigilance by workers such as security personnel.

Coming to the last two columns of the figure, one sees two trends. The top of the chart is coded to indicate *respond* and *recover* have no relationship to the terrorist's ability to *acquire, process,* and *weaponize* BW material. The bottom two rows, corresponding to *scenario development* (planning) and *deployment*, are where we have the most opportunity to impact outcomes. As an example, sensors can be developed that facilitate both warning and treatment in real time. Better biosurveillance techniques and methodologies can be designed to reduce the time to detect outbreaks and attacks and establish the means and methods to prevent further infections. Many of these capabilities were discussed in detail in Chapter 3. Additionally, planning and exercises can be conducted to ensure that first responders, medical professionals, and public health specialists, as well as citizens, are able to respond effectively in a BW event.

Unfortunately, in most scenarios, the attacker has the initiative in determining the time and place of attack, complicating the ability of the defender to *prevent* and *protect*. An old military adage states, "He who protects everything, protects nothing." This sentiment remains operative for BW. It is both cost prohibitive and infeasible to attempt to *protect* and *prevent* against all types of attacks, or against the use of all types of pathogens in all types of scenarios. The result would be to turn the United States into a "BSL-4" nation, an infeasible outcome for a country that values civil liberties and basic human freedoms. Rather, guided by prudent assessments and based on the available resources, decisions must be made on what to protect and the level of acceptable risk.

We know from previous analysis that under the current nonproliferation and counterproliferation regimes containment of BW capabilities alone will not be a successful strategy. Certainly, measures can be put in place to mitigate against terrorist plots, but they are the least useful in the *prevent* category, more useful in the *protect* category, and the most useful in the *respond* and *recovery* categories.

We must further realize it is not feasible to attempt to put the biological genie back in the bottle. Biological advancements have already progressed too far. Their ability to benefit humankind is too great to retrench in this field. Rather, society must come to terms with the understanding that fundamental building blocks of our educational, public health, medical research, and veterinary systems have the potential to allow for the development of devastating biological weapons.

The previous statements of the potential for a bioterror attack were prepared considering our capabilities in the near future, say in 2010, and were made without the benefit of classified material. Additionally, should a radical technological change to the environment occur or additional information become available, these assessments are likely to change. For example, as designer pathogens that may be invisible to certain families of sensors proliferate, we can expect even greater difficulty in preventing and protecting against a bioattack. Likewise, if this methodology were used for analysis in the year 2030, a different assessment is likely to result. Certainly, if we have been spending our resources wisely and the technology allows for more-sensitive and more-timely sensors to be deployed, we would expect a "significant ability to affect" in more areas over time.

Finally, this structured approach in considering the BW question results in a more refined assessment of the threats we face and the potential for affecting outcomes in this critical area. Therefore, the author believes that assessments employing this methodology should be conducted periodically to understand the shift that is occuring.

Identifying Essential Capabilities

The basic premise of U.S. policy has been that America requires a set of capabilities for preventing, protecting, responding to, and recovering from a BW event, should it occur. Singly focusing efforts for keeping BW capabilities from entering the country or out of the hands of a terrorist will not serve to protect the American people. Likewise, having no sensor or monitoring capabilities and allowing a potential attack to come as a complete surprise until the first symptoms appear puts us in the position of playing defense in a one-sided game. Similarly, building a "BSL-4 nation" undermines the foundations on which our nation was founded and would go far beyond the threat before us.

Instead, we must have strategies that can negate the effects of a likely attack and make use of these types of systems less attractive to terrorists. In framing the issue, some experts argue that the focus on BW, especially in the aftermath of the Amerithrax attacks, has detracted from other more pressing medical needs such as research in cancer and HIV/AIDS. Conversely, the hue and cry associated with the 2001 Amerithrax attack, despite how relatively small and inconsequential the attack was in real terms, indicates the degree to which the issue is emotionally charged. Several questions define the subject for experts and policy makers. How much preparation is enough? What level of risk are we willing to assume? How much are we willing to sacrifice in terms of personal freedoms and liberties? And what can we afford?

For this analysis, we will focus on understanding the competitive aspect of BW looking at trade-offs between terrorists' capabilities and intent, and our level of effort to counter BW threats and attacks. Level of effort will serve as a metric for conducting this analysis, and level of funding will be the key index. The assumption will be that level of funding equates to effective and balanced expenditures commensurate with the spending levels.

In a unique approach, a game theory construct was used to examine this issue. These techniques seem ideally suited for use in this two-sided analysis of terrorists' potential for BW and our potential actions to counter these threats. They will allow us to delve into the motivating factors and moderating behaviors that drive the terrorists, as well as the actions and counteractions that the United States could take in addressing this complex issue. Game theory, simply put, is a distinct and interdisciplinary approach to the study of human behavior with mathematics, economics, and the other social and behavioral sciences being the disciplines most normally associated with this type of analysis. One source notes, "[Game theory] addresses the serious interactions using the metaphor of a game: in these serious interactions, as in games, the individual's choice is essentially a choice of a strategy, and the outcome of the interaction depends on the strategies chosen by each of the participants."[15]

For our purposes, game theory allows for a rational expression of outcomes based on the motivations of the actors involved. The capabilities and intentions of the potential bioterrorist can be pitted against the actions and counteractions we might take to arrive at a set of consequences. These results are depicted in a payoff table (or matrix) normally expressed as numerical values, where each cell in the matrix has two values, one corresponding to each of the actors involved in the game. In this analysis, given the uncertainty of outcomes and attempting to consider conclusions that are more strategic, the payoffs will be expressed as favorable, neutral, or negative outcomes.[16]

In our game, we will look at four possible terrorist actions: (1) divest of BW capabilities, (2) demonstrate interest only, but do not conduct a BW attack, (3) conduct a small-scale BW attack, and (4) conduct a large-scale BW attack. U.S. efforts in this game in countering BW will include (1) a minimal level of effort, (2) a low level of effort, (3) a medium level of effort, or (4) a high level of effort. The levels of effort for the United States have been tied to the resourcing of biodefense and are further compared to the spending of more than $8 billion as of 2008.[17] Detailed explanations for each of the categories are provided in Table 4–1. Using this approach, we will attempt to understand the motivations of the actors involved and apply a level of rationality to the actions each might decide to take. For example, the intersection of the terrorist *divesting of BW capabilities* and the United States making *minimal effort to counter BW* forms a set of payoffs, one for each of the actors. Doing this across all four of the terrorist and U.S. potential actions forms a matrix with sixteen sets of possible outcomes.

The stratagem can be explained as follows: A terrorist would decide on a strategy to pursue by considering assessments, including capabilities and intentions. A certain payoff value would be possible, based on both his strategy and the strategy of the opposition (in this case, the United States). Likewise, the United States would decide to pursue a strategy. The value of that selection would be linked to the strategy pursued by the bioterrorist. The goal for each actor is to identify a strategy that provides the greatest potential for achieving his goals and objectives.

The strength of this analysis is to allow us to look not only at the capabilities and intentions of the terrorists, but also at the actions we can take to counter a terrorist BW threat. Previously, we discussed the five steps of the terrorists BW model and the potential for us to counter these activities through the homeland security doctrine of prevent, protect, respond, and recover. Our game theory approach builds on this previous analysis as well as on the earlier efforts to understand how capabilities and intentions have been factors within a historical context.

To provide more granularity to the analysis, we will examine three different categories of terrorists: traditional, waning, and apocalyptic (Table 4–2). The *traditional terrorist* relies on a range of activities from political to violence in pursuit of his objectives, yet is sensitive to retaining the support of its constituents. In this formulation, an action by the traditional terrorist results in a counteraction by the United States, and vice versa. The trade-offs continue as a series of actions and counteractions. An example is AQI following the U.S.-led invasion in Iraq in 2003. AQI attacked coalition forces, waged an insurgency, and attacked innocent people through bombings, attacks, and kidnappings. When the level of violence became too high for the populace to accept, AQI lost support and

TABLE 4-1 Explanation of the Game Theory Strategies

ACTOR	CATEGORY	DEFINITION
Terrorist	Divest of BW capabilities	Includes (1) divesting of all BW capabilities and intentions for those terrorists that have been involved in these types of activities, or (2) continuing to not demonstrate interest for those terrorists that have no active program or have never sought to acquire these capabilities.
	Demonstrate interest only, but do not conduct a BW attack	Includes all forms of BW in the steps necessary to acquire BW up to the deployment phase of the model. It can include planning, however no active measures for perpetrating an attack such as target reconnaissance would be conducted.
	Conduct a small-scale BW attack	An attack against an area target with BW capabilities that causes mortality and morbidity of less than one thousand. Normally, such an attack would employ noncontagious pathogens using such agents as anthrax or tularemia.
	Conduct a large-scale BW attack	A BW attack that causes mortality and morbidity in excess of one thousand people. Attack could be perpetrated using contagious or noncontagious pathogens.
United States	Minimal effort toward countering BW	Would see a return to pre-Amerithrax attack BW spending levels of less than $500 million per year. Would leave the United States with the current capabilities frozen as they are today with no modernization plans. This level of funding would essentially leave us unprepared for either a small- or large-scale attack.
	Low level of effort	Reduction of current counter-BW spending to less than $4 billion per year. This represents a 50 percent reduction over 2008 spending. Would freeze the current BioWatch, BioSense, and BioShield programs at existing levels with no further enhancements. Would essentially leave the United States unable effectively to a large-scale attack and put at risk preparedness and response for a small-scale attack.
	Medium level of effort	Increase 2008 levels of BW funding slightly to more than $10 billion per year. Continue modernization of the BioWatch, BioSense, and BioShield programs. Continue to raise visibility of counter-BW efforts. Would improve biosurveillance and response efforts, allowing for a coherent response to a small-scale attack, but with limited capacity for large-scale attack protection or response.
	High level of effort	Double BW spending to $16 billion per year. Aggressively field new generation BioWatch, BioSense, and BioShield capabilities. Raise the level of visibility for BW to make it a key policy issue for national security. Would provide capabilities for successfully managing a small-scale attack and would better prepare for a large-scale attack.

adjusted its tactics to reduce civilian casualties. An overwhelming majority of terrorist groups fall into this category of traditional terrorist.

TABLE 4-2 Terrorist Categories

Category	Description	Example
Traditional	• Conduct a range of activities from political activities to violence • Support of populace and constituents key • Represents the majority of terrorists	al-Qaeda
Waning	• Looking to achieve their objectives through political, social, and economic means • Use of violence contrary to their objectives • Support of populace and constituents paramount	IRA
Apocalyptic	• Very small number of these types • High violence as part of their strategy • No negotiation possible	Aum Shinrikyo

The *waning terrorist* began by using a range of activities from political to violence in pursuit of objectives, but over time has begun to move toward becoming a political organization and therefore tending away from violence. Terrorist organizations in this group are therefore less likely to become involved in BW because doing so would detract from the progress they have made in becoming political entities. The waning terrorist also is keenly focused on maintaining support from their constituents. An example of a waning terrorist group is the IRA.

Finally, *apocalyptic terrorists* include terrorists that have an ideology and intentions that will make involving them in any sort of action-counteraction game a near impossibility. The term "apocalyptic" is not necessarily intended to identify these terrorists as moving toward the apocalypse in a literal sense, but rather to indicate they have high violence strategies they will undertake, regardless of the actions of their adversary. Apocalyptic groups are insular and internally focused, using any and all available means to achieve their desired outcomes. An example would be Aum Shinrikyo, which would not have been dissuaded by any actions taken by the Japanese government or lack of support from the populace for their cause. Importantly, there are very few groups within this categorization of apocalyptic terrorists.

The first analysis will examine the outcomes for the traditional actor terrorist. As we have stated, this terrorist will be influenced by a number of different factors, making the outcomes across the solution space highly variable and subject to an action-counteraction solution. Several impor-

	TERRORIST ("Traditional")			
Actions	Divest	Demonstrate Interest Only	Attack (Small)	Attack (Large)
Minimal Effort Toward Counter BW	N– N–			
Low Level of Effort	N+ N–	N–		
Medium Level of Effort	N+ N+		N– N	
High Level of Effort		N–	N+ N–	N

UNITED STATES

Favorable / Neutral, Favorable / Neutral / Neutral, Negative / Negative

FIGURE 4-4 Game Theory Payoff Matrix for the Traditional Terrorist

tant assumptions serve to guide this analysis. First, the traditional terrorist wants to gain notoriety its cause. That need for notoriety becomes a driving factor in the actions it undertakes. Violence and the means used serve as tools, but they are not the ends of the strategy. Gaining and maintaining support from the traditional actor's constituency is important, and therefore plays a key role in the manner in which the terrorist acts, becoming both a motivating factor and moderating influence for the terrorist. The results are provided in the payoff matrix in Figure 4-4.

For the traditional terrorist, divesting of all BW capabilities and intentions would make him less of a perceived threat and therefore would likely lead to no increase in visibility for his cause. Therefore, the outcome for the traditional terrorist would be "neutral negative" for where the United States had minimal or low level of effort. The terrorist payoff of "neutral favorable" for the U.S. medium level of effort reflects that, despite divesting of capabilities and intentions in BW, the United States makes a significant commitment in terms of policy, programs, and spending. As the U.S. level of effort goes to high, which would represent a doubling of the current effort, the terrorist payoff changes to "favorable," reflecting that, despite the terrorist's divestiture in BW capabilities, the United States had "wasted resources" by overspending against a nonexistent threat.

Examining the payoff from the U.S. perspective for the terrorist divesting of BW, we see an interesting relationship. If the United States puts minimal effort toward countering BW and the terrorist divests of BW capabilities, and intentions, the result is "neutral negative" for the United States. This assessment is based on the perception that, at these levels, the government would fail to demonstrate the capability to mount an effective biodefense posture, which would be seen as imprudent.

As the level of effort goes up to low, the U.S. outcome moves to "neutral favorable," indicating the measures taken and the level of support would be seen as prudent. The same rating would be gained from the medium level of effort. In both these cases the rationale would be that an appropriate level of effort commensurate with the threat would have been undertaken. As the level of effort goes to high, the assessment changes to "negative" because the United States' expenditure can be thought of as being wasted if the traditional terrorist has divested of his BW capabilities.

In the second case where the traditional terrorist demonstrates interest only, one sees a different payoff structure for both sides. For the terrorist, demonstrating interest includes actions such as public pronouncements, attempts to develop BW capabilities and perhaps even having a BW capability, but stops short of using these capabilities in an attack. In all cases, the increased exposure translates to "favorable" outcomes for the terrorist for each of the strategies undertaken by the United States.

From the U.S. perspective, in the case where the terrorist demonstrates interest in BW and the United States puts forth minimal effort, the government will be seen as weak and even imprudent for failing to take actions to anticipate, deter, dissuade, detect, and perhaps preempt the terrorist. Until the level of spending and capabilities is seen to reflect reasonable and prudent expenditures, the outcome will be "negative" or "neutral negative" at the minimal and low levels of spending, respectively, from the U.S. perspective.

The case where the terrorist demonstrates interest and the United States puts forth a medium level of effort reflects a "favorable" outcome for both. The terrorist gains notoriety for his cause, which results in an expenditure of resources. The U.S. government is seen as taking prudent measures to protect the population against a possible BW attack. As the level of effort rises, overexpending resources can begin to change the outcome from the U.S. perspective from "favorable" at the medium level to "neutral negative" at the high level of effort, because the effort is once again disproportionate to the threat.

In the third case where the terrorist perpetrates a small-scale attack, the payoff structure changes yet again. Several notes are in order at this point. The payoff structure will likely be highly influenced by the targets selected. If a "military" target were selected, the traditional terrorist's supporters would likely not take great issue and may even express support. However, if an elementary or high school were attacked with a BW weapon, the traditional terrorist would likely lose support and even gain condemnation for the attack and perhaps even for his overarching cause. Despite the targeting question raised above, we assess the small-scale attack scenario as being "favorable" for the terrorist if the United States were to put forth minimal effort or a low level of effort. As the U.S. effort increases to medium, the terrorist payoff becomes "neutral." The attack would be less successful and mounting such an attack would introduce a degree of risk for the terrorist. At the U.S. high level of effort, a small-scale terrorist attack would be assumed to not be successful. Therefore, the assessment would be downgraded to "neutral negative" from the terrorist's perspective.

An important caveat: these ratings for a small-scale attack assume the attack was both against a perceived "just" target and the lack U.S. of preparation contributed to considerable casualties, but still below the one thousand threshold. Of course, the international norms against the use of WMDs, in particular BW, introduces a degree of risk because one could easily argue any use of BW would be considered irresponsible by the terrorist's supporters and therefore not worth the risk. Furthermore use of BW would likely result in a greatly increased level of effort against the terrorist. Certainly, in an age where there are other conventional capabilities that could be used to achieve desired outcomes commensurate with a small-scale bioattack, resorting to BW would seem to be crossing an important and risky threshold. This would be even truer should the agent be a highly contagious pathogen with the potential to threaten populations indiscriminatingly.

In looking at the payoffs from the small-scale attack scenario from the U.S. perspective, if the United States were to make minimal effort or only a low level of effort and an attack were launched, both strategies would be perceived as "negative" outcomes. In each, the result likely would be measured in increased casualties and a failure by the government to take prudent measures to protect citizens, property, and interests. If the U.S. government puts forth a medium level of effort and there is a small-scale attack, the outcomes are likely to be perceived as "negative neutral," assuming the preparations were reasonably effective and only moderate numbers of casualties resulted. The reasoning behind not raising the rating to "favorable" is that any use of biological weapons would likely be seen as a failure to prevent such an attack from occurring.

If the United States puts forth a high level of effort and there is a small-scale attack, the outcome from the U.S. perspective would be "neutral favorable." This is assuming the high level of effort has resulted in a system that is successful in monitoring and detecting the attack, that the response and recovery assets perform appropriately, and that there are few casualties. Of course, it is hard to imagine any conditions in which there was a BW attack on the United States that we would consider to have a "favorable" outcome.

The final strategy from the traditional terrorist's perspective is a large-scale attack. An implicit assumption is that a large-scale attack is not directed against a point target such as a military base, but rather is an area attack that indiscriminately affects a mix of military, governmental, and civilian targets. Based on the concern discussed previously about a traditional terrorist desire to gain and maintain support for his cause, a large-scale attack with significant casualties, including civilians, would likely be perceived as uniformly "negative." Additionally, such an attack would most likely result in a significant retribution that could become an existential threat to the traditional terrorist.

From the U.S. perspective, any large-scale attack would be considered almost uniformly "negative" because it would mean that we had failed to detect, deter, and preempt the BW threat. Only where the United States undertook a high level of effort could one remotely consider the outcome as "neutral," and only then if the U.S. response and recovery had been highly effective and casualties extremely low.

We will not go through the same exhaustive analysis for the waning and apocalyptic terrorists. The graphical assessment and some conclusions are worthy of discussion, however. Figure 4–5 provides the payoff matrix.

In the case of the waning terrorist, the only action he can take that results in a "favorable" outcome from his perspective is divestiture of all BW capabilities and intentions. This could include public denouncements of WMDs including BW, as well as divestiture of all developed capabilities. From the U.S. perspective, any outcome that would result in a waning terrorist demonstrating interest in or conducting an attack (either small scale or large scale) would have to be assessed as uniformly "negative." Only the portion of the payoff matrix where the United States makes a low level of effort and the waning terrorist divests of BW capabilities and intentions would be assessed as resulting in a "favorable" outcome. This would be seen as a prudent investment. For the United States, the higher the expenditure, the more effort is "wasted" guarding against the nonexistent threat posed by waning terrorists. Of course, this concept of waste is subjective: many would argue that efforts to improve biosurveillance and therefore prepare for a manufactured or natural biological event could be

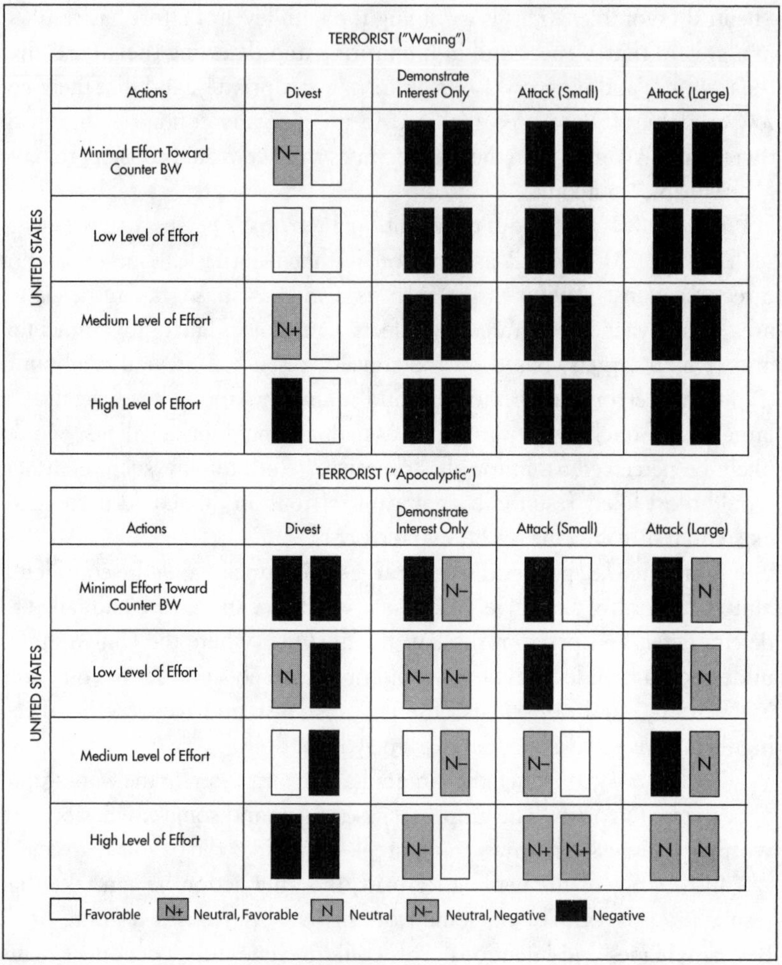

FIGURE 4–5 Payoff Matrix for the Waning and Apocalyptic Terrorists' BW Capabilities

considered resources well spent. Still, for our game we will consider these expenditures to be excessive and therefore imprudent.

In the case of the apocalyptic terrorist, the strategy employed by the waning terrorist is inverted. It is through an attack that the apocalyptic terrorist begins to achieve his goals. Divesting is therefore seen as a "negative" outcome. Demonstrating interest only is seen as "neutral-negative" for all strategies except where the U.S. put forth a high level of expenditure which would be seen as "favorable," as more resources would have been expended that were excessive and not commensurate with the threat. For the small-scale attack category, the greater the success of the attack, the more "favorable" the perceived outcome. Only in the case of a high level of effort by the United States does the assessment change to "neutral favorable." In the case of a large-scale attack, the payoff matrix depicts a "neutral" rather than "favorable" outcome because the assessment adjusts for the difficulties associated with a small, insular group attempting to conduct a successful large-scale attack. Almost by definition, the apocalyptic terrorist would encounter more technical and operational challenges in perpetrating the larger attack.

From the U.S. perspective, spending levels need to be perceived as commensurate with the threat. In the case of the apocalyptic terrorist divesting of BW or demonstrating interest only, the United States resourcing at the medium level is the most favorable. For the small-scale attack, the outcome would be considered "negative" for the minimal and low levels and "neutral negative" for the medium level of effort, assuming a robust response and recovery. Using the same philosophy as previously discussed, any large-scale attack could not be considered "favorable" from the U.S. perspective because, once again, an attack of this magnitude would imply there was a failure to deter, dissuade, prevent, and protect the populace from such an event. Therefore, the assessment for the large-scale attack would be at best "neutral" at the high level of effort from the U.S. perspective, again assuming a vigorous response and recovery.

The discussion of game theory with regard to BW terrorism is useful for working through the motivations of the terrorists and the potential for engaging to successfully eliminate terrorist BW programs, deter and dissuade attacks, monitor the environment, respond, and recover. However, one must be mindful that terrorism is a "low-probability, high-consequence" event. Predicting terrorist attacks and understanding intentions will always be problematic because the number of variables is virtually infinite: where to attack, the means to use, the time to attack, and so on. This is why the Los Alamos analysis, which became the basis for the DHS Bioterrorism Risk Assessment, needed to consider 35 million discrete scenarios to examine the range of outcomes across the twenty-two pathogens they considered.

In the analysis of the potential for a bioterrorist attack, the most likely scenario is an attack by a traditional terrorist rather than by a waning or apocalyptic terrorist. This assertion is made for several reasons. First, most terrorists fall into the category of traditional terrorists, and groups within this category would have a propensity toward the use of violent techniques if assessed to be within their interests. Conversely, the waning terrorist would tend away from the use of violence and certainly would tend away from the use of BW. Also, the number of terrorists in this category is comparatively small. Likewise, for the apocalyptic terrorists, while they would likely follow high-violence strategies, the number of this type of terrorist is small, making an attack from one of these terrorists extremely unlikely.

Second, the insular nature of the apocalyptic terrorist mandates a smaller cell with less outside interaction and therefore less reach for developing a complex BW capacity. It does not mean developing these capabilities will be impossible for the apocalyptic terrorist. Instead, it means the probability of success diminishes for this group. Additionally, such a group would have a more difficult time conducting a large-scale attack such as the scenario posited as part of the Atlantic Storm exercise, which considered a simultaneous release of smallpox in six locations.

The analysis described above has an important artificiality that must be noted. The world of terrorism is highly complex, with three types of terrorists existing simultaneously. In our analysis, we have considered each type in isolation. In looking at the likelihood of the outcomes, we find the traditional terrorist outcome is by far the most likely to consider for planning purposes. The waning and apocalyptic each have extremely low probabilities of occurrence. Therefore, given the numbers of apocalyptic terrorists and the motivations of the waning terrorist, we can essentially approximate the payoff analysis across all terrorists using the traditional actor payoff matrix.

In thinking about the payoff outcomes we have developed, another useful question is whether an equilibrium point exists. In game theory, such a point is called the Nash Equilibrium, a solution concept developed by John Forbes Nash. The Nash Equilibrium describes a point at which each player is assumed to know the equilibrium strategies of the other players, and no player has anything to gain by changing his own strategy (i.e., changing unilaterally). Therefore, at Nash Equilibrium each player is making the best decision he or she can, taking into account the decisions of the others. Of note, this point does not necessarily mean the best cumulative payoff for all players involved.

For our analysis, and using the payoff matrix from the traditional terrorist, we observe an apparent equilibrium point at the intersection of the U.S. medium level of effort and the terrorist demonstrating interest only. To explain this further, consider that the strategy of the United States is essentially known through policies, programs, and funding levels, and that it corresponds approximately to the medium level of effort. Of course, some elements of our programs, such as classified aspects of our efforts, are not necessarily known. Likewise, we know from history some terrorists have demonstrated interest in BW, but we also know (as they surely have assessed) a WMD attack introduces an extremely high degree of risk with potentially existential ramifications for the terrorists. Therefore, in considering the Nash Equilibrium for our analysis, the intersection of the U.S. medium level of effort and terrorists demonstrating interest appears to define a point at which the risk and rewards are in balance and the players have little to gain by changing their respective strategies.

Just as with the previous methodology, the author would like to stress the outcomes are less important to the findings than the use of a structured methodology for examining the actions-counteractions of terrorists and U.S. policy makers. Obviously, the assessments depicted are highly sensitive to the timeframes considered, changes in the security environment, and biotechnology developments.

Previously, in looking at what history had taught us about the potential for a terrorist BW attack, a diagram was introduced. Figure 4–2 depicted the probability of a viable attack as a function of the capabilities and intentions of the terrorist. In addition, we stated that knowledge was a critical factor in any "viable attack" and that the capabilities and intentions of the terrorists were integral to the manner in which the five-step model developed previously could be used.

Figure 4–6 has been modified in several ways. The y-axis now depicts the probability of a success rather than viability of the attack. The function has been modified to depict the capabilities and intentions of the terrorists as well as our ability to prevent, protect, respond, and recover (P/P/R/R, in the equation). In this way, the graph becomes a two-sided depiction of the probability of a successful terrorist BW attack. Added to the figure is the concept of security strategies that can be brought to bear to affect the likelihood of a successful attack.

The elliptical figure is meant to reflect the trends in biotechnology in which increasingly more-critical capabilities are proliferating and becoming readily available, coupled with the trends in (1) *globalization*, where more people are gaining access to knowledge and information as well as developing the propensity for disenfranchisement and ultimately for conflict to resolve issues, and (2) *terrorism*, where we have observed a propensity toward more attacks, a higher level of violence, and more-spectacular means to perpetrate the attacks.

We have previously presented the idea of a two-sided analysis that compared the five steps required for terrorists to develop a BW capability (acquire, process, weaponize, develop scenario, and deploy) with the

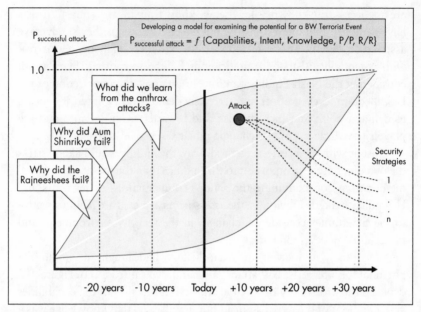

FIGURE 4-6 Examination of the Potential for a Successful Bioterror Attack

homeland security doctrine's four components (prevent, protect, respond, and recover). The relationship between these two frameworks provides an interesting opportunity to further analyze the potential for a bioterror attack and isolate the major factors that will likely determine success or failure, should an attack be launched.

The concept of using a probabilistic approach has been discussed previously, most notably in the discussion of the Los Alamos model in Chapter 2. For our purposes, we are interested in examining the individual terms of the probabilistic equation to gain an appreciation for the policy implications.

Conducting a successful bioterror attack is based on the probability of the terrorist to develop BW capabilities and successfully launch an attack and our opposing capacity to negatively influence and limit such an attack scenario, or if this fails, to respond and recover quickly. Reducing this to a probabilistic outcome expressed as the product of probabilities yields the following equation:

$$P_{Success} = [(P_{Capabilities} * P_{Intentions}) * P_{Knowledge}] * [(1 - P_{P/P/R/R})]$$

where

Probability of a Successful Attack = $P_{Success}$
Probability of a Terrorist Attaining Capabilities
     (Acquisition, Processing, Weaponizing) = $P_{Capabilities}$
Probability of a Terrorist Having the Intentions
     (Scenario Development and Deployment) = $P_{Intentions}$
Probability of a Terrorist Having the Knowledge = $P_{Knowledge}$
Probability of a Successfully Prevention, Protection, Response, and Recovery = $P_{P/P/R/R}$

This equation can further be expressed in its component parts, written as,

$$P_{Success} = [(P_A * P_P * P_W * P_S * P_D) * P_K] * [(1 - P_{PRE}) * (1 - P_{PRO}) * (1 - P_{RES}) * (1 - P_{REC})]$$

Due to the proliferation of biotechnology and the knowledge in this field, we must assess that the U.S. government's ability to positively affect the likelihood of either attaining the technical capabilities ($P_{Capabilities}$) or knowledge ($P_{Knowledge}$) is becoming extremely limited. Of course, this assessment is highly pathogen dependent, meaning it will remain either too difficult to acquire the necessary seed stock of certain pathogens or it will be beyond the capacity of a terrorist to process or weaponize certain pathogens. Therefore, the best opportunity to influence terrorist actions with regard to BW is to focus on the intentions represented by the term $P_{Intentions}$.

Turning to the right-hand side of the equation—the part we can influence directly through our efforts—we see a similar analysis. The ability to prevent a terrorist from acquiring, processing, and weaponizing a BW weapon is limited, and tends toward zero. One can see that as the probability of preventing a terrorist (P_{PRE}) from developing these technical capabilities approaches zero, the term $(1 - P_{PRE})$ goes to 1, meaning there is little significant prevention counterweight that can be employed.

We do have a greater capability to protect (P_{PRO}), although this too will become more challenging as the nexus between globalization, terrorism, and biotechnology continues to provide an increasing capability to the terrorists and a greater number of potential threat scenarios and possible targets to protect.

As we have discussed, we have significant ability to develop robust response and recovery programs. Therefore, the probability of a successful response and recovery—P_{RES} and P_{REC}, respectively—will be influenced directly by our actions.

Given trends in proliferation of biotech capabilities and information, and projecting toward the 2020–30 timeframe, the equation for the probability of success for the terrorist can be rewritten as follows:

$$P_{Success} = [(P_S * P_D)] * [(1 - P_{PRO}) * (1 - P_{RES}) * (1 - P_{REC})]$$

In this equation, the terms that begin to approach 1.0 (a near certainty of occurring) have been removed from the left-hand side of the equation, leaving only those that can be affected, or the scenario development and deployment aspects of terrorists actions integral to intent. Likewise, the terms with a probability approaching 0 (in this case, P_{PRE}) in the right-hand side of the equation have been allowed go to this asymptotic level as well. In this way, we are able to isolate and focus on only those terms we expect will be important in the 2020–30 timeframe while eliminating those we probably will not have the capacity to influence.

The policy implications of this revised equation are quite interesting: they imply efforts must be focused on influencing terrorists' intentions with regard to BW, rather than on significant additional efforts for preventing terrorists from developing and acquiring these capabilities. Actions taken to influence intentions—such as making clear that any bioterror act will be considered a cause for unequivocal and massive retaliation against the perpetrators—must form a basis for our future strategy. In this way, we must place at great risk anything terrorists hold dear. Taking this a step further, this must become a global strategy designed to make BW an abhorrent tactic that civilized people will not tolerate and make clear that all nations will cooperate unequivocally should such an attack be perpetrated. In this way, the threshold becomes absolute.

This discussion is not meant to imply efforts, including the AG or the Proliferation Security Imitative (PSI), should be discontinued. Rather, we must recognize the severe limitations inherent in attempting to control the proliferation of these types of technologies.

In turning to the counterweights, including protection, response, and recovery, we must recognize that policies, procedures, training, and education will be extremely important to our efforts. Sensors and standoff measures have an important role, but will not prove sufficient in reducing the probability of a successful bioterror attack. Enhanced biosurveillance that reduces the time between the first cases and a definitive determination that an attack has occurred must be the highest propriety. Additionally, technology will eventually lead to designer antibiotics and antivirals with dramatic implications for treating exposed individuals. Until these enhanced drugs are available, a significant window of vulnerability will exist.

The message to be conveyed is that trends in globalization, terrorism, and biotechnology all point toward an increase in the propensity for a successful attack and that actions taken by the United States to reduce these vulnerabilities within the framework of national (including homeland) security will be important for reducing the likelihood of a successful bioterror attack.

An in-depth analysis of the strategies for mitigating potential terrorist BW attacks is well beyond the scope of this analysis, but some important conclusions emerge that warrant reiteration by way of a summary of this chapter.

- The threshold for terrorists to successfully develop biological weapons has been greatly reduced by trends in biotechnology and globalization. We can expect these trends to continue for the foreseeable future.
- A terrorist BW program does not require the same amount of rigor as a state program. Several events and studies combine to conclude terrorists will be able to gain BW capabilities in the future, if they do not have them already.
- The BWC, which does little with regard to tangibly eliminating state programs, is even less effective against terrorist programs. Other nonproliferation efforts such as those by the AG or the PSI face similar challenges in attempting to moderate against these types of programs.
- A potential bioterrorist will not have access to the full range of capabilities (i.e., all pathogens, contagious biological material, and so on), but likely would be able to develop a viable BW capability and perpetrate an attack. In this regard, a small-scale attack is far more likely than a large-scale attack. These probabilities will continue to increase based on globalization and biotechnology proliferation.
- International norms that moderate state behavior by deterring and dissuading states from acquiring and employing biological weapons must be used to deter and dissuade terrorists by convincing would-be bioterror perpetrators they would lose support from their constituents if they use BW. Another important strategy in this regard is to convince the potential bioterrorist the use of these capabilities would represent an existential threat.

Our game theory analysis indicates the strongest position from both the perspective of the United States and the terrorists with regard to BW is for the United States to continue to develop affordable, full-range capabilities to limit terrorist BW capability and for terrorists to continue to demonstrate interest in these capabilities, without acquiring or employing them. An attack introduces risk for the terrorist because the potential for a loss of support from their constituents and the possibility that any type of attack could become an existential threat to the group that perpetrated such an attack.

CHAPTER FIVE

Conclusion

I n some regards, the question of bioterrorism is a race against time. A certain inevitability undergirds the question of whether bioweapons will be used by terrorists in some sort of attack (either a small- or large-scale attack) at some point in the future. With the proliferation of technologies, equipment, and knowledge, the advantage for the immediate future will shift in favor of the potential bioterrorist. This proliferation of technical capabilities exposes a dangerous seam and contributes to a greater likelihood of a bioterror attack, making concentration on influencing terrorists' motivations and intentions paramount in our efforts to protect the United States.

We are in a period when the state-of-the-art in biotechnology is increasing at an extraordinary pace. It is probably only a matter of time before advances will greatly reduce the threats posed by both natural and manufactured disease. Some experts, such as futurist Raymond Kurzweil, believe these advances are imminent, while others see the introduction of nanotechnology as a mainstream endeavor in the 2020 to 2030 timeframe as a key delineation point. Despite the question of timing, a point of widespread agreement is the certainty that advances in biotechnology will change the way we think about disease, and in some cases will eliminate diseases altogether.

Globalization will continue to define the world as greater numbers of people will be exposed to the effects of the expansion of human connectedness. With this growth will come enormous benefits as well as inevitable tensions and conflicts, including likely intensification of terrorist activities. While the numbers of attacks may drop once U.S. military operations in Iraq and Afghanistan end, the global reach of the new wave of terrorists will continue to be an increasing threat.

Despite the potential for more and increasingly violent attacks, we must remain mindful that terrorism is not today and will likely not be in the future an existential threat. Terrorism is not on par with the threat the United States and former Soviet Union faced during the height of the Cold War, nor is terrorism on par with the threats the United States faced during World War II. This is not to imply that we should not be concerned with terrorism or that someday it might not become an existential threat. Clearly, the potential for ever-increasing deadly capabilities to fall into the hands of dangerous individuals and groups who seek to harm innocent people on behalf of their ideologies, perceived past injustices, land apportionment, or religious beliefs is expanding. Furthermore, we know that the number of attacks and the casualties from those attacks is continuing to rise.

We also know with certainty that globalization, terrorism, and biotechnology form a potential deadly nexus that we must address. The thresholds for developing more-deadly and more-pervasive biological threats are being lowered at a rapid pace well before laws, regulations, and guidelines can be established to deal with the issues. Just as with virtually all other technologies, at some point we are likely to see these biotech capabilities used in an attack. As the technology matures and becomes more readily available, these attacks are likely to become large scale.

Given the lowering of thresholds for biotechnology and the dual-use nature of BW capabilities, it follows that affecting terrorists' intentions with respect to biological weapons must be more about what can be done to change the motivations and intentions of the potential bioterrorist than about attempting to retard or eliminate proliferation of biotechnology knowledge and capabilities. In this regard, our efforts must be designed to ensure our communications with regard to BW are clear and unequivocal. They must present an existential threat to the terrorists and reinforce that BW is not acceptable under any circumstances.

Some have asserted that the term "weapons of mass destruction" (WMD) is not relevant, and is even grossly misleading. Perhaps this is so. However, a major benefit that accrues from this lumping of capabilities is establishment of a major threshold we must continue to enforce. In fact, we must do everything possible to ensure the psychological thresholds that constrain terrorist behavior remain in place with regard to all WMDs, including biological weapons.

An inherent difficulty in preparing for a BW attack is the number of different pathogens and scenario combinations possible. Furthermore, unlike with conventional weapons where significant amounts of weapons (or material) may be required for an attack, the magnitude of the threat we face from bioterror is not necessarily proportional to the amount of biological material that would be required for a successful attack. Stated more directly, a relatively small amount of highly contagious pathogenic biological material can have an absolutely devastating effect on global society.

The increased visibility for biodefense has been important to improving our readiness posture in this area, but the enormity of the requirements mandates that spending be increased in key areas such as biosurveillance. Annual U.S. spending has gone from $500 million prior to the Amerithrax attacks to more than $8 billion in 2008. This increase was necessary given our initial posture in 2001, but is it still reasonable today? The author believes the answer is unequivocally "yes."

In fact, some areas even require significant increases. In particular, we are largely unprepared for a mass casualty event—either natural or manufactured—within our medical system, which continues to function with a focus on individual treatment at the expense of rapidly developing trends for assessing the health of the overall population in real time. Wherever possible, we must work to close the gap between exposure and definitive determination of an outbreak, because this presents an important window of opportunity to treat and warn that will ultimately save lives and reduce suffering.

Training, exercises, and equipping first responders and government leaders have been increased, but more must be done here as well. While not possible to make all within the response and recovery systems BW experts, we must ensure they have enough knowledge to rapidly detect anomalies so the right experts can be brought in and appropriate and timely decisions made.

We can also be assured that the solutions to these emerging vulnerabilities will not be found in national programs alone. The problems are global, requiring national and international solutions. What happens in distant lands truly can have a major impact on the United States. The swine influenza outbreak in 2009 provides a relevant example of how connectedness and globalization can magnify the worldwide impact while reducing the time it takes for contagious diseases to spread and for governments to act.

We must also be wary of the biohacker. Just as we have seen with computers and digital communications, it is not inconceivable that an individual can conduct "experiments" or misuse science with catastrophic effects. Just as we have seen with legitimate scientific study, the potential for negative outcomes is possible. As technology continues to become more widely available, the chances of this misuse increase, as do potential negative consequences.

This analysis has been about globalization, terrorism, and biotechnology. As was pointed out, though, the results can be generalized to fields other than biotechnology experiencing rapid growth. As the history of technology has demonstrated, even capabilities developed for purely peaceful purposes have found, over time, a use in the hands of those wishing to exploit the technology for nefarious purposes. Biotechnology has been and will be no different.

An area that has not received much scrutiny as part of this analysis is agroterrorism, or attacks against the food supply, targeting plants and animals as well as the supply chain. This omission has been by design: this entire area deserves a comprehensive treatment and would easily be a subject for follow-on work. However, in the research for this analysis, the topic has not been considered, except as it relates to human disease. In fact, many of the pathogens that have been discussed are epizoonotic, meaning they are diseases of animals that can be transmitted to humans. Recently, threats to the food supply have received considerable attention. An example from naturally occurring disease is the jalapeño pepper salmonella outbreak in 2008 in the United States. This and other similar events have demonstrated the potentially devastating economic consequences associated with naturally occurring or terrorist threats to the food supply, as well as the potential for mortality and morbidity from such threats.

Most literature indicates our food supply chain is largely unprotected at many points within the system, making agroterrroism a significant concern. Even a single incidence of a disease such as bovine spongiform encephalopathy (BSE)—known as mad cow disease, and the cause of Creutzfeldt-Jakob disease in humans would cripple our livestock industry for years and result in immeasurable economic losses. Aside from the first-order effects on the food supply, the potential for a disease to jump species from animals to humans has been and continues to be cause for great concern and demonstrates the importance of controlling zoonotic disease.

Policy Recommendations

Policy recommendations in a number of different areas are in order as we consider ways to prevent a potential bioterror event and protect the United States from such an event. Should our efforts fail, we also consider ways to ensure a rapid response and recovery, and a return to a normal way of life.

First, the game theory methodology should be repeated periodically, as new information becomes available. A useful exercise would be for the biodefense community and IC to periodically employ this approach using the classified and most up-to-date data to determine the most appropriate levels of funding and programs. A great deal can be learned about the actions and counteractions that can be taken to prevent a bioterror attack using game theory. In fact, such a methodology is ideally suited to bioterror in the future as the center of gravity moves away from the question of capabilities and toward intentions and motivations.

Concerning biodefense, there is a major policy gap that we need to close. In looking at the component parts of the system for developing a BW capability, the technical thresholds have been reduced, making the potential for developing such a weapon far more likely. The area where we seem to have the most leverage is in influencing motivations and intentions. Still, the community remains divided on the issue of the potential for a bioterror attack, with some saying an attack is imminent and others saying the threat is overstated. A more coherent assessment needs to be established.

Some experts argue the term "WMD" has no relevance and should be eliminated from our lexicon. This would be a significant mistake, in that one of the most effective tools we have in the fight against bioterror is the considerable stigma attached to the use of WMDs. To try and unpack the term and have different ways of speaking about nuclear, chemical, biological, radiological, and explosive capabilities would confuse the issue. The term "WMD" appears to have established an important invisible threshold that we need to ensure stays extremely high. The lack of historical precedents points to this threshold. Under no condition would we want to have any ambiguity with regard to our resolve concerning the use of any of these systems.

Some have questioned whether spending to date on biodefense programs such as BioWatch, BioShield, and BioSense have been implemented at the expense of more-pressing health needs. On the contrary, these programs must be expanded to include all forms of disease and environmental impacts. We must develop a broad capability to provide detect-to-treat *and* detect-to-warn systems. Biosurveillance will be essential for us to protect against a wide variety of issues, including naturally occurring threats to our agriculture and food supply.

In this regard, we must develop sensor systems that can reduce the time to detect a release, allowing for clearing an area rapidly to prevent additional exposure and infection. Most early-detection systems in use today still have a requirement for lengthy harvesting of the deployed kits, evaluation at lab testing facilities, and definitive testing to determine if an attack has occurred. Therefore, many of these systems are "detect-to-treat" rather than "detect-to-warn" systems. This was certainly understandable given the technology when these systems were first developed. However, as capabilities for detection and rapid identification become more readily available, we must develop systems that compress the amount of time between initial release and definitive identification. This could become even more challenging in the future: "designer" pathogens could complicate and confound sensor detection mechanisms. This underscores the need for thinking differently about the issue. Perhaps instead of attempting to have sensors that identify a pathogen, we should be thinking about measuring differences in air quality and dispatching teams to investigate when anomalies are detected.

Achieving a larger percentage of definitive diagnoses in hospitals and clinics in less time will require changes to the medical culture as well as structural changes and technical enhancements. Some have discussed the possibility of developing a "zebra" chip that would provide a greater range of diagnostic capabilities in a single diagnostic toolkit. Training and decision support systems will also need to be examined to determine what aids can be provided to health-care professionals. Decision support systems should also be incorporated into the realm of medical diagnosis to bring this field into the Information Age.

We must continue to work toward development of broad spectrum antibiotics and antivirals that will be effective across a number of bacterial and viral pathogens. It is easy to make this statement, but challenging to follow through. A delicate balance exists between drugs attacking the deadly pathogens that could also, perhaps, harm the individual by shutting down key normal biologic processes.

Advanced biotechnology will for a period give the advantage to the attacker with the potential for the development of bioengineered pathogens that will be a significant threat in the near future. To mitigate this threat, we must begin an aggressive program to find prophylaxis and treatments to augment our nonspecific immune systems to rapidly detect and attack all non-self entities that invade.

A major proliferation pathway has become the scientists and laboratory workers working in facilities that deal with especially dangerous pathogens. In the aftermath of the 2001 Amerithrax attacks, the number of BSL-3 and -4 facilities grew significantly. If one combines this growth with the number of international facilities and the even less positive control in many of these facilities, we have a recipe for a very dangerous, even deadly, outcome. This lack of accountability is not only a cause for concern, but also serves as a stimulus to close this proliferation window. A reevaluation must examine not only the number of facilities, but also the processes, procedures, and capabilities used; security; and the standards for workers.

Related to the issue above is the unfettered proliferation of information concerning the development and processing of BW material. Limiting the information already available will be difficult, but we must take prudent measures to not divulge state-of-the-art technical and procedural material. This will not be popular among scientists. This lowering of thresholds represents a major issue for biodefense, however. As one expert reminds us, "Information will kill us in the techno-terrorist age."

Exercises and training at the international and national (i.e., federal, state, and local) levels have already improved response capabilities and understanding of the issues that we would confront in the event of a naturally occurring or manufactured biological event. This must continue and be incorporated into virtually all localities, obviously with a major focus on areas assessed to be at the greatest risk.

In addressing complex policy issues such as bioterror, decision makers should endeavor to include more-rigorous analytical techniques whenever possible. The use of the game theory matrices was intended to provide such an analytical framework for developing a greater understanding of the issue as well as to allow for conducting sensitivity analyses to understand the limits of the problems and solutions we face in this area.

Many attempt to reduce the bioterror question to one of technical capabilities and the ability to gather the necessary resources. The author believes the question of bioterror must be less about these technical issues and more about the psychological motivations that will either make more or less likely the potential for a bioterror attack. Understanding these motivations will provide a foundation for developing more-appropriate strategies in this Age of Biotechnology.

APPENDIX A

Acronyms and Abbreviations

AG	Australia Group
Amerithrax	Anthrax attacks in the United States, October and November 2001
AQI	al-Qaeda in Iraq
ATCC	American Type Culture Collection
BMBL	Biosafety in Microbiological and Biomedical Laboratories
BSE	Bovine spongiform encephalopathy
BSL	Biosafety level
BW	Biological warfare
BWC	Biological Weapons Convention
CBP	Customs and Border Protection
CCL	Commerce Control List
CDC	Centers for Disease Control and Prevention
CIA	U.S. Central Intelligence Agency
CIDRAP	Center for Infectious Disease Research and Policy
CNS	Center for Nonproliferation Studies
COP	Common operational picture
CRS	Congressional Research Service
CSA	Covenant, the Sword, and the Arm of the Lord
CTR	Cooperative Threat Reduction
CW	Chemical warfare
CWC	Chemical Weapons Convention
DHS	U.S. Department of Homeland Security
DNA	Deoxyribonucleic acid
DoD	U.S. Department of Defense
DOS	U.S. Department of State

DTRA	Defense Threat Reduction Agency
EIF	Entry into force
EMAC	Emergency Management Assistance Compact
EU	European Union
FARC	Revolutionary Armed Forces of Colombia
FAS	Federation of American Scientists
FBI	Federal Bureau of Investigation
FCDA	Federal Civil Defense Administration
FDA	Food and Drug Administration
FEMA	Federal Emergency Management Agency
GAO	Government Accountability Office
GDP	Gross domestic product
GPHIN	Global Public Health Intelligence Network
GWOT	Global war on terror
HHS	Department of Health and Human Services
HPS	Hantavirus pulmonary syndrome
HSC	Homeland Security Council
HSI	Homeland Security Institute
HSPD	Homeland Security Presidential Directive
IC	Intelligence Community
IED	Improvised explosive device
IMS	Ion mobility spectrometry
IRA	Irish Republican Army
ISID	International Society for Infectious Diseases
JHU	Johns Hopkins University
LIDAR	Light detection and ranging
LD	Lethal dose
LTTE	Liberation Tigers of Tamil Eelam
MIIS	Monterrey Institute of International Studies
MNT	Molecular nanotechnology
NATO	North Atlantic Treaty Organization
NBACC	National Biodefense Analysis and Countermeasures Center
N/CP	Nonproliferation and counterproliferation
NCPC	National Counterproliferation Center
NCTC	National Counterterrorism Center
NDU	National Defense University
NEC	National Emergency Council
NIH	National Institutes of Health
NPS	Naval Postgraduate School

NRDM	National Retail Data Monitor
NRF	National Response Framework
NRP	National Response Plan
NSABB	National Science Advisory Board for Biosecurity
NSC	National Security Council
NSHS	National Strategy for Homeland Security
NSRB	National Security Resource Board
NSS	National Security Strategy
OCD	Office of Civil Defense
OCDM	Office of Civil and Defense Mobilization
OCDP	Office of Civil Defense Planning
OEP	Office of Emergency Planning
OTA	Office of Technology Assessment
PCR	Polymerase chain reaction
PDD	Presidential Decision Directive
P.L.	Public Law
PLO	Palestine Liberation Organization
PPE	Personal protective equipment
ProMED	Program for Monitoring Emerging Diseases
PSA	Partnership for a Secure America
PSI	Proliferation Security Initiative
R&D	Research and development
RNA	Ribonucleic acid
RNAi	RNA interference
SALT	Strategic Arms Limitation Talks
SAP	Select Agent Program
SARS	Severe acute respiratory syndrome
SAW	Surface Acoustic Wave (SAW)
SIPRI	Stockholm International Peace Research Institute
SNS	Strategic National Stockpile
SUNY	State University of New York
TRADOC	U.S. Army Training and Doctrine Command
UN	United Nations
UPMC	University of Pittsburg Medical Center
URF	Underground Revolutionary Front
USDA	U.S. Department of Agriculture
UTMB	University of Texas Medical Branch
WHO	World Health Organization
WMD	Weapons of mass destruction
WMD-CST	Weapons of Mass Destruction—Civil Support Teams

APPENDIX B

Dark Winter Exercise Findings

From University of Pittsburgh Medical Center website http://www.upmc-biosecurity.org/website/events/2001_darkwinter/findings.html (4 February 2008)

1. An attack on the United States with biological weapons could threaten vital national security interests. Massive civilian casualties, breakdown in essential institutions, violation of democratic processes, civil disorder, loss of confidence in government, and reduced U.S. strategic flexibility abroad are among the ways a biological attack might compromise U.S. security.

2. Current organizational structures and capabilities are not well suited for the management of a BW attack. Major fault lines exist between different levels of government (federal, state, and local), between government and the private sector, among different institutions and agencies, and within the public and private sectors. These disconnects could impede situational awareness and compromise the ability to limit loss of life, suffering, and economic damage.

3. There is no surge capability in the U.S. health-care and public health systems, nor in the pharmaceutical and vaccine industries. This institutionally limited surge capacity could result in hospitals being overwhelmed and becoming inoperable, and it could impede public health agencies' analysis of the scope, source, and progress of the epidemic; their ability to educate and reassure the public; and their capacity to limit casualities and the spread of disease.

4. Dealing with the media will be a major immediate challenge for all levels of government. Information management and communication (e.g., dealing with the press effectively, communication with citizens, and maintaining the information flows necessary for command and control at all institutional levels) will be a critical element in crisis and consequence management.

5. Should a contagious bioweapon pathogen be used, containing the spread of disease will present significant ethical, political, cultural, operational, and legal challenges.

Smallpox, because of its high case-fatality rates and transmissibility, represents one of the most serious BW threats to the civilian population. In 1980, the World Health Assembly announced smallpox had been eradicated and recommended all countries cease vaccination. Although labs in two countries still officially store smallpox samples (the United States and Russia), its reappearance would almost certainly indicate an intentional outbreak.

Aerosol release of smallpox virus disseminated among a relatively small population could result in a significant epidemic. Evidence suggests the infectious dose is very small. Several factors are cause for concern: the disease has historically been feared as one of the most serious of all pestilential diseases; it is physically disfiguring; it bears a 30 percent case-fatality rate; there is no treatment; and it is communicable from person to person. Smallpox vaccination ceased in this country in 1972, and vaccination immunity acquired before that time has undoubtedly waned. Prior to eradication, data on smallpox outbreaks in Europe indicated victims had the potential to infect ten to twenty other people. However, there has never been a smallpox outbreak in such a densely populated, highly mobile, unvaccinated population such as exists today.

In 1947, in response to a single case of smallpox in New York City, 6,350,000 people were immunized (500,000 in one day), including President Harry Truman. After the disease had disappeared from Yugoslavia for four decades, a single case of smallpox emerged in 1972. There are two ways to control a smallpox epidemic—vaccine and isolation. Yugoslavia's Communist president, Josip Broz (Tito), used both. He instituted a nationwide quarantine, and immunized the entire country of 20 million people using vaccine supplied by the WHO.

Estimates of the current U.S. supply of smallpox vaccine range from 7 million to 12 million doses. This stock cannot be immediately replenished, since all vaccine production facilities were dismantled after 1980, and renewed vaccine production is estimated to require at least twenty-four to thirty-six months. The CDC contracted with Acambis Inc. of Cambridge, Massachusetts, to produce 40 million doses of new vaccine after the ACAM2000 live, vaccinia virus smallpox vaccine was licensed for use in the United States by the FDA in August 2007.

CDC Categories

CATEGORY A	CATEGORY B	CATEGORY C
The U.S. public health-care system and primary health-care providers must be prepared to address various biological agents, including pathogens rarely seen in the United States. High-priority agents include organisms that pose a risk to national security because they • can be easily disseminated or transmitted from person to person; • result in high mortality rates and have the potential for major public health impact; • might cause public panic and social disruption; and • require special action for public health preparedness.	Second highest priority agents include those that • are moderately easy to disseminate; • result in moderate morbidity rates and low mortality rates; and • require specific enhancements of CDC's diagnostic capacity and enhanced disease surveillance.	Third highest priority agents include emerging pathogens that could be engineered for mass dissemination in the future because of • availability; • ease of production and dissemination; and • potential for high morbidity and mortality rates and major health impact.

CATEGORY A	CATEGORY B	CATEGORY C
Anthrax (*Bacillus anthracis*) Botulism (*Clostridium botulinum* toxin) Plague (*Yersinia pestis*) Smallpox (*Variola major*) Tularemia (*Francisella tularensis*) Viral hemorrhagic fevers (*filoviruses* [e.g., Ebola, Marburg] and *arenaviruses* [e.g., Lassa, Machupo])	Brucellosis (*Brucella species*) Epsilon toxin of *Clostridium perfringens* Food safety threats (e.g., Salmonella species, *E. coli* 0157:H7, *Shigella*) Glanders (*Burkholderia mallei*) Melioidosis (*Burkholderia pseudomallei*) Psittacosis (*Chlamydia psittaci*) Q fever (*Coxiella burnetii*) Ricin toxin from *Ricinus communis* (castor beans) *Staphylococcal enterotoxin B* Typhus fever (*Rickettsia prowazekii*) Viral encephalitis (*alphaviruses* [e.g., Venezuelan equine encephalitis, eastern equine encephalitis, western equine encephalitis]) Water safety threats (e.g., *Vibrio cholerae, Cryptosporidium parvum*)	Emerging infectious diseases such as Nipah virus and hantavirus

Source: CDC website at http://emergency.cdc.gov/agent/agentlist-category.asp#a.

APPENDIX D

Select Agents and Toxins

7 CFR Part 331, 9 CFR Part 121, and 42 CFR Part 73

HHS AND USDA SELECT AGENTS AND TOXINS

Abrin
Cercopithecine herpesvirus 1 (Herpes B virus)
Coccidioides posadasii
Conotoxins
Crimean-Congo haemorrhagic fever virus
Diacetoxyscirpenol
Ebola virus
Lassa fever virus
Marburg virus
Monkeypox virus Foot-and-mouth disease virus
Reconstructed replication competent forms of the 1918 pandemic influenza virus containing any portion of the coding regions of all eight gene segments (Reconstructed 1918 Influenza virus)
Ricin
Rickettsia prowazekii
Rickettsia rickettsii
Saxitoxin
Shiga-like ribosome inactivating proteins
South American Haemorrhagic Fever viruses
    Flexal
    Guanarito
    Junin
    Machupo
    Sabia
Tetrodotoxin
Tick-borne encephalitis complex (flavi) viruses
    Central European Tick-borne encephalitis
    Far Eastern Tick-borne encephalitis
    Omsk Hemorrhagic Fever
    Russian Spring and Summer encephalitis
Variola major virus (Smallpox virus) and *Variola minor* virus (Alastrim)
Yersinia pestis

OVERLAP SELECT AGENTS AND TOXINS

Bacillus anthracis
Botulinum neurotoxins
Botulinum neurotoxin producing species of *Clostridium*
Brucella abortus
Brucella melitensis
Brucella suis
Burkholderia mallei (formerly *Pseudomonas mallei*)
Burkholderia pseudomallei (formerly *Pseudomonas pseudomallei*)
Clostridium perfringens epsilon toxin
Coccidioides immitis
Coxiella burnetii
Eastern Equine Encephalitis virus
Francisella tularensis
Hendra virus
Nipah virus
Rift Valley fever virus
Shigatoxin
Staphylococcal enterotoxins
T-2 toxin
Venezuelan Equine Encephalitis virus

USDA SELECT AGENTS AND TOXINS

African horse sickness virus
African swine fever virus
Akabane virus
Avian influenza virus (highly pathogenic)
Bluetongue virus (Exotic)
Bovine spongiform encephalopathy agent
Camel pox virus
Classical swine fever virus
Cowdria ruminantium (Heartwater)
Goat pox virus
Japanese encephalitis virus

Lumpy skin disease virus
Malignant catarrhal fever virus
(Alcelaphine herpesvirus type 1)
Menangle virus
Mycoplasma capricolum/ M.F38/M.
      mycoides Capri (contagious caprine
      pleuropneumonia)
Mycoplasma mycoides mycoides
      (contagious bovine pleuropneumonia)
Newcastle disease virus (velogenic)
Peste des petits ruminants virus
Rinderpest virus
Sheep pox virus
Swine vesicular disease virus
Vesicular stomatitis virus (Exotic)

USDA PLANT PROTECTION AND QUARANTINE (PPQ) SELECT AGENTS AND TOXINS

Candidatus Liberobacter africanus
Candidatus Liberobacter asiaticus
Peronosclerospora philippinensis
Ralstonia solanacearum race 3 biovar 2
Schlerophthora rayssiae var *zeae*
Synchytrium endobioticum
Xanthomonas oryzae pv. *oryzicola*
Xylella fastidiosa (citrus variegated
      chlorosis strain)

Selected U.S. Laws, Executive Orders and Directives, and International Treaties

Selected Laws

1. *Pandemic and All-Hazards Preparedness Act* (CRS Summary, P.L. 109–417. Signed into law December 19, 2006). This act "reauthorizes the Public Health Security and Bioterrorism Preparedness and Response Act; identifies the Secretary of Health and Human Services (HHS) as the lead federal official responsible for public health and medical response to emergencies including a flu pandemic; establishes standard of preparedness from state-to-state; and, requires individual states to meet performance standards developed by the Secretary of HHS." In addition, the legislation moves management of the SNS from the CDC to the office of the assistant secretary for public health emergency preparedness at HHS.

2. *USA PATRIOT Improvement and Reauthorization Act of 2005* (P.L. 109–177. Signed into law March 9, 2006). This act was intended as a renewal of sixteen sunset provisions scheduled to expire December 31, 2005. These provisions were part of the Uniting and Strengthening America by Providing Appropriate Tools Required to Intercept and Obstruct Terrorism Act (USA PATRIOT Act) of 2001. Signed into law October 26, 2001, by President George W. Bush as P.L. 107–56.

3. *Project BioShield Act* (CRS Summary, P.L. 108–276. Signed into law July 21, 2004). This act "amend[s] the Public Health Service Act to provide protections and countermeasures against chemical, radiological, or nuclear agents that may be used in a terrorist attack against the United States by giving the National Institutes of Health contracting flexibility, infrastructure improvements, and expediting the scientific peer review process, and streamlining the Food and Drug Administration approval process of countermeasures." According to

the CRS Summary, the secretary of HHS is authorized to "expedite procurement [of qualified countermeasures] to respond to pressing research and development needs by: (1) using simplified procurement procedures for products and services that cost more than the simplified acquisition threshold; (2) allowing other than full and open competition in certain instances; (3) increasing the micropurchase threshold to allow the Secretary to use those procedures; and (4) limiting review of the Secretary's procurement decisions."

4. *Smallpox Emergency Personnel Protection Act* (CRS Summary, P.L. 108–20. Signed into law April 30, 2003). This act "provide[s] benefits and other compensation for certain individuals with injuries resulting from administration of smallpox countermeasures." According to the CRS Summary, the secretary of HHS is "to create a smallpox vaccine injury table identifying adverse effects that shall be presumed to result from the administration of (or exposure to) a smallpox vaccine and the time period in which the first symptom of each such adverse effect must occur for such presumption to apply."

5. *Public Health Security and Bioterrorism Preparedness and Response Act* (CRS Summary, P.L. 107–188. Signed into law June 12, 2002). This act "improve[s] the ability of the United States to prevent, prepare for, and respond to bioterrorism and other public health emergencies." It authorizes money for the federal, state, and local governments to evaluate public health emergency preparedness and plan and conduct additional preparations for public health emergencies. The act also addresses provisions concerning the control of biological agents and toxins; safety and security measures concerning food, drug, and water supplies; and development of countermeasures against bioterrorism. A section of this act is known as the Agricultural Bioterrorism Protection Act and "directs the Secretary of Agriculture to establish and maintain a list of each biological agent and each toxin that the Secretary determines has the potential to pose a severe threat to animal or plant health, or to animal or plant products."

6. *Uniting and Strengthening America by Providing Appropriate Tools Required to Intercept and Obstruct Terrorism Act (USA PATRIOT Act)* (CRS Summary, P.L. 107–56. Signed into law October 26, 2001). This act "deter[s] and punish[es] terrorist acts in the United States and around the world [and] enhance[s] law enforcement investigatory tools." The act also "prescribes penalties for knowing possession in certain circumstances of biological agents, toxins, or delivery systems, especially by certain restricted persons."

7. *Chemical Weapons Convention Implementation Act* (CRS Summary, P.L. 105–277. Signed into law October 21, 1998). This act is a division of the Omnibus Consolidated and Emergency Supplemental Appropriations Act, 1999, and implements the CWC. According to the CRS Summary, the act requires DOS, designated the U.S. National Authority by the president, to act as liaison for the Organisation for the Prohibition of Chemical Weapons (OPCW) and the CWC; makes developing, acquiring, transferring, stockpiling, possessing, or using chemical weapons illegal; and requires inspection of chemical plants by the Organisation for the Prohibition of Chemical Weapons.

8. *Antiterrorism and Effective Death Penalty Act* (CRS Summary, P.L. 104–132. Signed into law April 24, 1996). This act "deter[s] terrorism, provide justice for victims, provide for an effective death penalty, and for other purposes." According to the CRS Summary, the law makes the acts of threatening, attempting, or conspiring to use a biological weapon a federal crime; broadens the definition of biological weapons to include components of infectious substances, toxic materials, and recombinant molecules; and authorizes the secretary of HHS to regulate how biological agents are to be identified as potential threats and how they are to be transferred.

9. *Biological Weapons Anti-Terrorism Act* (CRS Summary, P.L. 101–298. Signed into law May 22, 1990). This act implements the BWC and protects the United States from biological terrorism by prohibiting certain conduct pertaining to biological weapons, including knowingly developing, producing, stockpiling, transferring, acquiring, retaining, or possessing any biological agent, toxin, or delivery system for use as a weapon, or knowingly assisting a foreign state or any organization to do so.

Executive Orders and Directives

1. *Public Health and Medical Preparedness* (HSPD-21. Signed into law October 18, 2007). "This directive establishes a National Strategy for Public Health and Medical Preparedness (Strategy), which builds upon principles set forth in Biodefense for the 21st Century (April 2004) and will transform our national approach to protecting the health of the American people against all disasters."

2. *Medical Countermeasures Against Weapons of Mass Destruction* (HSPD-18. Signed into law January 31, 2007).

It is the policy of the United States to draw upon the considerable potential of the scientific community in the public and private sectors to address our medical countermeasure requirements relating to CBRN threats. Our Nation will use a two-tiered approach for development and acquisition of medical countermeasures, which will balance the immediate need to provide a capability to mitigate the most catastrophic of the current CBRN threats with long-term requirements to develop more flexible, broader spectrum countermeasures to address future threats. Our approach also will support regulatory decisions and will permit us to address the broadest range of current and future CBRN threats.

3. *Biodefense for the 21st Century* (HSPD-10, aka National Security Presidential Directive 33 (NSPD-33). Signed into law April 28, 2004). By evaluating biodefense programs and initiatives, Biodefense for the 21st Century continues those efforts by identifying future priorities and actions and integrating the work of national and homeland security, medical, public health, intelligence, diplomatic, and law enforcement communities. The classified version contains specific directions on how departments and agencies are to implement this biodefense program.

4. *Defense of United States Agriculture and Food* (HSPD-9. Signed into law January 30, 2004). Defense of United States agriculture and food "establishes a national policy to defend the agriculture and food system against terrorist attacks, major disasters, and other emergencies." Fulfilling the policy requires recognition of important agriculture and food infrastructure and ensuring their protection; development of mechanisms that provide early warning to threats; reduction of weaknesses during production and processing; enhancement of both product screening procedures; and response and recovery.

5. *Further Amendment to Executive Order 12958, as Amended, Classified National Security Information* (Executive Order 13292. Signed into law March 25, 2003). While Executive Order 12958 established that scientific matters not be considered for classification unless it relates to national security, Executive Order 13292 extends that consideration to include scientific matters relating to defense against transnational terrorism.

6. *Implementation of the Chemical Weapons Convention and the Chemical Weapons Convention Implementation Act* (Executive Order 13128. Signed into law June 25, 1999). This executive order designates DOS as the United States National Authority (USNA) for the CWC and CWC Implementation Act. The responsibilities assigned

to the National Authority include coordinating the implementation of the provisions of CWC and the CWC Implementation Act with other federal agencies. In addition, the secretary of the U.S. Department of Commerce is to impose and enforce restrictions on the importation of chemicals into the United States as required by the CWC.

7. *National Policy on the Transfer of Scientific, Technical, and Engineering Information* (National Security Decision Directive 189. Signed into law September 21, 1985). "Establishes national policy for controlling the flow of science, technology, and engineering information produced in federally funded fundamental research at colleges, universities, and laboratories." That policy indicates products of research remain unrestricted to the maximum extent possible. If national security requires control of that research, then that research will be controlled through classification.

8. *Renunciation of Certain Uses in War of Chemical Herbicides and Riot Control Agents* (Executive Order 11850. Signed into law April 8, 1975). Through this executive order, the United States renounced first use of herbicides in war except for controlling vegetation within and around U.S. bases and installations, and their defensive perimeters. The United States also renounced first use of riot control agents in war except in defensive military mode to save lives in certain specific situations.

9. *United States Policy on Toxins* (National Security Decision Memorandum 44. Signed into law February 20, 1970). In the United States Policy on Toxins memorandum, the United States renounced the offensive production, stockpiling, and use of chemical and biological toxins and confined the military research in toxins to defensive purposes. Document acquired from the National Security Archive at The George Washington University.

10. *United States Policy on Chemical Warfare Program and Bacteriological/Biological Research Program* (National Security Decision Memorandum 35. Signed into law November 25, 1969). Through this memorandum, the Chemical and Biological Warfare Program was split into two entities: the Chemical Warfare Program and the Biological Research Program. The objective of the Chemical Warfare Program was to deter other nations from using their chemical weapons. Regarding the Biological Research Program, the United States renounced the use of biological weapons, lethal and otherwise, and focused its research on defensive purposes. Document acquired from the National Security Archive at The George Washington University.

Federal Agency Rules, Proposed Rules, and Notices

1. Possession, Use, and Transfer of Select Agents and Toxins-Reconstructed Replication Competent Forms of the 1918 Pandemic Influenza Virus Containing Any Portion of the Coding Regions of All Eight Gene Segments (Submitting agency is CDC, Federal Register 70 FR 61047, October 20, 2005).

   We [the CDC] are adding reconstructed replication competent forms of the 1918 pandemic influenza virus containing any portion of the coding regions of all eight gene segments to the list of HHS select agents and toxins. We are taking this action for several reasons. First the pandemic influenza virus of 1918–19 killed up to 50 million people worldwide, including an estimated 675,000 deaths in the United States. Also, the complete coding sequence for the 1918 pandemic influenza A H1N1 virus was recently identified, which will make it possible for those with knowledge of reverse genetics to reconstruct this virus. In addition, the first published study on a reconstructed 1918 pandemic influenza virus demonstrated the high virulence of this virus in cell culture, embryonated eggs, and in mice relative to other human influenza viruses. Therefore, we have determined that the reconstructed replication competent forms of the 1918 pandemic influenza virus containing any portion of the coding regions of all eight gene segments have the potential to pose a severe threat to public health and safety.

2. *Agricultural Bioterrorism Protection Act of 2002* (Possession, Use, and Transfer of Biological Agents and Toxins) (Submitting agency is Animal and Plant Health Inspection Service, Federal Register 70 CFR 13242, March 18, 2005). "We [the Animal and Plant Health Inspection Service] are adopting as a final rule, with changes, an interim rule that established regulations governing the possession, use, and transfer of biological agents and toxins that have been determined to have the potential to pose a severe threat to public health and safety, to animal health, to plant health, or to animal or plant products. This action is necessary to protect animal and plant health, and animal and plant products."

3. Possession, Use, and Transfer of Select Agents and Toxins rule. "This document establishes a final rule regarding possession, use, and transfer of select agents and toxins. The final rule implements provisions of the Public Health Security and Bioterrorism Preparedness and Response Act of 2002 and is designed to protect public health and

safety. In a companion document published in this issue of the Federal Register, the U.S. Department of Agriculture (USDA) has established corresponding final rules designed to protect animal and plant health and animal and plant products."

International Treaties

1. *Chemical Weapons Convention* (Opened for signature January 13, 1993. Entered into force April 29, 1997. Ratified by the United States April 25, 1997. Submitting agency was CDC. Federal Register 70 FR 13293, March 18, 2005). The state parties of the CWC agree not to develop, produce, acquire, stockpile, retain, transfer, or use chemical weapons. State parties also are to destroy their chemical weapons and chemical weapons production facilities and not use riot control agents in warfare. More information on the CWC can be found at the website for the Organisation for the Prohibition of Chemical Weapons (www.opcw.org).

2. *Biological and Toxin Weapons Convention* (Opened for signature April 10, 1972. Entered into force March 26, 1975. Ratified by the United States March 26, 1975). The signatories to BWC agree not to develop, produce, stockpile, or acquire biological agents outside of peaceful purposes, and weapons and equipment designed to use biological agents for hostile reasons. More information on the BWC can be found at the Biological and Toxin Weapons Convention website (www.opbw.org).

3. *Geneva Protocol* (Opened for signature June 17, 1925. Entered into force February 8, 1928. Ratified by the United States January 22, 1975). The Geneva Protocol is also known as the Protocol for the Prohibition of the Use in War of Asphyxiating, Poisonous or Other Gases, and of Bacteriological Methods of Warfare. It restates the prohibition on use of poisonous gases previously laid down by the Versailles and Washington treaties, and adds a ban on bacteriological warfare. When they ratified or acceded to the protocol, some nations—including the United Kingdom, France, and the former Soviet Union—declared it would cease to be binding on them if their enemies, or the allies of their enemies, failed to respect the prohibitions of the protocol. The U.S. position is that the protocol does not apply to the use in war of riot-control agents and herbicides.

Source: FAS website: http://www.fas.org/programs/ssp/bio/ resource/legislation.html#uslegise (accessed June 1, 2008).

Game Theory (Example)

Game theory has its early roots in the fields of mathematics and economics. In fact, many of the principles on which game theory rests were based on John von Neumann's prior work dealing with his proof of the minimax theorem in 1928. Mathematician von Neumann and economist Oskar Orgenstern were attempting to find a more effective way to solve certain types of economic problems. They realized that, in some areas of analysis, the classical mathematical approaches were not adequate to explain behaviors and outcomes. This was particularly true in questions of economic strategy when actors faced multiple choices, each with very different potential risks and rewards. To better explain complex economic issues of strategy, they developed a theory of games, which has since become a significant area of study that we now call simply "game theory."

While the original use of game theory was for examining behaviors and outcomes related to economic decisions and choices, the field of study has broadened to include virtually all aspects of human behavior and decision making. For example, in a 1970 article, the author described the potential for employing game theory in development of corporate strategies in such areas as "the airline competition, coalition formation to apply political pressure, plant location, product diversification, and conglomerate absorption."[1]

In the area of national security, game theory has been used by the military in examining positions for an international arms control negotiation involving conventional weapons in Europe. More recently, game theory has been used by the DHS in examining the potential for a bioterror attack.

In yet another example that some might consider trivial, one reference cites the use of game theory for such activities as trivial as deciding on travel arrangements. Despite the simplicity of the question, it entails the same fundamentals of decision making as the much more complex questions of economics and national security. In hurricane season, would the traveler be better planning a vacation to the Caribbean or to the mountains? What are the risks and rewards? How does one sort through the various options? Personal preferences feature prominently in the decision. Cost might be an option. The use of game theory can provide the basis for decisions large and small.

Perhaps the most famous example associated with game theory is the "Prisoner's Dilemma."[2] The illustration was created to demonstrate the difficulty of analyzing" certain kinds of games. This simple explanation has since given rise to a vast body of literature in subjects as diverse as philosophy, ethics, biology, sociology, political science, economics, and, of course, game theory. The story is as follows: Two burglars, Bob and Al, are captured near the scene of a burglary and are questioned separately by the police. Each has to choose whether to confess and implicate the other. If neither man confesses, then both will serve one year on a charge of carrying a concealed weapon. If each confesses and implicates the other, each will go to prison for ten years. However, if one burglar confesses and implicates the other, and the other burglar does not confess, the one who has collaborated with the police will go free, while the other burglar will go to prison for twenty years on the maximum charge. The strategies in this case are confess or do not confess. The payoffs (penalties, actually) are the sentences served. We can express all this compactly in a payoff table that is standard in game theory (Table F–1).

Prisoner		Al	
	Strategy	Confess	Don't Confess
Bob	Confess	10, 10	0, 20
	Don't Confess	20, 0	1, 1

TABLE F–1 Prisoner's Dilemma

The table is read as follows: Each prisoner chooses one of the two strategies. In effect, Al chooses a column and Bob chooses a row. The two numbers in each cell tell the outcomes in prison sentences for the two prisoners when the corresponding pair of strategies is chosen. The number to the left of the comma tells the payoff to the person who chooses the rows (Bob) while the number to the right of the column tells the payoff to the person who chooses the columns (Al). Thus (reading down the first column) if they both confess, each gets ten years, but if Al confesses and Bob does not, Bob gets twenty and Al goes free.

How to solve this game? What strategies are rational if both men want to minimize the time they spend in jail? Al might reason as follows: "Two things can happen: Bob can confess or Bob can keep quiet. Suppose Bob confesses. Then I get twenty years if I don't confess, ten years if I do. In that case it's best to confess. On the other hand, if Bob doesn't confess, and I don't either, I get a year. In that case, if I confess I go free. Either way, it's best if I confess. Therefore, I'll confess."

But Bob can and presumably will reason in the same way—in which case they go to prison for ten years each. If they had acted "irrationally," and kept quiet, they each could have gotten off with one year each.

This same story, using different names, values, and crimes, has been told millions of times to illustrate the complexities associated with multi-dimensional decision making under conditions of uncertainty. The technique seems ideally suited to questions of the potential for a bioterror attack.

Notes

Chapter 1. The 21st-Century Environment

1. *Encarta Encyclopedia* online, s.v. "Globalization," http://encarta.msn.com/encnet/refpages/search.aspx?q=globalization.
2. National Intelligence Council, "Mapping the Global Future," 10–12.
3. Ibid., 14–15.
4. From a briefing as part of the Biodefense curriculum at George Mason University, Fairfax, VA. The briefing was part of the class, "Biosurveillance–BIOD 610."
5. Hoffman, *Inside Terrorism*, 3, 5.
6. Ibid., 7.
7. Ibid., 7, 11.
8. Ibid., 7, 11, 14, 17–18.
9. Rapoport, "The Four Waves of Rebel Terror and September 11."
10. Tucker, "What's New about the New Terrorism and How Dangerous Is It?"
11. Manuel Perez-Rivas, "Bush Vows to Rid the World of 'Evil-Doers.'" Perez-Rivas's article reports on President George W. Bush's address to a Joint Session of Congress on Terrorist Attacks, delivered September 20, 2001.
12. Stern, *Terror in the Name of God*, 254.
13. Victoroff, "The Mind of the Terrorist."
14. Stern, *Terror in the Name of God*, 142–143.
15. Victoroff, "The Mind of the Terrorist," 142–143.
16. Richardson, *What Terrorists Want*.
17. Lake, "Rational Extremism."
18. U.S. Army, "A Military Guide to Terrorism," 3–3 to 3–4.
19. Tucker, "What's New about the New Terrorism," 11.
20. Stern, "The Protean Enemy," 7.
21. Cordesman, *Terrorism, Asymmetric Warfare, and Weapons of Mass Destruction*, 18.
22. Johnston's Archives, "Statistics on Terrorism."
23. Ibid. See Appendix L in that document for the raw data.
24. DOS, "Annex of Statistical Information."
25. Jones and Libicki, *How Terrorist Groups End*, 18–19, xv–xvi, 20–21.
26. CRS, "Terrorism and National Security," 1.
27. Ibid.
28. Ibid.

29. A number of sources were consulted in developing this characterization, including the MILNET, "Terrorist Group Profiles"; DOS, "Country Reports on Terrorism"; and the Center for Defense Information (CDI) Terrorism Project, "List of Known Terrorist Organizations."
30. Rapoport, "The Four Waves of Rebel Terror and September 11."
31. Cronin, "Behind the Curve," 43.

Chapter 2. Biotechnology and Biowarfare: Two Sides of the Same Coin?

1. Byrd and Powledge, *Microbiology*, 7.
2. Barry, *The Great Influenza*, 6–7.
3. NRC and the IOM, *Globalization, Biosecurity, and the Future of the Life Sciences*, 49.
4. Computer chips have been doubling in processing speed every eighteen months for several decades. This phenomenon is known as Moore's Law, after semiconductor pioneer Gordon Moore, who first predicted it in 1965. This constant increase in processing speed has helped fuel the microelectronic and information revolutions.
5. Carlson, "The Proliferation of Biotechnologies."
6. *McLaughlin Hour with John McLaughlin,* February 17, 2008.
7. DoD, "Militarily Critical Technologies List Part II."
8. NRC and IOM, *Globalization, Biosecurity, and the Future of the Life Sciences.*
9. Ibid., 19.
10. Ibid., 20.
11. GlobalSecurity.org, "Weapons of Mass Destruction."
12. NRC and IOM, *Globalization, Biosecurity, and the Future of the Life Sciences*, 23.
13. Ibid., 24–25.
14. Infoplease, "Life Expectancy at Birth by Race and Sex, 1930–2005."
15. Murphy and Nathanson, "Emergence of New Viral Infections."
16. WHO, "Summary of Probable SARS Cases."
17. "The global death toll from the SARS epidemic reached 745 on Wednesday with the cumulative cases of infection totaling 8,240, the World Health Organization (WHO) said. The disease's mortality rate rose to 9.04%, topping the 9%-mark for the first time. The mortality rate hovered around 4% when the epidemic began to draw worldwide attention in March." (*Asian Economic News* online, June 2, 2003.)
18. Joby Warrick, "Custom-Built Pathogens Raise Bioterror Fears," *Washington Post,* July 31, 2006.
19. NRC and IOM, *Globalization, Biosecurity, and the Future of the Life Sciences*, 32.
20. Robert Baker, "Toxins," George Mason University, Fairfax, VA, Winter 2007–08, class notes.
21. Cirincione, Wolfsthal, and Rajkumar, *Deadly Arsenals*, 9–10.
22. NRC and IOM, *Globalization, Biosecurity, and the Future of the Life Sciences*, 47.
23. Rothfeder, "Biological Warfare."
24. Parliamentary Office of Science and Technology, "Bio-Terrorism."
25. DoD, "Militarily Critical Technologies List Part II."
26. Robert Baker, "Bacterial Toxins," George Mason University, Fairfax, VA, Fall 2007, class notes.
27. NRC and IOM, *Globalization, Biosecurity, and the Future of the Life Sciences,* 46–47, cited from GlobalSecurity.org, "Proliferation: Threat and Response Briefing."
28. Ibid., 46–47, cited from Block, "Living Nightmares."
29. Robert Baker, George Mason University, Fairfax, VA, personal communication.

30. Alibek, *Biohazard*, 259–261.
31. NRC and IOM, *Globalization, Biosecurity, and the Future of the Life Sciences*, 50–51.
32. Ibid.
33. Leitenberg, "An Assessment of Biological Weapons Threat." Leitenberg also lists from four references for the states that are believed to have had a BW program at the time of each analysis.
34. Ibid.
35. Salerno, Gaudioso, Frerichs, and Estes, "A BW Risk Assessment," 34, 27.
36. Guillemin, *Biological Weapons*, 54–56.
37. Alibek, *Biohazard*.
38. Margold, Tom and Jeff Goldberg. *Plague Wars*. NY, New York: St. Martin's Griffin, 1999, 74.
39. Parliamentary Office of Science and Technology, "Bio-Terrorism."
40. Alibek, *Biohazard*, 160.
41. The Nunn-Lugar program includes the development of programs for scientists of the former Soviet Union that provide for using the scientists' knowledge for peaceful purposes and shun returning to the development of BW.
42. U.S. Congress, "Technologies Underlying Weapons of Mass Destruction," 83.
43. FAS, "Introduction to Biological Weapons."
44. DoD, "Militarily Critical Technologies List Part II," II-3–3; II-3–7.
45. Ibid., II-3–9, 3–12.
46. NRC and IOM, *Globalization, Biosecurity, and the Future of the Life Sciences*, 57.
47. *Encarta Encyclopedia online*, s.v. "Deterrence," http://encarta.msn.com/encnet/refpages/search.aspx?q=deterrence.
48. DoD, "Dictionary of Military and Associated Terms."
49. Joint Chiefs of Staff, "National Military Strategy," 16.
50. Nunn-Lugar, "Nunn-Lugar Cooperative Threat Reduction Program."
51. BWC, "Convention on the Prohibition of the Development, Production and Stockpiling."
52. Arms Control Association, "The BWC at a Glance."
53. Zilinskas, *Biological Warfare*, 150. Zilinskas cites 142 parties and another eighteen nations that have signed the treaty but not ratified it.
54. Cordesman, *The Challenge of Biological Terrorism*, 15.
55. Cirincione et al., *Deadly Arsenals*, 11.
56. Zilinskas, *Biological Warfare*, 150.
57. Cordesman, *The Challenge of Biological Terrorism*, 15. The seventeen countries were Bulgaria, China, Cuba, Egypt, India, Iran, Iraq, Israel, Laos, Libya, North Korea, Russia, South Africa, South Korea, Syria, Taiwan, and Vietnam.
58. Leitenberg, *Assessing the Biological Weapons and Bioterrorism Threat*, 35.
59. Gronvall, "A New Role for Scientists," 1, 4.
60. Ibid., 5.
61. Guillemin, *Biological Weapons*, 195.
62. The use of the phrase "some degree of control" is used to express the degree to which the former Soviet Union was able to prevent accidental releases and even control insider threats could be debated. The accidental release of anthrax at Sverdlovsk in 1979, an incident that killed sixty-six people and launched a plume that traveled one hundred kilometers downwind, is an example of at least one major incident where biological weapons capabilities caused a major catastrophe.
63. Nunn-Lugar, "Nunn-Lugar Cooperative Threat Reduction Program."
64. Enemark, "United States Biodefense," 34.
65. Rosenberg, "Defending against Biodefence," 1.

66. Biological and Chemical Weapons: History of the U.S. Offensive Biological Warfare Program, Stimson Center, at http://www.stimson.org/cbw/?sn=CB2001121275.
67. Ibid.
68. Fact Sheet: Project Shipboard Hazard and Defense (SHAD), Office of the Special Assistant, Under Secretary of Defense (Personnel and Readiness) for Gulf War Illnesses, Washington, D.C., Version 09-13-2001.
69. Fact Sheet: Deseret Test Center, Office of the Secretary of Defense (Health Affairs), Washington, D.C., Version 10-09-2002.
70. A Department of Defense briefing by Michael E. Kilpatrick, Deputy Director, Deployment Health Support Directorate, indicates that 134 tests were planned from 1963 to 1973 with 46 conducted, 62 cancelled, and 26 with the status unknown.
71. Carroll, *Lab 257*, 14–15.
72. Stimson Center.
73. Some of the secrecy is due to the ongoing litigation by veterans who were exposed to various agents during these tests and are claiming disabilities as a result. Additionally, a number of conspiracy theorists believe that the U.S. offensive and defensive programs have caused several outbreaks including West Nile Virus and HIV/AIDS. No evidence exists to support these accusations.
74. Enemark, "United States Biodefense," 36.
75. Bhattacharjee and Salama, "Libya and Nonproliferation."
76. NRC and IOM, *Globalization, Biosecurity, and the Future of the Life Sciences*, 83.
77. Alibek, *Biohazard*. No specific references are provided; the book in its entirety provides a description of the Soviet's massive program, particularly in the period after the signing of the BWC.
78. Gerstein, "Biotechnology and Bioterrorism."
79. For more on this topic, see Tucker, *Toxic Terror*.
80. Stern, "The Protean Enemy," 7.
81. Randall, "Bioterrorism, Public Health and the Law."
82. Salerno et al., "A BW Risk Assessment," 49.
83. DOS, "Transforming Diplomacy to Combat WMD Terrorism."
84. Hoffman, *Inside Terrorism*, 209.
85. Russell, "Framing Globalization, the Nexus, and WMD Proliferation."
86. Zilinskas, "Possible Terrorist Use of Modern Biotechnology Techniques."
87. Ibid., 2.
88. Leitenberg, *Assessing the Biological Weapons and Bioterrorism Threat*, 11.
89. Ibid.
90. GAO, "Biological Weapons," 12.
91. RAND, "First Annual Report of the Advisory Panel."
92. RAND, "Fifth Annual Report of the Advisory Panel."
93. The FBI was preparing to indict Dr. Ivins after two years of focus on his activities, but he committed suicide within days of the indictment being issued.
94. Salerno et al., "A BW Risk Assessment," 36.
95. The MIIS maintains a database on terrorist incidents that was used in the study.
96. Zilinskas, "Final Report and Commentary," 6.
97. This is particularly noteworthy when one considers there were almost 14,500 terrorist attacks in 2007 (DOS data), with not one being a BW attack.
98. Dejban, "Bioterrorism and Islamists Extremism, Reality and Myth," 164–168. Another particularly important source in examining the topic of bioterror is Tucker, *Toxic Terror*. The compendium examines twelve uses or attempted uses of terrorist BW and chemical warfare, and provides information on the manner

in which the weapons were acquired and the results of each effort (table in *Toxic Terror*, 250–251, Table 14.1). In this work, see Table 2–4, which extracts information pertaining only to the incident, motivation or objective, agents, and outcome.

99. Tucker, *Toxic Terror*.

100. Ibid., 240. While Tucker's book does not include discussion of the Amerithrax attacks in the United States because it was published a year prior, one cannot begin to understand the current state of preparations or rhetoric concerning BW and in particular the potential for terrorists to gain access to these weapons without considering what has been learned as a result of this event. A detailed account of these attacks, provided in Cole, *The Anthrax Letters*, clearly articulates the panic, uncertainty, and uncoordinated actions taken in the immediate aftermath.

101. Randall, "Bioterrorism, Public Health and the Law."

102. Ibid.

103. Cole, *The Anthrax Letters*, viii–ix.

104. Center for Nonproliferation Studies (CNS), "Al-Qaida Reported Attempts to Acquire Biological Weapons.

105. Ibid.

106. Ibid.

107. Snyder and Pate, "Tracking Anthrax Hoaxes and Attacks."

108. Clark, *Bracing for Armageddon?* The table reflects a synopsis of the information Clark provides on pages 149–159.

109. Ibid., 157. Quoting Smithson and Levy, "Ataxia," 282.

110. CRS, *Terrorist Motivations of Chemical and Biological Weapons Use*, CRS-2.

111. Ibid., CRS-3. Quoting Falkenrath, Newman, and Thayer, *America's Achilles' Heel*, 31–46.

112. In summarizing the potential for terrorist BW use and in particular acquisition of BW material, one CRS publication provides an outstanding synopsis, calling the information "contradictory and sketchy." The reference notes many allegations of terrorist attempts to acquire these capabilities, but few that have been verified. Groups falling into this category (besides al-Qaeda) include the PLO, the Red Army Faction, Hezbollah, the Kurdistan Workers' Party, German neo-Nazis, and the Chechens. See CRS, *Terrorist Motivations of Chemical and Biological Weapons Use*, CRS-2–3; Falkenrath et al., *America's Achilles's Heel*, 31–46.

113. Spencer and Scardaville, "Understanding the Bioterrorist Threat."

114. CIDRAP website, www.cidrap.umn.edu.

115. ProMED website, www.promedmail.org.

116. Dire, "CBRNE–Biological Warfare Agents."

117. Robert Baker, "Toxins," George Mason University, Fairfax, VA, Spring 2008, class notes.

118. DoD, "Militarily Critical Technologies List Part II."

119. Kosal, "Art or Bioterrorism?"

120. Jerry Seper, "Secret Project Manufactured Mock Anthrax," *Washington Times*, October 26, 2001.

121. Edward Hammond, Director of the Sunshine Project in Austin, TX, tracks bioweapons and biodense issues.

122. Petro, "Intelligence Support to the Life Science Community."

123. Clark, *Bracing for Armageddon?*, 170.

124. Randall Larsen (USAF, Ret.), "Biodefense Colloquium," George Mason University, Fairfax, Virginia, lecture notes.

125. Stern, "Dreaded Risks and the Control of Biological Weapons," 99.

126. Allen-Mills and Mahnaimi, "Al-Qaeda Seeks Toxins for Biowarfare Attack," *Sunday Times*, Tel Aviv, January 2, 2005.
127. Ibid.
128. Enemark, "Biological Attacks and the Nonstate Actor," 913.
129. Disease resulting from many biological pathogens begins with nonspecific influenza-like symptoms.
130. Stern, "Dreaded Risks and Control of Biological Weapons," 99.
131. Stern, *Terror in the Name of God*, 173, 185.
132. Enemark, "Biological Attacks and the Nonstate Actor," 914, is discussing a model developed by Daniel Gressang.
133. Ibid., 916.
134. Tucker, *Toxic Terror*, Page 10.
135. Stern, "Dreaded Risks and Control of Biological Weapons," 99.
136. Ibid., 102–103.
137. Ibid., 102–107.
138. CRS, *Terrorist Motivations of Chemical and Biological Weapons Use.*
139. Leitenberg, "An Assessment of Biological Weapons Threat to the United States" 12.
140. Lake, "Weaponization Is Just a Buzz Word."
141. Ibid., 6.
142. Leitenberg, brief of his Army War College Strategic Studies Institute publication, *Assessing the Biological Weapons and Bioterror Threat.*
143. Stern, "Dreaded Risks and Control of Biological Weapons," 102–103.
144. Ackerman and Moran, "Bioterrorism and Threat Assessment," 5.
145. Wilson, "How DHS Currently Manages Risk."
146. Zilinskas, "Final Report and Commentary," 8.
147. DHS, *Bioterrorism Risk Assessment*, 5–8.

Chapter 3. Homeland Security and Biodefense

1. DHS, *Civil Defense and Homeland Security*, 4–22.
2. Cordesman, *Terrorism, Asymmetric Warfare, and Weapons of Mass Destruction*, 7.
3. CDC, "Emergency Preparedness and Response."
4. CDC, "National Select Agent Registry."
5. CDC, "BMBL Section II: Principles of Biosafety," 4.
6. Ibid.
7. Ibid.
8. Mantell, "Growth of Biosafety Labs Poses Unknown Risks."
9. Warner, "Biosafety Lapses Prompt Government Review."
10. Roos, "Lab Lapses Sparked Anthrax False Alarm."
11. GAO, *Biosafety Laboratories.*
12. USDA, "Fact Sheet: Cartagena Protocol on Biosafety."
13. Office of Biotechnology Activities website, www.biosecurityboard.gov.
14. Stern, "Dreaded Risks and Control of Biological Weapons," 111, 112.
15. U.S. Congress, *Homeland Security Act of 2002.*
16. White House, "Homeland Security." These same objectives are contained in several recent policy documents, including White House, "National Strategy for Combating Terrorism."
17. HHS, "HHS Plan to Combat Bioterrorism."
18. Ibid.
19. Personal communication, based on a commercial contract for services supporting the New Brunswick, New Jersey, Hospital.

20. Joby Warrick, "The Secretive Fight Against Bioterror" *Washington Post*, July 30, 2006.
21. FAS, "NSPD: George W. Bush Administration."
22. White House, "HSPD-21: National Strategy for Public Health and Medical Preparedness."
23. Office of the Director of National Intelligence, News Release No. 9–05, December 21, 2005.
24. DHS, *National Planning Scenarios.*
25. CRS, *DHS's Risk Assessment Methodology*, 20–21.
26. FEMA, "Overview of Stafford Act Support to States."
27. Clark, *Bracing for Armageddon?*, 178. Note that no rationale was given for botulism in 2008 in the original source.
28. Crosby, *The American Plague*, 254.
29. Johnson, *The Ghost Map.*
30. Wagner, Gresham, and Dato, "Case Detection, Outbreak Detection, and Outbreak Characterization."
31. Ibid., 35.
32. David Siegrist, "Biosurveillance," George Mason University, Fairfax, Virginia, Winter 2007–08, class notes. Siegrist presented a model outlining the "Stages of Clinical Disease."
33. Cole, *The Anthrax Letters*; Cordesman, *The Challenge of Biological Terrorism*, 17–22.
34. Wagner and Aryel, *The Handbook of Biosurveillance*, 20–22.
35. Personal communication with Director Julie Gerberding of the CDC, October 2006.
36. DHS, "HSPD-8 Overview: Planning Scenarios." These scenarios were first released with the HSPD-8 document.
37. Wagner and Aryel, *The Handbook of Biosurveillance*, 468, 380.
38. Brewster, Rudell, and Lesser, "Emergency Room Diversions."
39. Bagley, "Hospital to Double Emergency Room Size."
40. Hatchett, "Community Planning for Pandemic Influenza."
41. White House, "National Strategy for Combating Terrorism." These same objectives are contained in White House, "National Strategy for Homeland Security" published in October 2007.
42. White House, *9/11: Five Years Later.*
43. DoD, "Militarily Critical Technologies List Part II," II-3–27.
44. Commission on the Prevention of Weapons of Mass Destruction Proliferation and Terrorism, "World at Risk."
45. Change.gov, "Agenda: Homeland Security."
46. Bernstein, *International Partnerships to Combat Weapons of Mass Destruction*, 24.
47. "Atlantic Storm: Interactive."
48. Gerstein, "Preparing for a Pandemic."
49. PSA, "WMD Report Card Release."

Chapter 4. Examination of the Potential for a Bioterror Attack

1. Center for National Policy, "WMD Terrorism."
2. CNS, "Al-Qaida Reported Attempts to Acquire Biological Weapons."
3. Ibid.
4. Carrie Johnson, Joby Warrick, and Marilyn W. Thompson, "Anthrax Dryer a Key to Probe: Suspect Borrowed Device from Lab," *Washington Post*, August 5, 2008, p. A01.

5. List of symptoms is from Weinstein and Alibek, *Biological and Chemical Terrorism.*

6. Alibek, *Biohazard,* 89.

7. Purkin, "Biowarfare Lessons," 14.

8. Data on tularemia is from Weinstein and Alibek, *Biological and Chemical Terrorism,* 106–107.

9. Robert Baker, "Viral Agents," George Mason University, Fairfax, VA, Fall 2007, class notes.

10. The term "viable attack" is being used in lieu of "successful attack" because this implies terrorists could successfully achieve the requirements embedded in the five-step process. The potential for a "successful" attack must also consider the U.S. government's potential to thwart an attack and respond and recover. This will be discussed in more detail later in this chapter.

11. Stern, *Terror in the Name of God,* 255.

12. For this study, a large-scale BW attack is one that causes mortality and morbidity in excess of one thousand people. Such an attack could be perpetrated using contagious or noncontagious pathogens.

13. "Possible Consequences of the Misuse of Biological Sciences."

14. The term "red team" is associated with wargaming and assessment of options to examine potential scenarios through the eyes of the enemy. By doing this, one learns not to evaluate scenarios from one's own perspective, but rather to understand what might be best strategy from the standpoint of an adversary.

15. Drexel University, "Preface: Game Theory."

16. Volumes have been written about the topic. While a complete elaboration of game theory goes well beyond the scope of this effort, it is useful to understand how the fundamentals of this technique work. In this regard, Appendix F provides a more in-depth explanation of game theory and an example for the reader.

17. Joby Warrick, "The Secretive Fight against Bioterror," *Washington Post,* Sunday, July 30, 2006.

Appendix F. Game Theory (Example)

1. Davis, *Game Theory,* pp. xiv.

2. Drexel University, "Preface: Game Theory."

Selected Bibliography

Ackerman, Gary A., and Kevin S. Moran. "Bioterrorism and Threat Assessment." Center for Nonproliferation Studies, Monterey Institute of International Studies, The Weapons of Mass Destruction Commission, Report No. 22, 2006.

Alibek, Kenneth. *Biohazard*. New York: Random House, 1999.

Arms Control Association. "The BWC at a Glance." July 2008. http://www.armscontrol.org/factsheets/bwc (accessed April 29, 2009).

Asian Economic News (online). "SARS mortality rate tops 9%, death toll reaches 745: WHO," June 2, 2003. http://findarticles.com/p/articles/mi_m0WDP/is_2003_June_2/ai_102670109 (accessed May 12, 2008).

"Atlantic Storm: Interactive." http://www.atlantic-storm.org/flash/flash.htm (accessed June 8, 2008).

Atlas, Ronald M., and Malcolm Dando. "Biosecurity and Bioterrorism: Biodefense Strategy, Practice, and Science." doi:10.1089/bsp.2006.4.276, 4, no. 3 (2006). http://www.liebertonline.com/doi/abs/10.1089/bsp.2006.4.276?cookieSet=1&journalCode=bsp (accessed November 7, 2008).

Bagley, Chris. "Hospital to Double Emergency Room Size." *The Californian*, July 6, 2005. http://www.nctimes.com/articles/2005/07/07/news/californian/21_59_297_6_05.txt (accessed February 26, 2008).

Barry, John M. 2004. *The Great Influenza*. New York: Penguin Books.

Bernstein, Paul. *International Partnerships to Combat Weapons of Mass Destruction*. Washington, DC: National Defense University Press, National Defense University, 2008.

Bhattacharjee, Anjali, and Sammy Salama. "Libya and Nonproliferation." CNS Research Story, December 24, 2003. http://cns.miis.edu/pubs/week/031223.htm (accessed May 21, 2008).

Biological Weapons Convention (BWC). "Convention on the Prohibition of the Development, Production and Stockpiling of Bacteriological (Biological) and Toxin Weapons and on Their Destruction." Entered into force March 26, 1975. http://www.fas.org/nuke/control/bwc/text/bwc.htm (accessed October 25, 2008).

Block, Steven M. "Living Nightmares: Biological Threats Enabled by Molecular Biology." In *The New Terror: Facing the Threat of Biological and Chemical*

Weapons, edited by S. D. Drell, A. D. Sofaer, and G. D. Wilson. Stanford, CA: Hoover Institution Press, 1999.

Brewster, Linda R., Liza Rudell, and Cara S. Lesser, "Emergency Room Diversions: A Symptom of Hospitals under Stress." Issue Brief No. 38 (May 2001). Center for Studying Health System Change, Washington, DC.

Byrd, Jeffrey J., and Tabitha M Powledge. *Microbiology.* New York: Penguin Group, 2006.

Caplan, Bryan. "Terrorism: The Relevance of the Rational Choice Model." Department of Economics and the Center for Public Choice, George Mason University, Fairfax, VA, May 2005.

Carlson, Rob. "The Proliferation of Biotechnologies." *Biosecuirty and Bioterrorism: Biodefense Strategy, Practice and Science* 1, no. 3 (2003).

Carroll, Michael Christopher. *Lab 257.* New York: Harper Collins, 2005.

Center for Defense Information (CDI) Terrorism Project. "List of Known Terrorist Organizations." http://www.cdi.org/terrorism/terrorist-groups.cfm (accessed November 3, 2008).

Center for National Policy. "WMD Terrorism: The Biological Threat." October 23, 2008. http://www.cnponline.org/ht/display/ContentDetails/i/7761 (accessed January 25, 2009.

Center for Nonproliferation Studies (CNS) at the Monterey Institute for International Studies (MIIS). "Al-Qaida Reported Attempts to Acquire Biological Weapons." From outside publications by CNS staff, Chart: Al-Qa'ida's WMD Activities, by Weapons of Mass Destruction Terrorism Research Program (WMDTRP). http://cns.miis.edu/pubs/other/sjm_cht.htm. May 13, 2005 (accessed May 20, 2008).

Centers for Disease Control and Prevention (CDC). "BMBL (Biosafety in Microbiological and Biomedical Laboratories) Section II: Principles of Biosafety." http://www.cdc.gov/OD/ohs/biosfty/bmbl4/bmbl4s2.htm (accessed May 25, 2008).

Centers for Disease Control and Prevention (CDC). "Emergency Preparedness and Response." http://emergency.cdc.gov/agent/agentlist-category.asp#a (accessed May 18, 2008).

Centers for Disease Control and Prevention (CDC). "National Select Agent Registry." http://www.cdc.gov/od/sap/docs/salist.pdf (accessed May 18, 2008).

Change.gov. "Agenda: Homeland Security." http://change.gov/agenda/homeland_security_agenda/ (accessed January 16, 2009).

Cirincione, Joseph, Jon B. Wolfsthal, and Miriam Rajkumar. *Deadly Arsenals: Tracking Weapons of Mass Destruction,* rev. ed. Washington, DC: Carnegie Endowment for International Peace, 2005.

Clark, William. *Bracing for Armageddon?: The Science and Politics of Bioterrorism in America.* New York: Oxford University Press, 2008.

Cole, Leonard. *The Anthrax Letters: A Medical Detective Story.* Washington, DC: National Academies Press, 2003.

Commission on the Prevention of Weapons of Mass Destruction Proliferation and Terrorism. "Report: World at Risk." December 3, 2008. http://www.preventwmd.gov/report/ (accessed May 2, 2009).

Congressional Research Service (CRS). *The Department of Homeland Security's Risk Assessment Methodology: Evolution, Issues and Options for Congress.* Washington, DC: CRS, 2007.

Congressional Research Service (CRS). "Terrorism and National Security: Trends and Issues." Brief to Congress, updated September 8, 2005. Congressional Printing Office, Washington, DC. http://www.fas.org/irp/crs/IB10119.pdf (accessed May 2, 2009).

Congressional Research Service (CRS). *Terrorist Motivations of Chemical and Biological Weapons Use: Placing the Threat in Context*. Washington, DC: CRS, 2003.

Congressional Research Service (CRS). *Terrorists and Suicide Attacks*. Washington, DC: CRS, 2003.

Cordesman, Anthony H. *The Challenge of Biological Terrorism*. Washington, DC: Center for Strategic and International Studies, 2005.

Cordesman, Anthony H. *Terrorism, Asymmetric Warfare, and Weapons of Mass Destruction: Defending the U.S. Homeland*. Washington, DC: Praeger Security International, 2002.

Crenshaw, Martha. "The Causes of Terrorism." *Comparative Politics* 13, no. 4 (1981): 379–399.

Cronin, Audrey Kurth. "Behind the Curve: Globalization and International Terrorism." *International Security* 27, no. 3 (2002/2003): 30–58.

Crosby, Molly Caldwell. *The American Plague*. New York: Penguin Publishing Group, 2006.

Davis, Col. Jim A., USAF. "The Looming Biological Warfare Storm: Misconceptions and Probable Scenarios." *Air & Space Power Journal*, Spring 2003. http://www.airpower.maxwell.af.mil/airchronicles/apj/apj03/spr03/davis.html (accessed September 25, 2008.

Davis, Jim A., Col. USAF, and Anna Johnson-Winegar. "The Anthrax Terror: DoD's Number-One Biological Threat." http://www.airpower.au.af.mil/airchronicles/apj/apj00/win00/davis.htm (accessed May 2, 2009).

Davis, Morton D. *Game Theory*. New York: Dover Publications, 1997.

Dejban, Saced S. "Bioterrorism and Islamists Extremism, Reality and Myth." PhD diss., George Mason University, Fairfax, VA, 2007.

Dire, Daniel J. "CBRNE–Biological Warfare Agents," *eMedicine Journal* 2, no. 7 (2001): §2.

Drexel University. "Preface: Game Theory." http://william-king.www.drexel.edu/top/eco/game/game.html (accessed July 20, 2008).

Encarta Encyclopedia online. http://encarta.msn.com/encyclopedia.

Enemark, Christina. "Biological Attacks and the Nonstate Actor: A Threat Assessment." *Intelligence and National Security*, 21, no. 6 (2006): 911–930.

Enemark, Christina. "United States Biodefense, International Law and the Problem of Intent." *Politics and Life Sciences*, 24, nos. 1–2 (2006): 32–34.

Falkenrath, Richard A., Robert D. Newman, and Bradley A. Thayer. *America's Achilles's Heel: Nuclear, Biological and Chemical Terrorism and Covert Attack*. Cambridge, MA: MIT Press, 1998.

Federal Emergency Management Agency (FEMA). "Overview of Stafford Act Support to States." http://www.fema.gov/pdf/emergency/nrf/nrf-stafford.pdf (accessed March 19, 2008).

Federation of American Scientists (FAS). "Introduction to Biological Weapons." http://fas.org/biosecurity/resource/bioweapons.htm (accessed January 11, 2008).

Federation of American Scientists (FAS). "National Security Presidential Directives [NSPD]: George W. Bush Administration." http://fas.org/irp/offdocs/nspd/ (accessed March 24, 2008).

Friedman, Thomas. *The Lexus and the Olive Tree.* Rev. ed. New York: Farrar, Straus and Giroux, 1999.

Friedman, Thomas. *The World Is Flat.* New York: Farrar, Straus and Giroux, 2005.

Gerstein, Daniel M. "Biotechnology and Bioterrorism—Two Sides of the Same Coin." Unpublished, CONF 795 Independent Study, George Mason University, Fairfax, VA, Fall 2007.

Gerstein, Daniel M. "Preparing for a Pandemic." *ICMA Press IQ Report* 39, no. 3 (2007).

Gerstein, Daniel M. *Securing America's Future: National Strategy in the Information Age.* Westport, CT: Praeger Security International, 2005.

GlobalSecurity.org. "Proliferation: Threat and Response Briefing." DoD News Briefing, November 25, 1997.

GlobalSecurity.org. "Weapons of Mass Destruction: Biological Warfare Agent Production." http://www.globalsecurity.org/wmd/intro/bio_production.htm (accessed August 20, 2007).

Government Accountability Office (GAO). "Biological Weapons: Effort to Reduce Former Soviet Threat Proposes Benefits, Offers New Risks." GAO/NSIAD-00–138 (April 2000).

Government Accountability Office (GAO). *Biosafety Laboratories: Perimeter Security Assessment of the Nation's Five BSL-4 Laboratories.* Washington, DC: GAO, 2008.

Gronvall, Gigi Kwik. "A New Role for Scientists in the Biological Weapons Convention." *Nature Biotechnology,* 23, no. 10 (2005).

Grover, Jonathan, "The Bioterrorist Threat in America: Is There Any Reason to Be Concerned?" *Johns Hopkins News-Letter,* September 13, 2002. http://media. www.jhunewsletter.com/media/storage/paper932/news/2002/09/13/Science/The-Bioterrorist.Threat.In.America.Is.There.Any.Reason.To.Be.Concerned-2248561. shtml (accessed September 11, 2008).

Guillemin, Jeanne. *Biological Weapons: From the Invention of State-Sponsored Programs to Contemporary Bioterrorism.* New York: Columbia University Press, 2005.

Hammond, Edward. In "Biodefense Research Raises Issues," by Ian Hoffman, June 7, 2007. http://www.starseedtv.com/content/biodefense_research_raises_issues.html.

Hatchett, Richard J., MD. "Community Planning for Pandemic Influenza." Briefing, National Institutes of Health, Washington, DC, April 19, 2006.

Henderson, Donald, Thomas Inglesby, and Tara O'Toole. *Bioterrorism: Guidelines for Medical and Public Health Management.* Chicago, IL: AMA Press, 2002.

Hoffman, Bruce. *Inside Terrorism.* New York: Columbia University Press, 2006.

Homeland Security Institute (HSI). *Underlying Reasons for Success and Failure of Terrorist Attacks: Selected Case Studies.* Arlington, VA: HSI, 2007.

Howard, Russell, James Forest, and Joanne Moore. 2006. *Homeland Security and Terrorism: Readings and Interpretations.* New York: McGraw-Hill, 2006.

Huntington, Samuel. *The Clash of Civilizations and the Remaking of the World Order*. New York: Simon & Schuster.

Infoplease. "Life Expectancy at Birth by Race and Sex, 1930–2005." http://www .infoplease.com/ipa/A0005148.html (accessed August 19, 2007).

Interpol. "The bioterrorism threat: strengthening law enforcement." January 6, 2008. http://www.interpol.int/Public/BioTerrorism/default.asp (accessed September 25, 2008).

Jenkins, Brian Michael. "Defining the Role of a National Commission on the Prevention of Violent Radicalization and Homegrown Terrorism." RAND, CT-285. Testimony presented before the House Committee on Homeland Security, Subcommittee on Intelligence, Information Sharing, and Terrorism Risk Assessment, June 14, 2007.

Johnson, Steven. *The Ghost Map*. New York: Riverhead Books, 2006.

Johnston's Archive. "Statistics on Terrorism." 2008. http://www.johnstonsarchive.net/ terrorism/intlterror.html (accessed May 2, 2009).

Joint Chiefs of Staff. "National Military Strategy to Combat Weapons of Mass Destruction." Chairman of the Joint Chiefs of Staff, Washington, DC, February 13, 2006.

Jones, Seth G., and Martin C. Libicki. *How Terrorist Groups End: Lessons for Countering al Qa'ida*. RAND Publication MG-741-RC. Santa Monica, CA: RAND.

Kennedy, Paul. *The Rise and Fall of the Great Powers*. New York: Random House, 1989.

Koch, Tom. *Cartographies of Disease*. Redlands, CA: ESRI Press, 2005.

Kosal, Margaret E. "Art or Bioterrorism? The Implications of the Kurtz Case," James Martin Center for Nonproliferation Studies, Monterey, CA, July 27, 2004. http://cns.miis.edu/stories/040727.htm (accessed November 1, 2008).

Kurzweil, Ray. *Fantastic Voyage*. Emmaus, PA: Rodale Press, 2004.

Lake, David A. "Rational Extremism: Understanding Terrorism in the Twenty-First Century." Dialog-IO 1–29. 2002. http://dss.ucsd.edu/~dlake/Reprints/ Rational%20Extremism.pdf.

Lake, Ed. "Weaponization Is Just a Buzz Word." February 20, 2003. http://www. anthraxinvestigation.com/weaponization.html (accessed September 25, 2008).

Leitenberg, Milton. *Assessing the Biological Weapons and Bioterrorism Threat*. Carlisle, PA: Strategic Studies Institute, U.S. Army War College, 2005.

Leitenberg, Milton. "Assessing the Biological Weapons and Bioterrorism Threat." Brief synopsis (n.d.). http://www.strategicstudiesinstitute.army.mil/pubs/display .cfm?PubID=639 (accessed August 16, 2008).

Leitenberg, Milton. "An Assessment of Biological Weapons Threat to the United States." A White Paper prepared for the Conference on Emerging Threats Assessment: Biological Terrorism, at the Institute for Security Technology Studies, Dartmouth College July 7–9, 2000.

Mantell, Ruth. "Growth of Biosafety Labs Poses Unknown Risks." *Market Watch*, October 5, 2007. http://www.marketwatch.com/story/unchecked-growth-in-biosafety-labs-poses-unknown-human-risk-gao (accessed May 24, 2008).

Matthews, Robert. "A Model Legislation for the Implementation of the Biological Weapons Convention and UN Security Council Resolution 1540." First Interpol

Global Conference on Preventing Bioterrorism, Lyon, France, March 1–2, 2005. http://www.interpol.int/Public/BioTerrorism/Conferences/Presentations/RobertMathews.pdf (accessed October 16, 2008).

McLaughlin Hour with John McLaughlin. NBC, New York. Air date February 17, 2008, 12:00 p.m. (pre-taped Friday, February 15).

Memorial Institute for the Prevention of Terrorism website. http://www.mipt.org.

MILNET. "Terrorist Group Profiles." http://www.milnet.com/tgp/tgpndx2.htm (accessed May 2, 2009).

Mousseau, Michael. "Market Civilization and Its Clash with Terror." *International Security* 27, no. 3 (2002/2003): 5–29.

Murphy, Frederick, and Neal Nathanson. "Emergence of New Viral Infections: Implications for the Blood Supply." *Semin Virol 5* (1994): 87–102.

National Intelligence Council. "Mapping the Global Future." Report of the National Intelligence Council's 2020 Project. GPO, Superintendent of Documents, Pittsburgh, PA, December 2004.

National Research Council (NRC) and Institute of Medicine (IOM). *Globalization, Biosecurity, and the Future of the Life Sciences.* Committee on Advances in Technology and the Prevention of Their Application to Next Generation Biowarfare Threats. Washington, DC: National Academies Press, 2006.

National Science Advisory Board for Biosecurity (NSABB) website. http://www.biosecurityboard.gov/ (accessed May 25, 2008).

Nunn-Lugar, "Nunn-Lugar Cooperative Threat Reduction Program." http://nunn-lugar.com/.

Office of the Director of National Intelligence. "ODNI News Release No. 9-05," December 21, 2005. http://www.fas.org/irp/news/2005/12/dni122105.pdf (accessed June 1, 2008).

Osborne, Michael W. "Managing Risk and Dual-Use Technologies: The Case of Biotechnology." Briefing from the Director, Organisation for Economic Co-operation and Development (OECD) International Futures Program, at a conference in Tokyo, December 2, 2005.

Parliamentary Office of Science and Technology (United Kingdom). "Bio-Terrorism." *Postnote* no. 166 (November 2001). http://www.parliament.uk/post/pn166.pdf (accessed May 16, 2008).

Partnership for a Secure America (PSA). "WMD Report Card Release." http://www.psaonline.org/article.php?id=393 (accessed May 2, 2009).

Perez-Rivas, Manuel. "Bush Vows to Rid the World of 'Evil-Doers.'" CNN.com, September 16, 2001. http://archives.cnn.com/2001/US/09/16/gen.bush.terrorism/.

Petro, James B. "Intelligence Support to the Life Science Community: Mitigating Threats from Bioterrorists." https://www.cia.gov/library/center-for-the-study-of-intelligence/csi-publications/csi-studies/studies/vol48no3/article06.html (accessed May 2, 2009).

Pipes, Daniel. "God and Mammon: Does Poverty Cause Militant Islam?" *National Interest* (Winter 2002).

"Possible Consequences of the Misuse of Biological Sciences." From conference sponsored by UNESCO International School for Science and Peace, Villa Olmo, Como, Italy, December 3–6, 1997. http://www.unesco.org/science/wcs/meetings/eur_como_97.htm (accessed May 2, 2009).

Purkin, Helen E. "Biowarfare Lessons, Emerging Insecurity Issues, and Ways to Monitor Dual-Use Biotechnology Trends in the Future." Institute for National Security Studies, United States Air Force Academy, Colorado Springs, CO, September 2005, 14.

RAND. "Fifth Annual Report of the Advisory Panel to Assess Domestic Response Capabilities for Terrorism Involving Weapons of Mass Destruction: Forging America's New Normalcy: Securing Our Homeland, Preserving Our Liberty." http://www.rand.org/nsrd/terrpanel/volume_v/volume_v.pdf (accessed December 2003).

RAND. "First Annual Report of the Advisory Panel to Assess Domestic Response Capabilities for Terrorism Involving Weapons of Mass Destruction: Assessing the Threat, December 15,1999." http://www.rand.org/organization/nsrd/terrpanel/ html (accessed November 7, 2008).

Randall, Vernellia R. "Bioterrorism, Public Health and the Law." University of Dayton, Ohio. http://academic.udayton.edu/health/syllabi/ bioterrorism/3bioterror/bioterror05.htm (accessed May 12, 2008).

Rapoport, David C. "The Four Waves of Rebel Terror and September 11." *Anthropoetics* 8, no. 1 (2002). http://www.anthropoetics.ucla.edu/ap0801/terror. htm (accessed May 2, 2009).

Richardson, Louise. *What Terrorists Want: Understanding the Enemy, Containing the Threat.* New York: Random House, 2006.

Roos, Robert. "Lab Lapses Sparked Anthrax False Alarm in Idaho." *CIDRAP* [Center for Infectious Disease Research and Policy] *News,* September 11, 2008. http://www.cidrap.umn.edu/.

Rosenberg, Barbara Hatch. "Defending against Biodefence: The Need for Limits." *Disarmament Diplomacy*, February–March, no. 69 (2003): 1.

Rothfeder, Jeffrey, "Biological Warfare." *Popular Science*, March 2005. http://www .popsci.com/popsci/medicine/10b7c4522fa84010vgnvcm1000004eecbccdrcrd. html (accessed December 11, 2008).

Russell, James. "Framing Globalization, the Nexus, and WMD Proliferation." DOS presentation at the NPS conference on Terrorism, Transnational Networks and WMD Proliferation: Indications and Warning in an Era of Globalization, July 2006. http://www.ccc.nps.navy.mil/events/recent/Presentations/Russell%20 WMD%20I&W%20Brief.pdf.

Salerno, Reynolds M., Jennifer Gaudioso, Rebecca L. Frerichs, and Daniel Estes. "A BW Risk Assessment: Historical and Technical Perspectives." *The Nonproliferation Review*, Fall (2004): 25–43.

Smithson, Amy, and Leslie-Anne Levy. "Ataxia: The Chemical and Biological Threat and the U.S. Response." Stimson Center Report No. 35, Henry L. Stimson Center, Washington, DC, October 2000, 282.

Snyder, Laura, and Jason Pate. "Tracking Anthrax Hoaxes and Attacks." James Martin Center for Nonproliferation Studies, May 20, 2002. http://cns.miis.edu/ stories/020520.htm (accessed May 2, 2009).

Spencer, Alexander. 2006. "Questioning the Concept of New Terrorism." *Peace Conflict & Development*, 8 (January 2006).

Spencer, Jack, and Michael Scardaville. "Understanding the Bioterrorist Threat: Facts and Figures." The Heritage Foundation, October 11, 2001. http://www.heritage. org/Research/HomelandSecurity/BG1488.cfm#pgfId=1159547.

Stern, Jessica. "Dreaded Risks and the Control of Biological Weapons." *International Security* 27, no. 3 (Winter 2002/2003): 89–123.

Stern, Jessica. "The Protean Enemy." *Foreign Affairs,* July/August 2003.

Stern, Jessica. *Terror in the Name of God: Why Religious Militants Kill.* New York: HarperCollins, 2003.

Tilly, Charles. "Terror, Terrorism, Terrorists." *Sociological Theory* 22, no. 1 (2004): 5–13.

Tucker, David. "What's New about the New Terrorism and How Dangerous Is It?" *Terrorism and Political Violence* 13, no. 3 (2001).

Tucker, Jonathan B. *Scourge: The Once and Future Threat of Smallpox.* New York: Atlantic Monthly Press, 2001.

Tucker, Jonathan B., ed. *Toxic Terror: Assessing Terrorist Use of Chemical and Biological Weapons.* Cambridge, MA: MIT Press, 2000.

U.S. Army. "A Military Guide to Terrorism in the Twenty-First Century." Fort Leavenworth, KS: U.S. Army Training and Doctrine Command (TRADOC) Intelligence Support Activity, August 2007.

U.S. Congress. *Homeland Security Act of 2002.* H.R. 5005, §101. Executive Department: Mission, November 2002. http://www.pfir.org/2002-hr5005 (accessed May 22, 2008).

U.S. Congress. "Technologies Underlying Weapons of Mass Destruction." OTA-BP-ISC-115, Office of Technology Assessment (OTA). Washington, DC: GPO, December 1993.

U.S. Department of Agriculture (USDA). "Fact Sheet: Cartagena Protocol on Biosafety." DOS, July 21, 2003. http://www.fas.usda.gov/info/factsheets/biosafety.asp (accessed May 23, 2008).

U.S. Department of Defense (DoD). "Dictionary of Military and Associated Terms." http://www.dtic.mil/doctrine/jel/doddict/data/a/00429.html (accessed February 3, 2008).

U.S. Department of Defense (DoD). "Militarily Critical Technologies List Part II: Weapons of Mass Destruction Technologies: Biological Weapons Technology." DoD, Office of the Under Secretary of Defense for Acquisition, Logistics and Technology (February 1998). http://www.fas.org/irp/threat/mctl98-2/.

U.S. Department of Health and Human Services (HHS). "HHS Plan to Combat Bioterrorism and Other Public Health Emergencies." HHS Bioterrorism Council website. http://www.hhs.gov/aspr/opeo/documents/hhsplncombat.html (accessed June 1, 2008).

U.S. Department of Homeland Security (DHS). *Bioterrorism Risk Assessment: A Call for Change, Committee on Methodological Improvements to the Department of Homeland Security's Biological Agent Risk Analysis.* Washington, DC: National Research Council.

U.S. Department of Homeland Security (DHS). *Civil Defense and Homeland Security: A Short History of National Preparedness Efforts.* Washington, DC: DHS, 2006 (September).

U.S. Department of Homeland Security (DHS). DHS, "HSPD-8 Overview: Planning Scenarios." http://www.ojp.usdoj.gov/odp/assessments/hspd8.htm (accessed February 26, 2008).

U.S. Department of Homeland Security (DHS). *National Planning Scenarios*. Washington, DC: DHS, April 2005. http://media.washingtonpost.com/wp-srv/nation/nationalsecurity/earlywarning/NationalPlanningScenariosApril2005.pdf (accessed May 2, 2009).

U.S. Department of State (DOS). "2007 Report on Terrorism." National Counterterrorism Center, Washington, DC, April 2008. http://wits.nctc.gov/reports/crot2007nctcannexfinal.pdf (accessed October 28, 2008).

U.S. Department of State (DOS). "Annex of Statistical Information." National Counterterrorism Center, 2007. http://www.state.gov/s/ct/rls/crt/2007/103716.htm (accessed July 18, 2008).

U.S. Department of State (DOS). "Country Reports on Terrorism." Released by the Office of the Coordinator for Counterterrorism, April 30, 2008. http://www.state.gov/s/ct/rls/crt/2007/103714.htm (accessed October 15, 2008).

U.S. Department of State (DOS). "Transforming Diplomacy to Combat WMD Terrorism." Briefing presented at the Naval Postgraduate School conference on Terrorism, Transnational Networks and WMD Proliferation: Indications and Warning in an Era of Globalization, July 2006. http://www.ccc.nps.navy.mil/events/recent/Presentations/HarbaughPresentationtoAccompanyNPSRemarks.pdf (accessed May 10, 2008)

U.S. Department of State (DOS). "U.S. Efforts to Combat Biological Weapons Threat." Fact Sheet by DOS for a conference in Geneva, Switzerland, by the U.S. Delegation to the Fifth Review Conference of the BWC, November 14, 2002.

Victoroff, Jeff. "The Mind of the Terrorist: A Review and Critique of Psychological Approaches." *Journal of Conflict Resolution* 49, no. 1 (2005): 3–42.

Wagner, Andrew Moore, and Ron Aryel, eds. *The Handbook of Biosurveillance*. Burlington, MA: Academic Press (Elsevier), 2006.

Wagner, Michael M., Louise S. Gresham, and Virginia Dato. "Case Detection, Outbreak Detection, and Outbreak Characterization." In *The Handbook of Biosurveillance*, edited by Andrew Moore Wagner and Ron Aryel, 27–50. Burlington, MA: Academic Press (Elsevier), 2006.

Warner, Susan. "Biosafety Lapses Prompt Government Review." *The Scientist*, 2007. http://www.the-scientist.com/news/print/53626 (accessed January 11, 2008).

Weinstein, Raymond S., and Kenneth Alibek. *Biological and Chemical Terrorism: A Guide for Health-Care Providers and First Responders*. New York: Thieme, 2003.

White House. *9/11: Five Years Later: Successes and Challenges*. Washington, DC: White House, 2006.

White House. "Homeland Security." http://www.whitehouse.gov/infocus/homeland/nshs/2007/sectionV.html (accessed June 1, 2008).

White House. "HSPD-21: National Strategy for Public Health and Medical Preparedness." Washington, DC: White House, October 18, 2007. http://www.fas.org/programs/ssp/bio/resource/documents/hspd-21.pdf (accessed May 2, 2009).

White House. "National Security Strategy of the United States." Washington, DC: White House, March 2006. http://www.whitehouse.gov/nsc/nss/2006/ (accessed October 2, 2008).

White House. "National Strategy for Combating Terrorism." Washington, DC: White House, September 2006.

White House. "National Strategy for Homeland Security." Washington, DC: White House, October 2007.

White House. "Strengthening the International Regime against Biological Weapons: President's Statement." Washington, DC: White House, November 1, 2001. http://www.whitehouse.gov/news/releases/2001/11/20011101.html (accessed August 15, 2008).

Wilson, Alyson. "How DHS Currently Manages Risk." Los Alamos National Laboratory brief, Los Alamos, NM. http://www.samsi.info/200708/risk/ppp/presentations/1004/samsi_risk_wilson.ppt#272 (accessed March 28, 2008).

World Economic Forum. "Global Risks 2007: A Global Network Report." World Economic Forum, Geneva, January 2007. http://www.weforum.org/pdf/CSI/Global_Risks_2007.pdf (accessed December 12, 2007).

World Health Organization (WHO). "Summary of Probable SARS Cases with Onset of Illness from 1 November 2002 to 31 July 2003." Concluding report, April 21, 2004. http://www.who.int/csr/sars/country/table2004_04_21/en/index.html (accessed August 2, 2008).

Zanders, Jean Pascal. "Assessing the Risk of Chemical and Biological Weapons Proliferation to Terrorists." *The Nonproliferation Review*, Fall 1999.

Zilinskas, Raymond A., ed. *Biological Warfare: Modern Offense and Defense.* Boulder, CO: Lynne Reiner, 2000.

Zilinskas, Raymond A. "Final Report and Commentary: Bioterrorism Threat Assessment and Risk Management Workshop." Presentation to the U.S. Department of Energy, Monterey Institute of International Studies, CA, June 24, 2003.

Zilinskas, Raymond A. "Possible Terrorist Use of Modern Biotechnology Techniques." Proceedings for the Conference on Biosecurity and Bioterrorism, Istituto Diplomatico "Mario Toscano" Villa Madama, Rome, Italy, September 18–19, 2000. http://www.mi.infn.it/~landnet/Biosec/zilinskas1.pdf (accessed May 16, 2008).

Index

About the Author

DANIEL M. GERSTEIN is strategist and policy expert with a PhD in Biodefense. He has served in the security and defense fields in a variety of strategic and operational assignments dealing with national strategy, arms control, international negotiations, and conflict analysis. A resident of Alexandria, VA, he is the author of *Securing America's Future, Leading at the Speed of Light,* and *Assignment Pentagon.*